Library Off-Site Shelving

Library Off-Site Shelving

Guide for High-Density Facilities

Danuta A. Nitecki
Curtis L. Kendrick

Editors

2001
Libraries Unlimited, Inc.
Englewood, Colorado

Courtesy of Yale University.

Libraries Unlimited, Inc.
P.O. Box 6633
Englewood, CO 80155-6633
1-800-237-6124
www.lu.com

Library of Congress Cataloging-in-Publication Data

Library off-site shelving : guide for high-density facilities / Danuta A. Nitecki, Curtis L. Kendrick, editors.
    p. cm.
  Includes bibliographical references and index.
  ISBN 1-56308-885-1
    1. Library storage centers--United States. 2. Library storage centers--United States--Case studies. 3. Library materials--Storage--United States. I. Nitecki, Danuta A. II. Kendrick, Curtis L.

Z675.S75 L53 2001
021--dc21

                  2001029624

Contents

List of Contributors

Kenneth E. Carpenter
Assistant Director
Harvard University Library (retired)
> Ken Carpenter worked from the early 1990s to select books from Widener Library for storage at the Harvard Depository. This work was carried out in consultation with Harvard faculty.

Paul Conway
Head, Preservation Department
Yale University Library
> Paul Conway was a member of the faculty committee that proposed a shelving facility at Yale University. He served on three of the planning committees (facilities, selection, processing) for the Library Shelving Facility and continues as a member of the LSF Coordinators Group.

June L. DeWeese
Librarian IV
Head of the Access Services Division
Ellis Library, University of Missouri-Columbia
> June L. DeWeese is the librarian who supervises the on-site staff who are responsible for the day-to-day operations of the UM Libraries Depository, a storage facility which houses materials for the four campuses of the University of Missouri system. She was involved in the planning and construction phases of the building, in choosing equipment and furniture, in writing the guidelines for operation and service level agreement, and was responsible for hiring the original staff. She was involved in the planning for the reconstruction of the facility following a tornado during the first year of operation. She has 26 years of experience as a professional librarian.

Reese Dill
Dill & Company
Bedford, Massachusetts
> Reese Dill started his own firm, Dill & Company, in 1981. Dill & Company is a consulting firm, which specializes in the design and implementation of material handling and storage systems for manufacturers, distributors, and institutions. In 1985, Harvard University retained Dill & Company as part of a team including staff from the Harvard Library to first survey the existing methods of off-site book storage and then propose a system for the most efficient off-campus storage of 1 million volumes. Dill & Company proposed a system that involved sorting books by size and placing them into specially sized corrugated trays that were stored up to 30 feet high. This system was selected by Harvard for its first storage module, which was constructed in 1986. Since then, Dill & Company has designed five more modules for Harvard and similar high-density book storage systems for 16 other universities or institutions.

Joel J. Felber, J.D.
Ostrolenk, Faber, Gerb & Soffen, LLP
New York, New York

>   Joel Felber was a full-time systems analyst in Yale University's Library Systems
>   Office. During the implementation and opening of Yale's Library Shelving Facil-
>   ity, he was a member of the Facility's Software Selection Committee and later be-
>   came the Systems Office's coordinator for the Facility. He also contributed
>   programming to the Facility, and acted as Systems Office liaison between the Uni-
>   versity and the Facility's multiple third-party hardware and software vendors.

Lee Anne George
Publications Program Officer
Association of Research Libraries

>   Lee Anne George currently holds the position of Publications Program Officer at
>   the Association of Research Libraries. Previously, she was Librarian for Informa-
>   tion and Document Delivery Services for the Harvard College Library at Harvard
>   University. In that position she was responsible both for interlibrary loan and docu-
>   ment delivery services in the 11 Harvard College libraries in the Faculty of Arts and
>   Sciences and for coordinating the transfer of materials from the Widener Library
>   stacks to the Harvard Depository off-site storage facility. She oversaw all aspects of
>   the management of Harvard Depository Transfer and Linkage (HDTL) staff and
>   worked closely with cataloging units to develop procedures and record entry poli-
>   cies to ensure HDTL staff compliance with cataloging standards.

Helen R. Goldstein
Access Services Librarian
American University Library

>   As Head of Access Services at the American University Library, Helen Goldstein
>   manages the borrowing requests for material housed at the WRLC storage facility.
>   She also oversees many summer projects involving processing the material to be
>   sent to the storage facility. In addition, she is responsible for identifying material
>   from the library's general collection in the areas of psychology and women's and
>   gender studies to be sent to the WRLC storage facility.

Barbara Graham
Associate Director
Harvard University Library

>   Barbara Graham is the Associate Director of the Harvard University Library for
>   Administration and Programs. Her responsibilities include the Harvard Depository,
>   the University Archives, and the Weissman Preservation Center as well as adminis-
>   trative services, publications, and capital projects. In the mid-1980s she was part of
>   the original design team for the Harvard Depository.

Steven J. Herman
Chief of the Collections Management Division
The Library of Congress

>   Steven J. Herman currently serves as Chief of the Collections Management Divi-
>   sion at the Library of Congress, a position he has held since the Division was estab-
>   lished in 1978. In this position, he manages the Library's general collections, which
>   consist of 12 million books and bound periodicals, as well as other collections as-
>   signed to the division. He has been heavily involved with the Library of Congress's
>   off-site storage program for more than two decades, and has, for the past five years,

worked on the development and plan for operation of the Library's soon-to-be-opened facility at Fort Meade, Maryland. In this context, he has led and participated in groups to determine: service policies, criteria for determining what collections will be transferred, preservation issues, design and procurement of equipment and supplies, and staffing requirements.

Jeffrey L. Horrell
Associate Librarian of Harvard College for Collections
Harvard College Library
> Jeffrey Horrell oversaw the planning for the 1998-2000 Harvard Depository-Push project and ongoing selection of materials for the Harvard Depository for the HCL administration.

Bruce Hulse
Director of Library Services
Washington Research Library Consortium
> Bruce Hulse has been with the Washington Research Library Consortium since 1990. He was responsible for planning and implementing services at the WRLC storage facility, which began operations in April 1994, and continues to oversee the facility's daily operations. Mr. Hulse received his MLS from Columbia University.

Donald G. Kelsey
Library Facilities Planner
University of Minnesota Libraries
> Donald is the Facilities Planner for the University of Minnesota Libraries and most recently completed the Elmer L. Andersen Library, a facility combining an archives research center with a 1.5 million-volume library storage center. His private consulting practice as a library planner also includes the planning and management of large-scale library moves.

Curtis L. Kendrick
Director, Access Services Division
Columbia University Libraries
> As Assistant Director in the Harvard University Library, Curtis Kendrick was responsible for the management of the Harvard Depository. While at Harvard he oversaw two depository expansion projects, and the development of the Library Archival System inventory control system. Since coming to Columbia in 1998, he has played a lead role in the joint effort of Columbia, New York Public Library, and Princeton University to create a high-density shelving facility.

David F. Kohl
Dean and University Librarian
University of Cincinnati
> David has been active in the development and ongoing function of the Southwest Regional Depository (SWORD), one of five Ohio depositories established in association with the OhioLINK project, since 1991.

Mary C. LaFogg
Chief Collections Management Archivist
Manuscripts and Archives
Yale University Library

> Mary C. LaFogg served on the working group appointed by Yale's Provost and Vice President for Finance and Administration to consider the feasibility of a shelving facility, and the task force that formulated principles and guidelines for the selection of Library material for inclusion. She led the project implementation group that considered preparation issues for the transferal of material and services provided by the operation, participated in discussions regarding building design, and assisted in the choice of manager for the Library Shelving Facility (LSF), which opened in November 1998. As Chief Collection Management Archivist, she coordinated the efforts of Manuscripts and Archives in the transfer of two thirds of its holdings, over 68,000 items, to the LSF.

Ron Lane
Manager
Harvard Depository
Harvard University Library

> Ron Lane left a position with a major records storage firm to assume management of the Harvard Depository in 1989. Since that time, he has presided over an eight-fold increase in both the size and activity of the collections in his charge. He was a major contributor to the redesign of the system software, and introduced many new techniques to the daily workflow. The influence of his operation can be seen in a multiplicity of shelving facilities throughout the country.

Danuta A. Nitecki
Associate University Librarian
Yale University Library

> Danuta A. Nitecki was responsible for transforming the concept of a high-efficiency, off-campus library shelving facility into a reliable and effective service operation at Yale University. She chaired the Implementation Committee that coordinated the design of operations for the Yale University Library Shelving Facility that opened in November 1998. The LSF continues to be a unit within her administrative scope as she joins campus facilities staff to plan the building of the second shelving module to be completed by August 2002.

Lizanne Payne
Executive Director
Washington Research Library Consortium

> Lizanne Payne has served as Executive Director of WRLC since 1991, where she has overall responsibility for strategic planning and budgeting for all WRLC programs. She presided over implementation of the shared digital library system (now in its second generation), and oversaw design and construction of WRLC's off-site book storage facility in 1993. She is presently involved in planning for the likely expansion of the off-site storage facility sometime in the next few years.

Margaret K. Powell
Librarian
The Lewis Walpole Library
Yale University
> Margaret Powell served as the coordinator for selection (1997-2000) for the Yale University Shelving Facility while in a previous position (Librarian for Literature in English and Commonwealth Studies, Sterling Memorial Library, Yale University).

Bruce M. Scott
> Bruce Scott, of Russell Scott Steedle Capone Architects Inc., Cambridge, Massachusetts, was the architect for the Harvard, Yale, and Columbia/NY Public Library/Princeton Consortium off-site shelving facilities.

Deborah Slingluff
Head, Access Services
Milton S. Eisenhower Library
Johns Hopkins University
> Deborah Slingluff assumed responsibility for the Moravia Park Off-site Shelving Facility six months prior to its opening in November 1995. She continues to collaborate with University and Library personnel to oversee the renovation of the existing warehouse and to define and develop services, staff, and operations that support the shelving and retrieval needs of the University and its researchers.

Christine Weideman
Assistant Head
Manuscripts and Archives
Yale University Library
> Christine Weideman directed planning retreat for the move of departmental holdings to the Library Shelving Facility and developed the project plan.

1

The Paradox and Politics of Off-Site Shelving*

Danuta A. Nitecki and Curtis L. Kendrick

Many would consider off-site storage to be what economists call an inferior good. Who among us wouldn't prefer to build spacious new libraries with perfect climate control and adaptable infrastructure for future technological requirements right on campus? And once we adopt high-density off-site shelving the probability of ever seeing such libraries constructed on campus becomes remote.

Still, it is difficult to rationalize keeping books on campus that are used only once in a generation. Imagine a lecture hall or laboratory that was used only four times a century and it would seem like a waste of space. And yet, in our libraries, we have volumes that are used once every 25 years sufficient to fill countless labs and lecture halls. Housing for this type of material, it is increasingly being argued, can more effectively be provided in an off-site location where it is possible to provide better security and environmental controls that extend the useful life of our collections.

The contemporary approach to high-density storage was pioneered by Harvard in the mid-1980s. Other institutions soon followed, building on Harvard's experience and tailoring solutions to meet local needs; to name a few: Yale, Cornell, University of Pennsylvania, Johns Hopkins, Texas, Ohio, and the Library of Congress.

---

*There is no commonly held naming protocol for such facilities. We chose not to edit the terms used by contributors to this volume. For many these facilities are "storage" something—facilities, libraries, or warehouses. Some librarians feel that the naming of such facilities should avoid words that connote a warehouse role. Instead, some have assumed the strategy that this is another place to shelve library materials and hence use such names as the "shelving facility." The reader will find "storage" and "shelving" used interchangeably.

The elements of the program typically include:

♦ Store by size in stacks up to 30 feet high.

♦ Store in pH neutral trays—five sizes at two heights each.

♦ Access by bar code.

♦ Support operation with an inventory control system or modifications to library management system.

♦ Utilize order picker.

♦ Control climate—50 to 60 degrees, 35 to 50 percent relative humidity.

♦ Process to achieve near-zero error rate.

Historically, the central focus of research libraries has been on building collections. Service has been a second-order consideration, typically delivered at the convenience of the service provider. The success of off-site facilities hinges on our ability to deliver service excellence that is user-centered. To compensate for the fact that we have inconvenienced users by not building a new library on campus, we have to provide service that is:

♦ Fast

♦ Reliable

♦ Economical

♦ Sustainable

♦ Convenient

♦ Accurate

It is not atypical for services established in support of an off-site facility to be the best or among the best that a library offers. This leads to the "Paradox of Off-Site." We take our least used collections and then we:

♦ Inventory them.

♦ Ensure online bibliographic access.

♦ Develop a convenient way for users to request material, usually through the online catalog or Web.

♦ Pull collections from stacks and deliver them to a centralized pick-up point.

♦ Provide free copying and faxing.

♦ Implement sophisticated inventory control and operational procedures.

♦ Provide better security.

♦ Provide a far superior preservation environment relative to open stack libraries on campus.

The decision to move collections to a high-density shelving facility represents a fundamental change in how research libraries operate. Off-site shelving is an enterprise-wide endeavor, affecting and involving all units within the library. It represents additional work. It represents change to how we do things. It is resisted.

Managing services typically has not been a priority for research libraries. Some resist taking a systemic view of how public services are provided. But a successful off-site program has service requirements that force us to change how we do business. Slowdowns in technical services processing, the protectiveness of selectors who embrace the notion of an off-site location only for *other* people's collections, the behavior of those frontline public service staff or students who are undertrained, misinformed, noncommunicative or surly—all these weaknesses in our traditional system of service support are exposed and become unacceptable. The off-site program's demand for precision and coordination cannot tolerate such shortcomings. Off-site shelving is an enterprise-wide initiative; it cuts across departmental lines. Moreover, as people start to realize the Paradox of Off-Site they begin to wonder why we can't provide a higher level of service for *all* of our collections, not just the materials stored remotely. The off-site program puts pressure on research libraries to improve services across the board, not solely in support of collections transferred to the high-density shelving facility.

Another form of resistance stems from the belief that off-site storage is misguided and that all of our collections should be in the same location. Arguments are advanced that transferring collections to a remote site destroys browsing and the wonder of serendipitous discovery. It is critical that discussions on these topics take place and involve librarians, administrators, and faculty because such conversations address the core issue of off-site storage being an inferior good. While it may take many forms, this is really the question, Why can't we build another library on campus? Until this issue is addressed and the decision made that the institution will not expand the library on campus, it will not be possible to gain widespread support for an off-site program. And the two main selling points in favor of off-site storage are the security and preservation benefit, and the excellent service that will be provided in support of the program.

What might be learned from the collective wisdom of those that have designed and managed an off-site shelving solution? That there are no single answers to questions about how to shelve library materials to best use space. That there are no standards yet by which to compare productivity, costs, or services offered by these facilities. But some best practices are emerging from which we propose the following set of assumptions and values for colleagues planning or already operating such facilities:

♦ Start early. It always takes longer than you think it will or should. This is particularly vital if you are considering a multi-institutional initiative.

♦ Recognize that the planning effort requires a significant staffing commitment.

♦ Get help. There are people who have been through this before and people who offer specialized expertise. Talk to them; use them; hire them.

♦ Project focus. An off-site initiative will typically involve new money, and librarians can quickly come to resemble a bunch of politicians standing around a pork barrel. Mission creep can occur and you can recognize it if your project focus is on space, but you start spending a lot of time talking about de-duping collections, digitizing tables of contents, or microfilming brittle collections. All of these could be part of the project, but if you decide they are not, then don't let them creep into your budget planning and negotiations.

♦ Involvement. Librarians need to be part of the design and construction team. This means going to a lot of meetings where people are talking about things you may not understand. But it is important to be at the table both to learn about the capabilities of this new form of library space and to temper the designers' creativity with the librarian's practical sense of what works. Beware that architects and engineers may come up with such ideas as skylights over collections (they leak), mechanical systems on the roof (they destroy the roof membrane and create leaks), or putting the operations supervisors in a separate building from the facility's processing staff (the isolation assumes the wrong management style). Research and unique collections should be housed in environments fostering their long-term preservation.

♦ Materials should be readily accessible for use by eligible readers.

♦ Browsing is a highly valued activity among researchers and the perception of it may even be more highly valued.

♦ No library has sufficient resources to address all its responsibilities and most seek to maximize the effectiveness of its resource allocations, including capital expenditures.

♦ The increased reliance on off-site shelving is an emerging theme in a shift in how readers think about sources of materials. This shift includes increased use of Inter-Library Loan, the World Wide Web, and Document

Delivery Suppliers. This shift is also predicated on our perception of our reader's diminished expectation that everything readers need will be under one roof and increased expectation that everything they need can be requested easily, reliably supplied, and delivered to a convenient array of locations or via a useful array of technologies.

♦ The requirements for the success of such facilities include zero tolerance for error, accuracy of placement and inventory control, and high user-focused service standards. These service standards typically include next day or quicker delivery, high availability rates, an ease of placing requests, and convenient communications for the user to be aware of the status of requests (e.g., ready for pick up, delayed delivery).

♦ To support these service standards, changes in library operations are required. These changes require integration of many activities—selection, system design, collection preparation, bibliographic controls, user assistance, retrieval services, and transport.

♦ While space is the catalyst for building facilities, off-site storage presents other opportunities beyond mitigating space problems. Chief among these collateral opportunities is a relatively low-cost option for extending the useful life of collections, buying time until solutions that are more comprehensive are technically and fiscally possible. In addition, the establishment of large-capacity stores of collections provides what may be a necessary piece of infrastructure in order for the promise of shared collection development to reach full fruition.

This volume addresses the planning, construction, and operating issues relating to such high-density library shelving facilities. In this collection of practical reports, our intent is to codify folklore into reference information for those planning or beginning to operate such facilities, as well as to explore with colleagues the opportunities for service improvements this collection management approach offers. We aim to capture in one volume some answers, both facts and opinions, to the more frequently asked questions about building and operating a library shelving facility. All authors contributing chapters write from experience and with expertise in some aspect of planning, designing, or operating such facilities.

The volume covers essential topics that address issues relating to the building, its operations, and serving the collections. It begins with a collection of five case studies discussing governance issues and cost models. Barbara Graham was instrumental in the planning and design of the original Harvard Depository Library, and continues to provide administrative direction and support to its operation. From this excellent historic perspective, she describes a client–owner model for off-campus shelving that may be unique in its cost-recovery objective. Deborah Slingluff reviews how the Johns Hopkins University library has conceived and operates its facility to serve a single university with multiple libraries. Two consortia models are described. David Kohl records how libraries in Ohio developed and now operate a state-funded program of off-site shelving and Lizanne Payne reports on the efforts of a voluntary association of libraries in the District of Columbia area to support and operate the Washington Regional Library Consortium. Finally to this section, Steven Herman introduces some of the early planning principles and issues addressed by the Library of Congress as it embarks on a program to consolidate several of its distributed off-site collections and build the first of a projected 13 modules at Fort Meade, Maryland.

Design and construction issues are addressed by three experts who first worked together to develop the Harvard Depository and since have continued to have direct experience designing other facilities, streamlining workflow designs, and creating necessary management infrastructures. Bruce Scott presents invaluable insights from an architect's perspective on the design and construction process. Reese Dill, an operations engineer who has consulted extensively in designing commercial warehouses and library shelving facilities, pairs with Ron Lane, the on-site manager of the Harvard Depository to describe operational issues that should be considered when designing a facility or trying to improve an existing one.

Off-site facilities provide an excellent opportunity to improve conditions for the preservation of library collections. Paul Conway assembles some of the profession's theory and research that influenced planning of the environment for the Yale University Library Shelving Facility, as well as insights gained from this experience.

Deciding what should be shelved in a separate off-site facility is not a simple task; it should be responsive to the attitudes and traditions of the community served. Insights from two different approaches to this important step are described. Kenneth Carpenter and Jeffrey Horrell report on the approach taken by the Widener Library at Harvard University, while Margaret Powell shares insights from the Yale University experience.

Once items are identified by intellectual content for transfer to an off-site shelving facility, they begin a transformation to be treated as valuable objects of a given dimension. Lee Anne George summarizes an important set of issues regarding bibliographic controls and physical handling in her essay on preparation for transfer, and Donald Kelsey and Curtis Kendrick describe the logistics of transporting materials to and from a facility. Joel Felber discusses the automation support developed to facilitate the inventory control, location, and retrieval of accessioned objects through essential computer equipment, peripheral tools, and software design. June DeWeese summarizes insights from experiences among several facility managers in her essay about accessioning and managing issues. Bruce Hulse highlights common service practices to retrieve and deliver items from a shelving facility and also reports initial findings of new services evolving from such facilities including the robotic retrieval and digitizing project underway at the Johns Hopkins University. Archivists Christine Weideman and Mary LaFogg take a collective view of operating issues from selection, through preparation, to retrieval, as they address concerns they have heard raised among their colleagues who manage archives and special collections in off-site environments.

Our intent is to present this volume as a reference book, knowing that we cannot answer all the questions readers might have when thinking about shelving materials off-site. In the tradition of excellent reference work, we hope to have also offered contacts and plenty of information for those interested in pursuing a topic further and to get more up-to-date data. Helen Goldstein has created a helpful bibliography of other relevant readings as well as Web sites to other dynamic sources of information. We encourage readers to pursue those sources that are of interest.

We hope that this collection of essays will be helpful to our colleagues who are faced with the challenge of planning and operating high-density shelving facilities. Our contribution as editors is relatively minor. Appreciation for all that is useful and good from this collection is owed to the individual authors of contributed chapters. We also wish to thank our institutions and their administrators not only for supporting our efforts to prepare this collection, but also for entrusting us with assignments to implement and administer shelving facilities from which we gained the experience that led us to this project.

Danuta A. Nitecki
Associate University Librarian
Yale University Library

Curtis L. Kendrick
Director
Access Services Division
Columbia University Libraries

October 2000

II. Governance Issues and Cost Models: Case Studies

2

The Harvard Depository
Client–Owner Model

Barbara Graham

Introduction

The Harvard Depository (HD) and its operation have exceeded the expectations of Harvard's library and university administrators on several counts, including its scale, intense use, and effectiveness. Harvard settled on a client–owner model as a logical extension of its decentralized management environment. The HD is funded for every aspect of its operation through fees paid by the libraries and departments of the University system that choose to use it and thus constitute its client base. Wholly owned as a subsidiary of the University and devoted to its library, archive, and records management needs, the HD is currently administered by the Harvard University Library, a department of the University's Central Administration. The administrative model has evolved since its inception in 1986, but its fundamental principles remain intact.

The 1984 decision of the Harvard University Library Director and the University's Central Administration to create an economical, preservation-conscious facility to meet the storage needs of Harvard's distributed library system was far-sighted. On an urban campus, critically constrained by a paucity of land and bound by certain scholarly traditions, the valence of geopolitics is often a defining variable in the equation. The issue of proximate access to the collections is not only a tradition ineluctably linked to research at Harvard, but a perceived *sine qua non* for vital research in many fields where the multiplicity of language, the age of materials, limited cataloguing, and the lack of indexing may combine to make information difficult to retrieve without the physical volume at hand. The reality of creating an unbrowsable and remote facility would mean that great attention to detail, accuracy, timely delivery, and consistent service would have to become the Depository's mandates.

9

The Depository's unusual stack configuration, which includes volumes stored by size, uncomfortably low temperatures, and 30-foot-high shelving racks, and its distance from the Harvard Yard, coupled with its structure as a client–owner model, unfolded a complex of operational issues which were impossible to calculate at the outset. Although in absolute terms, the Depository's overhead expense remains well below the cost of traditional library operations due to its efficiencies, small staff, and lack of on-site professional librarians, many challenges exist:

♦ the ability to predict the need in an accurate and timely manner for new modules in order to be prepared for transfers while not assuming new capital debt prematurely;

♦ the need to establish channels for client communication and the ability for the Depository to develop responsive service strategies;

♦ the "value engineering" in order to control costs and "commissioning" in order to ensure the quality of new construction;

♦ the consistent maintenance of the complex physical plant and its mechanical systems over time;

♦ an understanding of the constantly evolving operational and physical plant issues affected by scale, the unpredictability of client needs, and variability in the need for labor and its supply;

♦ the challenge of integrating, developing, and recognizing staff at an isolated site with the staff of the central campus;

♦ the development and implementation of emergency preparedness and recovery plans;

♦ the precautions needed to avoid "maximum foreseeable loss" events;

♦ the assistance for library and archives clients with cost projections in an effort to support their management of expenses which accrue to their budgets;

♦ the provision of accurate accounting of recovered costs and for brokered services on behalf of the clients.

Added to these operations management concerns is the need for Depository administrators to engage in the University Library System's efforts to enhance intellectual access, to provide a robust preservation program, and to develop new services in order to accommodate the logistics of having a growing proportion of the University's collections at a significant distance from campus.

Origins

The idea of a new facility was preliminarily discussed in early 1984. However, key responsibility for advancing the idea and the project was undertaken by the Director of the University Library and Carl Pforzheimer University Professor, Sidney Verba. Professor Verba and Harvard's Planning Group explored storage options in consultation with senior faculty librarians. These deliberations established the principles that were to serve as the underpinnings of the new facility. Synchronous with University deliberations, a study of library space had been commissioned by the Faculty of Arts and Sciences (FAS). The study was intended to examine various storage options, to project collection growth, and to estimate the time and costs involved in transferring collections, as well as to establish criteria for their selection for transfer for FAS libraries. This report concluded that though the complexity of scholarly needs and the demands of various disciplines would require a combination of responses such as compact shelving and proximate storage in some cases, a single, high-density facility promised the optimal long-term solution. Soon thereafter, Harvard's Planning Office identified a viable site outside of Boston. The facility's design benefited from the insightful advice of its early consultants—shelving experts drawn from the commercial storage field—as well as from visits to other institutions and storage facilities, most notably the Library of Congress, the National Archives, and the University of California's Richmond facility.

In spring 1985, a small Harvard team visited the University of California's Northern Regional Facility in Richmond, California. This site visit resulted in several key decisions related to the design of integrated shelving, the use of shelving containers both to avoid abrasion to the materials and to optimize storage density, and the integration of seismic design to ensure the facility's overall structural integrity.

Following the construction of its first unit, Professor Verba said:

> There is no single, simple solution to the major dilemma facing research libraries, that collections continue to grow while facilities do not. Yet the Harvard Depository, thoroughly researched and innovative, designed to provide the best possible environment for the secure preservation of materials, and with a mandate to be responsive to the needs of libraries and users, is a very welcome step toward housing safely and accessibly all of the University Library's collections.[1]

As new research findings emerged, the benefits of lower temperatures and humidity were confirmed. With advances in the technology of both building design and HVAC, the facility's climate moved away from seasonally cycled ranges to set points for temperature and humidity. Technology was also brought to bear on extending the life span of library materials. Harvard's intention was to create an aggressive preservation environment for its collections while working to keep costs reasonable for the libraries and archives using the facility.

Once plans were in place for the first module, the University's Central Administration provided funding to support development and construction. From the start, however, Harvard's libraries were advised that the cost of the facility would be borne by its users. The pricing schedule would account for both the amortized capital expense of the building and the cost recovery for its operation and a portion of its management. The facility would add a new budget line to many libraries, but the debt was to be mitigated through a multiyear subvention by the Central Administration in an effort to ease the transition and to encourage libraries to make use of the facility.

Growth

The first module began operation in 1986 and the second one was completed in 1991. By 1995, a third unit and a high-rise storage vault, suitable for film and other media, were added. The fourth module followed closely in 1996 and, like the others, reached capacity before its projected fill date. Each of these early modules had an area of 8,500 square feet and held between 2 and $2\frac{1}{2}$ million volumes or their equivalent. The two newest modules, completed in 1999, adopted a new expanded design that was initiated at Yale and added a combined 27,000 square feet of storage. Each of these 13,500-square-foot modules is capable of storing from 3 to $3\frac{1}{2}$ million volumes or their equivalent. In addition to scaling up the units, Harvard also chose to follow Yale's decision to adopt a turnkey environmental system for the latest modules. By fall 1999, the Harvard facility had grown to approximately 62,500 square feet of intensely used library and archival storage. Investments in on-site infrastructure, including upgrades in electrical capacity, a fire road, and a stored water supply, were also undertaken in the course of the unprecedented two-module expansion that almost doubled the facility's overall size in the course of one nine-month period.

Even in the midst of a fast-paced but disruptive construction project, the Depository staff accessioned and shelved over 600,000 items and retrieved over 100,000 items in 1999. Growth has averaged more than 20 percent in the past decade. HD's growing acceptance by the faculty is attributed in part to reliable daily service, virtually error-free retrievals of materials stored, and the promise of extending the life span of scholarly resources through climate control.

Organization and Administration

Harvard University's organizational structure is complex, and the Library system is no exception. Within Harvard's federalist arrangement, each major faculty library derives its budget through its faculty dean. The Harvard University Library is the name given both to the system of more than 90 libraries across the faculties of the institution and to the Central Administration department devoted to coordinating them and to providing a cadre of centralized services. It is headed by a senior faculty member who holds the Pforzheimer University Professorship in tandem with the title of Director of the University Library.

Moreover, the Director of the University Library is considered the official steward of the Library system's collections on behalf of the Harvard Corporation. Among the purposes of the Central Administration department called the Harvard University Library is to anticipate systems and services that libraries will need and to provide those services cost effectively.

In addition to the Harvard Depository and a core of administrative services including publications and institutional statistics, HUL programs include the Office for Information Systems, which administers and develops the HOLLIS (integrated library system) and the Library Digital Initiative; the Weissman Preservation Center and Special Collections Conservation Program; and the University Archives and Records Management Programs. In this latter capacity, the HUL not only administers the Harvard Depository but is also one of its major depositors. These programs are each aimed at adding value to scholarly research resources in terms of enhancing access, providing reliable and effective service to the libraries and their constituents, and ensuring the well being of the collections in perpetuity. Moreover, the programs are also engaged in asset and risk management on behalf of the University's library collections.

The Harvard Depository administration was the province of the Vice President for Administration in its early years. In the past several years, its management was assumed by the University Library in recognition of its core mission to steward the collections. As the centrality of the Depository has grown, the level of management assigned to it has also increased commensurately. In recent years, the Associate Director of the University Library for Administration and Programs has been responsible for the Harvard Depository's administration including its finance, planning efforts, capital projects, and operation. Within this office, the Assistant Director of the Harvard University Library for the Harvard Depository[2] focuses on daily HD operations and transfer planning, the inventory control system development, customer and new information services, assistance in budget preparation, and human resource management. The Assistant Director is the initial interface with all library clients and supervises the Depository facility manager,[3] whose core responsibilities include workflow design, inventory control, and supervision of the warehouse staff as well as an administrative staff member for customer service whose office is in Cambridge in proximity to the majority of clients.

There are 18 staff members based at the Depository with approximately eight to ten devoted to operations, four serving as couriers to drive or accompany two vans, an additional four to provide processing support and record keeping, and one for general office support. All but three of the on-site personnel are support staff and none is a professional librarian. The on-site staff is responsible for day-to-day function of the facility, including such duties as accessioning new materials, setting and loading warehouse shelves, retrieving and delivering materials to clients, refiling items to their shelves, and generating client activity and cost reports.

Client input is solicited though various means including periodic meetings of the major Harvard library participants within the HD Council and meetings with the head of the Records Management Program within the University Archives. The HD Council meets approximately four to six times a year to discuss operational issues, planning, preparing materials for transfer, and pending issues such as the status of ongoing projects and functions, client concerns, and the quality of services. In addition, the group discusses prospective services and is critical to their planning and implementation.

Operations decisions reflect the emphasis placed on cost-effectiveness and accountability by both the University's Central Administration and the client libraries of the Depository. Significant policy decisions such as those related to long-term clients or new directions are often the product of the combined deliberation of the associate and assistant directors in consultation with the Central Administration and the HD Council. Capital projects plans, such as expansion proposals, are advanced to the Central Administration by the Associate Director of HUL for Administration and Programs with the support of the HUL Director. These efforts are based on the distilled projections of space needs developed by the Assistant Director of the Harvard University Library for the Harvard Depository and the facility. In addition, the HD Council and the preservation officers of the Weissman Preservation Center of the Harvard University Library are consulted on issues related to the environmental conditions suitable for the storage of the collections and on other related matters, including construction and cleaning. HUL Administrators, systems specialists, and HD operations managers meet regularly to review the status of the inventory control system and to plan additional development in relation to cost and function.

Finance and Expense

As discussed earlier, the Harvard Depository is a fee-based, cost-recovery operation. The University's Central Administration secured the initial capital for the project and structured a favorable loan. However, library and archives participants were expected to absorb the amortized capital costs for each unit's construction as well as its ongoing operations from the start. To assist in the early years of the Depository, the Central Administration provided a subsidy to reduce the capital debt. This subvention mitigated the rate at which debt would accrue but did not affect the cost to libraries, archives, or records management operations. Annual increases in costs are intended to account for inflation and other annual incremental costs.

The plan adopted to achieve this mandate allocated capital costs to the most predictable variable of the equation—that of the storage fee. This plan allows library participants to control costs to some extent by determining the scale of their respective transfers for any given year. In turn, accessioning, retrieval, and courier costs are based largely on recovering labor and van expense on a direct-cost basis. This means that the libraries, Archives, and Records Management Program clients pay to store materials as well as paying for their retrieval, transport, delivery, and refiling upon return. In spite of these fees and costs to the University's libraries, the Harvard planning group estimated that the "costs of storing and retrieving materials from the depository are one-quarter to one-third that of either new library construction or of other comparable storage alternatives."[4] The most recent modules yield a construction cost of approximately

$1.20 per book based on 12.5 volumes per *billable storage foot*—far less than comparable costs for a traditional library.

A review of construction costs and capital debt over the past 14 years, though not insignificant, would confirm this conclusion. Each of the two most recent modules, constructed in 1999, amounts to approximately $4.2 million, exclusive of infrastructure investments at the site as well as improvements to the earlier modules. As noted above, the newest modules have one-half more capacity than earlier modules and thus realize new economies in storage costs.

During fiscal year 2000, the operating budget projections for the total facility (61,000 square feet) are estimated at less than $2 million exclusive of interest and amortization on the capital loan. Employment and labor costs, including benefits and temporary employment, account for about 47 percent of the operating budget. Utilities including electricity and gas account for about 14 percent; and maintenance and repairs, 14 percent. Administrative costs, including oversight of subcontractors and vehicle operation, are approximately 6 percent. Specialized supplies and other costs such as facilities improvements, systems development, and space alterations vary from year to year; however, these were estimated at 19 percent. Readers should note that the budget and financial model is particular to Harvard and is in no way to be construed as either a recommendation or a template for other institutions.

Conclusion

Like the ancient river Meander, the path of progress is seldom linear. The Depository facility was designed and constructed in response to the critical need for additional secure, economical, and environmentally sound library storage. The University Library strives to improve the operation and its cost-effectiveness for the libraries as well as to leverage advances in the relevant technologies to ensure the long-term well being of its library and archives collections.

The salient issues for the client–owner model of a remote Depository continue to include the stewardship of the collections and the capacity to provide error-free and timely service to its constituents consistently, while also containing the cost of their provision. Harvard University's decentralized physical plant and its fiscal practices create complexity for administrators. Programmatic approaches to staff integration and familiarizing librarians with the Depository's processes remain lynchpins in its success. The transfer of some older and unindexed library materials from the shelves of local libraries heightens the desirability of enhanced intellectual access, but does not readily lessen the cost associated with the effort. Such issues add to the somewhat invisible expense associated with remote facilities for the libraries, the users, and the Depository. In addition, these facilities require an extensive level of supervision and an ongoing commitment to maintenance, as well as to continuing improvement of the physical plant and its mechanical systems. The extent to which management monitoring and intervention are necessary is difficult to appreciate in the abstract but constitutes a major preoccupation through various levels of the parent organization.

However complex, the client–owner model does serve to focus the organization on the needs of its client libraries and to set priorities accordingly. While the economics of supporting the Depository's capital and operational costs may be burdensome for client libraries, it also serves to discourage casual use of the storage facility and adds to administrative accountability for the client, owner, and manager. In spite of the many continuing challenges, the efficiencies and long-term benefits of an integrated, environmentally sound, and responsive program for high-density storage are certain.

Notes

1.   B. Graham, "Firmitas, Utilitas, et Frugalitas," in *The Great Divide: Challenges in Remote Storage*, ed. James Kennedy and Gloria Stockton (Chicago: American Library Association, 1991), 29.

2.   The two most recent Assistant Directors of HUL for HD are Thomas Schneiter (since 1999) and Curtis Kendrick (1992–1998). Each has made valuable and unique contributions to the maturation and success of the facility.

3.   No description of the Harvard Depository is complete without reference to its long-time Facility Manager, Ron Lane, whose commitment to quality and ongoing improvements have been key to the Depository's performance record. Moreover, the supervisors, team leaders, and staff of HD are the critical resource in HD's ability to function.

4.   Barbara Graham, Curtis Kendrick, and Joseph Urtz. *The Design and Operation of Off-Site Storage Facilities in Support of Preservation Programs*, ed. Carlo Federici and Paola Munafo, International Conference on Conservation and Restoration of Archival and Library Materials, Erice, April 1996.

3

Milton S. Eisenhower Library of Johns Hopkins University

Deborah Slingluff

Introduction

The Milton S. Eisenhower Library of the Johns Hopkins University opened the Moravia Park Off-Site Shelving Facility in November 1995. The University leased an existing warehouse and renovated a portion of it as one component of a comprehensive space plan to house the Eisenhower Library's collections until 2020. The Eisenhower Library maintains the University's primary research collection and focuses services on students, faculty, and staff affiliated with the Schools of Arts and Sciences, Engineering, and Professional Studies in Business and Education. The Library also serves as a resource for the Schools of Medicine, Public Health, Advanced International Studies, and the Peabody Institute. The current building opened in 1964 and was designed for a collection of 1 million volumes.

During the early 1980s, the Library began to experience space problems. Aisles were narrowed to extend stack ranges, student study space was overtaken for stack space, and the shelves were bulging. Stacks in Gilman Hall, home of the original campus library, were at capacity with 250,000 items. In 1988 the entire Government Publications, Maps and Law Library moved from MSEL to space in the New Engineering Building. Krieger Hall was renovated in 1990 and provided space to move 6,050 linear feet of manuscripts and archival materials, as well as the Preservation Unit from the Eisenhower Library. As a result of these initiatives, the Eisenhower Library entered the 1990s with 1.5 million volumes of its collections shelved in the Library and 0.6 million volumes distributed among various campus spaces. An analysis of collection growth and available space projected that by FY1996 the Library would have exhausted its capacity to

17

improvise solutions to the problem of finding three-fourths mile of additional shelving space every year. The development of a long-term plan for collection growth became an operational necessity.

Space Planning

The Library's management team agreed that there were four key questions to address as the Library began to plan for new space.

♦ Will the library shelve a significant portion of the research collection away from the principal points of service?

♦ How will library services for the sciences be shaped?

♦ Will the Government Publications/Maps/Law department return to the Eisenhower Library?

♦ Will the Special Collections department be consolidated to create a cohesive unit?

Scott Bennett, then Library Director, argued that choices could not be "intelligently framed, usefully debated, or wisely decided without a reliable sense of the differences in costs associated with them."[1] The first step, therefore, was to model costs for various choices. Dr. Bennett charged a task force to provide a "model that states a set of reasonable assumptions about each of the four questions and provides the approximate costs associated with various courses of actions."[2] A short common assumption set was considered basic for all four questions. These assumptions addressed the community served, collection growth, and Special Collections and projected to the year 2020, reflecting the belief that the University should have a 25-year planning horizon for shelving its research collections and not need to confront unplanned shelving needs prior to 2020.

Assumptions about the community

♦ Changes in the faculty and student numbers will have no impact on the resolution of the four key issues.

Assumptions about collection growth

♦ The paper-based research collections will grow at an annual rate of 90 percent of the annual average volume growth rate observed between 1985 and 1990. The paper-based collections in Government Publications will grow at an 85 percent annual rate.

♦ Electronic formats and microform publications outside of Government Publications will grow at the same rate observed between 1985 and 1990. Government Publications in these formats will grow at a 115 percent annual rate.

♦ By 2020, the total shelving capacities of the Eisenhower Library, including its distributed sites, will be 90 percent occupied.

Assumptions about Special Collections

♦ The Special Collections Department of the Eisenhower Library will administer the University Archives.

♦ The George Peabody Library (an off-site collection) will be fully cataloged and weeded, yielding a 150,000-volume permanent collection.

♦ The manuscript collections will grow at 110 percent the rate observed between 1985 and 1990.

With these basic assumptions in place, a set of detailed assumptions was developed to define various possibilities within each of the four key questions. Cost estimates for each assumption included capital costs, the cost of shelving and furniture, and annual operating costs. To facilitate comparison among the choices, costs for each assumption were calculated to the year 2025 and presented as Net Present Value (NPV). Various combinations of assumptions were evaluated to determine Net Present Values for various "packaged" plans.

Decisions

1. Will the library shelve a significant portion of the research collection away from the principal points of service?
   The fundamental choice was between continuing to offer convenient, on-site access to the collection or access that imposes library staff at some level between the researcher and the material needed. Open-stack spaces allow users easy access to materials, contain staff costs since many operations are self-service, and acknowledge that having to wait to receive delivery of requested items may disrupt researchers' work. The principal disadvantage of open-stack design is that it requires more square feet of library space than other alternatives.
   Cost estimates were prepared for a variety of scenarios (see Table 1, page 20). Note the difference in the $7.9 million (NPV) cost to build an offcampus facility and the $23.3 million (NPV) price tag for an open-stack addition to the existing building. This dramatic difference resulted from differences in construction costs but even more so from differences in the operation and maintenance of plant ($14.50 psf on campus compared to $6.00 psf off campus). On a campus where space and dollars for new

buildings are at a premium, and in an educational environment where resources increasingly are distributed, the library indicated a preference for
an open-stack addition to the Eisenhower Library, but acknowledged that it
could make a remote site housing the least used parts of its collections
work well for most researchers. This confidence and the awareness of the
need for the university to invest in other academic programs resulted in the
recommendation to invest in off-campus space for what eventually would
be a major part of its library collections.

Table 1. New Shelving Space Cost Scenarios

MSEL New Shelving Space Cost Scenarios—1991 Arranged in Ascending Net Present Values*	
Smaller remote shelving facility (13,000 sf)	$ 6,076,774
Remote shelving facility—buy/build (27,000 sf)	$ 7,881,645
Remote shelving facility—lease (27,000 sf)	$ 9,216,751
Smaller MSEL addition (29,000 sf)	$12,377,678
Smaller underground shelving facility (18,200 sf)	$12,582,133
Underground shelving facility (33,000 sf)	$14,707,010
MSEL addition (54,000 sf)	$23,254,793

*1991 dollars were used as the base for calculating net present value to provide a basis for
comparing the total cost of each option to FY2025. The net present value rate (8%) and
the interest rate for debt service (7%) were provided by the University Treasurer's Office.
Cost estimates for each assumption included capital costs, the cost of shelving and furniture, and annual operating costs.

The decisions made on questions 2, 3, and 4 depended on the outcome of
question 1, and were made in the context of moving sizable portions of the
MSEL collection off-site.

2. How will library services for the sciences be shaped?
    This long-standing question was analyzed from a cost perspective.
The choice was between maintaining services centralized in the Eisenhower Library and building a new, relatively small science library elsewhere on campus for $13.9 million (NPV). This estimate underscored the
high cost for the convenience that branch libraries unquestionably offer
their users. The decision was made to continue to serve the science community from the Eisenhower Library.

3. Will the Government Publications/Maps/Law department return to the Eisenhower Library?

This question addressed the advisability of closing a branch library, as opposed to creating one. Ultimately, the decision was to integrate conceptually and physically the use of this material with the use of other Eisenhower Library material. It was hoped that this re-integration would save time and be more convenient for researchers. The return of these collections and services to the Eisenhower Library also freed space in the New Engineering Building for use by the School of Engineering.

4. Will the Special Collections department be consolidated to create a cohesive unit?

The Library's special collections and staff associated with them were at three widely spread Baltimore locations: Homewood, Evergreen, and the George Peabody Library. The library administration believed that a coherent special collections department would enrich teaching and research at Hopkins and would attract other uniquely valuable gifts to the University. The recommendation was to create a cohesive department either through construction of new space or the remodeling of the existing Eisenhower Library. Note that although portions of the Eisenhower Library have been renovated, to date, this recommendation has not been realized.

All four key questions involved decisions about library services as well as construction costs. Planning first centered on cost issues, since choices about services would benefit from comparative estimates of capital and operating costs. Other issues not addressed in the initial planning process included the critical need to improve reader accommodations in the Eisenhower Library and the costs of remodeling the existing building. Decisions on these issues affected the final cost of new library space and depended on the decisions made about the four key questions outlined above. To renovate the Eisenhower Library in order to improve the delivery of services, especially electronic information services; increase the number of good quality reader spaces; and maintain on campus a research collection of 1.25 million volumes, required that the Library transfer 450,000 volumes to off-site shelving during the initial year and approximately 40,000 each subsequent year. The Library administration felt confident that it could maintain an effective research strength collection on campus for a few years, but much less confident about the impact after the turn of the century. By not planning for additional space on campus, the Library and the University essentially were gambling on the impact of electronic resources on research activity.

Once the Library determined that a significant portion of its collections would be shelved off-site, the questions became how and where. In addition to the options presented in Table 1, two new options were investigated: digitization and commercial shelving/storage facilities. Based on the costs reported at Cornell for a pilot digitization project[3] a detailed study projected a cost of $2,007,730 to digitize and provide access to 43,000 volumes per year, the annual growth rate of the Eisenhower Library. Considering this high figure, costs were not even calculated for digitizing the initial 450,000 volumes to be moved. Shelving the collection with a commercial vendor at $405,500 per year initially appeared to provide a viable option. Since the University's intention was to eventually own a facility, subsequent cost studies revealed that once the Library retired any debt associated with acquiring its own facility, ownership became significantly more cost-effective. Another detraction of the commercial facility was its physical environment. Established for document-level storage for seven years, it had no climate controls in place and would not be appropriate for long-term shelving of library materials.

Leasing

On July 1, 1994, the University signed a 10-year lease with the option to purchase a 44,000-square-foot warehouse about 7 miles from the Eisenhower Library. At the end of five years, the University could opt to purchase the warehouse at the price of $900,000; at the end of the 10th year, the purchase price would be $750,000. The Eisenhower Library was designated as the lead occupant for the space and all costs for renovating and operating the entire facility were to be charged to the Library's budget. Since the Library planned to renovate the building in phases, beginning with a 14,000-square-foot renovation project, other space in the warehouse was available for use as high-grade storage space for other purposes. The University's real estate office agreed to lead the initiative to secure appropriate tenants for this space, with the approval of the Library and all rental income credited against the Library's budget. All leases included a clause allowing either party to break the lease with 90 days' notice. Note that the Library has maintained the shelving space for the shelving of library collections, and has been resolute in its refusal to store other types of materials in the conditioned space in the warehouse.

As the Library and the University began to come to terms with the decision to lease a warehouse to renovate for the off-site shelving of library collections, the Library investigated the possibility of partners in this initiative. Although Johns Hopkins University intended to manage the facility from the outset, Library staff created informational material and targeted area libraries to assess their interest in shelving materials at an off-site facility. The other separately administered JHU libraries particularly were invited to participate at the planning stages, with the goals of sharing costs and incorporating their requirements into the initial renovation, shelving, and operational plans for the facility. Shared costs would reflect the base cost of leasing the building, the cost of renovating to provide a good environment for materials and staff, and the costs of operating the facility. Reaction to these inquiries was disappointing but not unexpected. Some libraries reported no need for new space, some libraries were getting their own new space, some were using federal space, and for some cost was a concern. Since Eisenhower is one of only two research libraries in Maryland, and the District of Columbia area libraries already were being served by the Washington

Research Library Consortium facility, geographical location became a limiting factor in the possibilities for sharing space in the new facility.

With no prospect for external partners, the Eisenhower Library administrative staff worked with the University to secure funding for the renovation and on-going operations of the off-site facility. The University community shared the Library's goals of minimizing the inconvenience to readers of not finding materials on-site and minimizing the costs involved in selecting, processing, shelving, and servicing the off-site collections. Gift money supported the capital project, funding the first phase of renovations to the facility and including shelving, materials and wiring, moving and shifting costs for 450,000 volumes, as well as start-up staff costs for the first year (see Table 2). Using information gathered from existing facilities at other universities, the Library proposed an ongoing operational budget based on the yearly transfer of 40,000 volumes to the facility and servicing 3 percent of the entire off-site collection for user requests. Table 3, page 24, provides estimated costs for the first full year of operations, plus selected years to FY2003. Note that the savings from rent on the space the Library was occupying in the New Engineering Building begin in FY1998 and significantly decreased the annual operating funding needed to operate the facility in outlying years. Costs were projected through FY2003, at which time the annual operating funding is $108,000. Agreeing that the Library did not have sufficient funding to incorporate these costs into its existing operational budget, University administration added a new line to the Library's budget. This new funding was provided by the traditional sources of the Library's budget, that is, the President's discretionary fund, the Homewood Schools, endowment income and revenue income.

Table 2. Estimated Cost of Project

Estimated Cost of Project—Initial Year (1994 dollars)	
Warehouse renovation	$ 710,000
Shelving and related costs	$ 374,600
Materials and wiring	$ 272,500
Moving and shifting 450,000 volumes	$ 75,000
Start-up staff	$ 358,662
Total Project Costs	**$1,790,762**

Table 3. Estimated Annual Costs

Estimated Annual Costs (1998 dollars)	FY97	FY98	FY01	FY03
Rent	$140,000	$140,000	$140,000	$140,000
Property taxes	$ 22,000	$ 22,000	$ 22,000	$ 22,000
Plant operating & maintenance	$ 60,000	$ 62,000	$ 68,000	$ 72,000
Library operating	$145,000	$151,000	$171,000	$182,000
Internal credits—JHU libraries/archives	$ 8,000	$ 8,000	$ 10,000	$ 10,000
Total Annual Operating	$359,000	$367,000	$391,000	$406,000
Annual Savings and Revenues				
Savings—decreased rent on New Engineering	-0-	$ 99,000	$188,000	$188,000
Rental revenue— Other JHU renters	$ 30,000	$ 40,000	$ 40,000	$ 40,000
Rental revenue— Other	$ 27,000	$ 44,000	$ 70,000	$ 70,000
Total Annual Savings and Revenues	$ 57,000	$183,000	$298,000	$298,000
Annual Operating Funding Needed	**$302,000**	**$184,000**	**$ 93,000**	**$108,000**

Administrative Structure and Staffing

Following this extensive planning effort, the Moravia Park Off-Site Shelving Facility opened in November 1995 for the purpose of shelving and providing easy access to a significant portion of the Library's paper-based collections. Administrative responsibility rests with the Head of Access Services, who worked with a coordinating committee to establish initial policies and procedures. When the facility opened, the committee disbanded with the understanding that staff involved in the various processes would continue to communicate on an as-needed basis (see Figure 1). Material selection decisions are coordinated with the Library's Collection Development Committee; the transfer of materials is managed by Cataloging, Support Services, and Moravia Park staff. Significant budgetary or policy issues are discussed and resolved by the Library's management team, a group representing the administrative heads of the functional units of the library. In some cases, issues also are presented to the Library Advisory Committee for review, discussion, and decision.

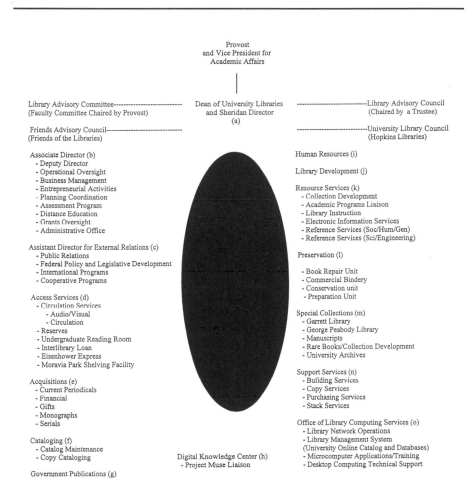

Provost
and Vice President for
Academic Affairs

Library Advisory Committee----------------------------
(Faculty Committee Chaired by Provost)

Dean of University Libraries
and Sheridan Director
(a)

----------------------------Library Advisory Council
(Chaired by a Trustee)

Friends Advisory Council------------------------------
(Friends of the Libraries)

----------------------------University Library Council
(Hopkins Libraries)

Associate Director (b)
 - Deputy Director
 - Operational Oversight
 - Business Management
 - Entrepreneurial Activities
 - Planning Coordination
 - Assessment Program
 - Distance Education
 - Grants Oversight
 - Administrative Office

Assistant Director for External Relations (c)
 - Public Relations
 - Federal Policy and Legislative Development
 - International Programs
 - Cooperative Programs

Access Services (d)
 - Circulation Services
    - Audio/Visual
    - Circulation
 - Reserves
 - Undergraduate Reading Room
 - Interlibrary Loan
 - Eisenhower Express
 - Moravia Park Shelving Facility

Acquisitions (e)
 - Current Periodicals
 - Financial
 - Gifts
 - Monographs
 - Serials

Cataloging (f)
 - Catalog Maintenance
 - Copy Cataloging

Government Publications (g)

Digital Knowledge Center (h)
 - Project Muse Liaison

Human Resources (i)

Library Development (j)

Resource Services (k)
 - Collection Development
 - Academic Programs Liaison
 - Library Instruction
 - Electronic Information Services
 - Reference Services (Soc/Hum/Gen)
 - Reference Services (Sci/Engineering)

Preservation (l)

 - Book Repair Unit
 - Commercial Bindery
 - Conservation unit
 - Preparation Unit

Special Collections (m)
 - Garrett Library
 - George Peabody Library
 - Manuscripts
 - Rare Books/Collection Development
 - University Archives

Support Services (n)
 - Building Services
 - Copy Services
 - Purchasing Services
 - Stack Services

Office of Library Computing Services (o)
 - Library Network Operations
 - Library Management System
 (University Online Catalog and Databases)
 - Microcomputer Applications/Training
 - Desktop Computing Technical Support

Figure 1. Organization Chart

Permanent on-site staff at Moravia Park initially consisted of two staff members, a supervisor, and an assistant. Eight temporary staff worked with them to process the initial year's 450,000 volumes. The two staff members serviced the collection and processed the incoming 40,000 volumes yearly until September 1998, when a permanent part-time assistant was added in order to offer delivery services on weekends.

Services

Services available from the facility were designed to minimize the impact on researchers needing materials housed off-site. For all requesters, article-length material is copied at the facility and delivered at no charge. Delivery options include print, fax, e-mail, and secure Web delivery. Physical materials are delivered to the Eisenhower Library twice daily, Monday through Friday; a single delivery on Saturday and Sunday began in September 1998. In November 1999, direct delivery from the facility to other JHU libraries was instituted as part of the JHU Libraries first coordinated courier service. For researchers desiring to work on-site, a corner of the workroom was designed and designated for public use. Very few people elect this option; it is much more convenient to have materials brought to campus.

Early in the life of the facility, an assumption about use of the shelving space was reexamined. The facility was designed to shelve print materials by size in trays on warehouse shelving 16 feet high. In order to complete the renovation of the Eisenhower Library's Audiovisual Center, a suggestion came forward to shelve a significant portion of the audiovisual (AV) collection at Moravia Park. An analysis of AV usage statistics revealed the least-used portions of this collection and after consultation with staff in cataloging, support services, and at Moravia Park, a proposal was advanced for consideration by the resource services librarians and the Library's management team. The proposal was accepted; sections of the Moravia stacks were reconfigured to house AV cabinets and new services were born. Microform materials are serviced in the same way as print materials, with the same delivery options. When the second bay of the facility is renovated for library use, space will be designed specifically to house AV materials. The current arrangement does not maximize the use of existing space.

Researchers at Hopkins and in the larger academic community are Moravia Park's ultimate customers, and services must be designed to meet their requirements. Feedback from users is gathered informally by the Resource Services Librarians who serve as liaisons to the academic departments, as well as by staff in the Circulation and Interlibrary Services units. The staff at Moravia Park also monitors the requests received for materials and is proactive in the design of new services. While there remain researchers who are unhappy with the decision to move materials off-site, there are seldom complaints about the services rendered from the facility.

CAPM:
Comprehensive Access to Printed Material

As substantial portions of the collection are moved to off-site shelving, it will become a greater challenge to minimize the impact on researchers. The Eisenhower Library is collaborating with the Johns Hopkins Whiting School of Engineering and several international corporations and foundations "to develop efficient (i.e., cost-effective), real-time, enhanced browsing and search capabilities, through a Web browser interface, to off-site materials by using a combination of robotics, automated systems, software and high-speed communication."[4] The Comprehensive Access to Printed Material (CAPM) project plans to provide real-time access to materials shelved at Moravia Park by transmitting scanned images to the researcher's desktop. The project envisions a robot retrieving material from the shelves and delivering it to a scanning station from which it will be delivered to the researcher's desktop. Two models are being considered for the scanning station, one employing robotics and one employing humans to turn pages upon request from the researcher at the desktop. Developers are confident in the technology necessary to support the project.

An economic feasibility study is in progress to inform developers about the market viability of the product. A cost analysis will document the costs of creating the system and project both one-time and ongoing costs for implementation. One-time costs may include reconfiguration of shelving to support robotic retrieval, the robot, page-turner, scanner, and any computer facilities. Ongoing costs include labor, maintenance, and supplies. A benefits survey will poll the potential user communities to assess the expected benefits of CAPM. Following these analyses, developers will have a better understanding of CAPM's viability in the library market.

Costs

The Library carefully monitors the costs for maintaining the Moravia Park facility. From FY1996 through FY1999, actual plant and operational costs have proven to be slightly less than anticipated. Revenues also have been slightly less than anticipated, so total annual operating expenses are slightly higher than budgeted. Data from FY1999 is representative of the first four years of operating the Moravia Park facility (see Tables 4 and 5, page 28). Note the impact that purchasing the facility would have on the budget, once the debt from acquiring the property is retired.

Table 4. Operating Expenditures (Revenue)

Cost Summary FY99	Budget	Revenues/ Expenditures	% of Total Expenditures
Rent	$140,000	$140,000	33%
Property taxes	$ 22,000	$ 22,000	5%
Plant operating & maintenance	$114,200	$104,159	25%
Library operating	$157,800	$157,256	37%
Expense subtotal	**$434,000**	**$423,415**	**100%**
Internal credits— JHU libraries/ archives/tenants	($ 60,000)	($ 61,388)	
Revenue— other tenants	($110,000)	($ 54,661)	
Total Annual Operating	**$264,000**	**$307,366**	

Table 5. Library Operating Expenditures FY99

Library Operating Expenditures FY99	% of total
Staff	83%
Supplies and materials	4%
Telecom & computing	3.1%
Contractual services	9.8%
Repairs & maintenance	0.1%

Purchase and Continuing Renovation

In June 1999, the Library recommended that the University exercise its option to purchase the Moravia Park facility. This decision slightly increased the yearly real estate costs from $162,000 per year to $167,000 per year and will retire real estate costs from the funding model in FY2007.

The Eisenhower Library has continued to offer to provide space for shelving materials from other JHU-affiliated libraries. In March 2000, the Welch Medical Library began the transfer of 90,000 volumes to the facility. Other JHU libraries also have plans to transfer materials to Moravia Park. As a result of these projects and the ongoing transfer of materials from the Eisenhower Library, the first shelving bay will be fully occupied during summer 2001. Plans are underway to renovate the second bay, with occupancy scheduled for July 2001. The $914,000 estimated for this project requires a short-term University loan, to be paid off over a five-year period.

Between the purchase of the warehouse and the renovation of the second bay, the Library is facing significant expenses during FY2000-FY2007. Note that these costs were included in the NPV evaluation that occurred in the early stages of the original planning process. The option of leasing a facility and renovating it as needed allowed the Library to proceed with the shelving of materials off-site at a time when purchasing a facility was not possible. Off-site shelving remains the most cost-efficient way to shelve and service a sizable portion of the Library's collection.

Notes

1. Scott Bennett, "New Library Space," memo to the Johns Hopkins University New Library Space Planning Committee, 19 November 1990, 2.

2. Ibid.

3. See Anne R. Kenney and Lynne K. Personius, "The Cornell/Xerox/Commission on Preservation and Access Joint Study in Digital Preservation . . . Digital Capture, Paper Facsimiles, and Network Access," Cornell University, 1992.

4. Sayeed Choudhury, "A Proposal for Comprehensive Access to Off-Site Library Print Materials," submitted to the Andrew W. Mellon Foundation by the Milton S. Eisenhower Library, The Johns Hopkins University, 11 May 1998. Available: http://dkc.mse.jhu.edu/CAPM

4

Cheaper by the (Almost Half) Dozen
The Ohio State-Wide Remote Storage System

David F. Kohl

Ohio's academic libraries in publicly supported institutions have, for over a decade, been developing a system of remote storage sites as a cost-effective and efficient solution to the problem of increasingly overcrowded library stacks. Presently there are five such sites in Ohio containing over 2 million volumes, a number which continues to grow rapidly. Probably most librarians will be surprised to learn that this remote storage program arose out of the same initiative which called forth OhioLINK. Consistently overshadowed by the spectacular growth and success of OhioLINK, a related initiative originally conceived as just a linking system of automation, the program of remote storage locations has received relatively little attention in the library literature. Nevertheless, it is innovative in design, state-wide in scope, and large in size.

Brief History

By the mid-1980s a pressing need for additional library space had developed on most of the campuses of state-supported higher education in Ohio. As the funding requests for new library facilities on campus after campus mounted so did resistance from the state legislature. The amount of capital money required was more than the legislature was willing to spend. In 1986 an imaginative group of librarians and academics working with the Ohio Board of Regents proposed a creative system of regional storage sites which would allow clusters of libraries in distinct geographic areas of the state to share remote storage space.

These regional storage sites would be linked to their parent institutions and to each other by means of a shared system of library automation. In all, five remote regional storage sites were proposed—essentially, one in each corner of the state and one in the middle. The libraries for all state-supported institutions of higher education would then be assigned to one of the nearby remote storage facilities. Through historical happenstance two institutions ended up with their own facilities—Ohio State University in the center of the state and Ohio University in the southeast corner of the state. (See Table 1 for institutions and facilities.)

Table 1. Depository Partnerships

◆ Northeastern Ohio Cooperative Regional Library Depository

> University of Akron
> Cleveland State University
> Kent State University
> NEOUCOM
> Youngstown State University

◆ Northwest Ohio Regional Book Depository

> Bowling Green State University
> University of Toledo
> Medical College of Ohio

◆ Ohio State University Library Book Depository

> Ohio State University

◆ Southeast Ohio Regional Library Depository

> Ohio University

◆ Southwest Ohio Regional Library Depository (SWORD)

> Miami University
> University of Cincinnati
> Wright State University
> (Central State University)

Even with the additional costs of the linking automation, the obvious savings of constructing 5 storage sites over local library construction in as many as 18 sites represented a powerful incentive. This incentive combined with the determined lobbying of a visionary Vice-Chancellor (later Chancellor) of the Board of Regents, Ms. Elaine Harriston, convinced the legislature to act. In the 1989-90 legislative session the original vision of OhioLINK as a system of remote storage sites was funded.

After a necessary period of planning the various depositories began to come online. The first was the Northeastern Ohio Cooperative Regional Library Depository (March 23, 1994), followed by the Southwest Ohio Regional Depository (September 6, 1994), the Ohio State University Library Book Depository (August 24, 1995), the Northwest Ohio Regional Book Depository (October 10, 1996), and concluding with the Southeast Ohio Regional Library Depository (opening in three staged phases running from January 15, 1996 through November 15, 1997). As of this writing, two of the depositories are almost full (Southwest Ohio and Ohio State) and plans are underway to add additional modules to each of these sites.

Key State-Wide
Depository Features

The first important point about this state-wide system of depositories is the unusual method by which the state has chosen to implement central funding—a mechanism which encourages a considerable degree of local involvement and autonomy. Although local involvement and control represents a philosophical choice made by the Board of Regents, it is powerfully reinforced by the method the state has chosen to disburse the monies underwriting the depositories' construction and operations. This method of disbursement also explains why the system of linking automation could develop almost independently of the depository system, becoming so important in its own right by providing library services and common electronic collections that its original function of simply linking libraries and depositories to each other has been reduced to relative insignificance.

The system of disbursing monies to the local depository projects is both clever and cost effective. Rather than set up a multitude of new offices for financial oversight at the local level, the legislature assigned different institutions of higher education to oversee the expenditure of specific depository funds. The funds for the Southwest depository, for example, were assigned to Miami University and so all expenditures for linking automation must go through Miami's financial offices and conform to Miami's financial procedures for expenditure of state funds. These "institutions of convenience" have no authority over or responsibility for policy choices nor do they have any voice in the purposes for which the money is to be spent. Their only role is to oversee procedural propriety in the expenditure of funds. Each depository library has been assigned an "institution of convenience" which receives a lump sum allocation of monies and which it in turn disburses through a large number of specific accounts to cover the construction and operating costs of the local depositories.

The second characteristic of the depository system is local governance by the associated library directors. While there is great variation in the degree of involvement by each site's library director, his or her role is generally to determine the kind of physical facility desired, establish policies, determine annual budget requests, hire a site manager, and oversee operations of the site. On some of these issues there can be considerable variability among sites. For example, while most directors have chosen to build new facilities on the Harvard model, one group decided to purchase and renovate the building of a used car dealership.

Within each associated library the director makes the final decision on how materials are selected for remote storage and for arranging initial processing of these materials. Each library director also serves on the Library Advisory Council, which is the highest-level library advisory group advising Tom Sanville, OhioLINK Executive Director, on the development and policies of OhioLINK automation. Thus the two related initiatives—the storage sites and the OhioLINK automation—are joined and coordinated by the role of the library directors.

The third characteristic, already mentioned, is the shared nature of the depositories. With the exception of Ohio State University and Ohio University, each depository serves to hold overflow materials from a number of different libraries. How members share depository space is decided by the directors of each depository and is quite varied. For instance, the members of one depository have preassigned all the depository space with each library having its own area, while the members of another depository have simply agreed on the number of volumes each member may send each month and let each institution's volumes be interfiled.

There is another level to this sharing as well. Materials in the depositories are directly available to all OhioLINK members on the same basis as if they were still in their local libraries. In three of the depositories, Central, Southwest and Northwest, material is available via OhioLINK automation and retrieved directly from the depository by the OhioLINK patron; the remaining two depositories, Northeast and Southeast, are still unlinked, requiring requests to be submitted in traditional ways. While linking the depositories into the larger OhioLINK system is a simple and perhaps obvious concept, putting it into practice is logistically complex. Depository software needs to interact smoothly with OhioLINK software while depository records need to retain their original ownership designation, reveal the items' depository location, contain two call numbers (library and depository), and be capable of being accessed and changed in real time (for circulation purposes).

SWORD
(Southwest Ohio Regional Depository)—
History and Features

Although each of the remote storage sites is unique, the Southwest Ohio Regional Depository (SWORD) is, generally speaking, a fairly representative depository to examine in detail. Originally serving as the regional depository for three schools—University of Cincinnati, Miami University (of Ohio), and Wright State University—a fourth school, Central State University, has in recent years been added to the site's storage program. The storage facility is based on the Harvard model and is essentially a three-and-a-half-story cube housing 30-foot-high stacks. Books are retrieved by staff on a mobile, electric cherry picker. Connected to the stacks is a delivery dock and storage area for the cherry picker plus a standard single-story work area.

The stack building includes 8,700 square feet with the site and building designed for adding on three more stack units of the same size. The stacks themselves are arranged in four rows of three-story (30-feet) stacks running 37 sections (about 166 feet) in length. Shelves are adjustable so they can be fine tuned to fit the size of the books being shelved. The on-site workspace for staff includes 6,741 square feet, which includes space for work area (tables, processing and scanning equipment, computers, book trucks, etc.), offices, conference room/scholars study area (for faculty or student use should they choose to work on-site), and a break room with a small canteen area. It also includes a 100-square-foot walk-in freezer for use in the disaster recovery of wet books.

The Middletown campus of Miami University was chosen to house the depository site since it is nearly equidistant from the three original libraries whose materials constitute the depository collection. Planning for the building was begun in 1988 with a two-level team consisting of the library directors from the three schools plus their key administrative assistants. Miami was chosen as the institution of convenience and consequently its director, Judith Sessions, and her administrative assistant, Dick Pettitt, as well as Miami's Facilities staff and their budgetary officers, have carried an extra share of the logistics part of the building burden.

As meetings among the directors and their assistants proceeded, both the California and the Harvard model were discussed. The space limitations of the site as well as the heating and cooling efficiency of the Harvard "cube" were strong arguments for the Harvard model. Subsequent visits to both Harvard and the University of Texas at Austin (which had also selected the Harvard model) convinced the directors that the Harvard model was preferable for Ohio. The year 1993 saw ground broken and in January of the following year, Ms. Sue Berry was hired as the Depository manager. On September 6, 1994 Miami University officially took possession of the building for the state and by October of that year the depository partners were loading materials into the building.

As designed and constructed, the Southwest Ohio Regional Depository has at least three notable architectural features. The first, common to all Harvard model depositories, is the need for what is called a superflat floor. Given the extraordinary height of the stack ranges and the heavy load they carry, it is crucial for their stability that they not lean even slightly. It was necessary not only for the architects to clearly specify this in bidding and construction documents but to emphasize its importance to compliance inspectors. For laymen, superflat means that from end to end and side to side the floor cannot vary in height by even the width of a dime.

The second feature was to purposely omit a sprinkler system. Even with a dry pipe system, the risk of accidentally activating the system was considered too high. The necessary variance from code was allowed for a number of reasons. The principal and underlying reason was that the strict temperature and humidity controls for the stacks area made it essentially an airtight structure. Any fire which got started would tend to suffocate itself. Secondly, tests showed that the local fire department could arrive on-site within a matter of minutes, responding to smoke and heat detectors which were installed. Thirdly, the work area where most of the on-site staff spend most of their time is physically distinct and separate from the stacks area. Fourth, the stack area is not a public area and not even that heavily used by on-site staff. And lastly, all mechanical equipment has been installed external to the stack building; even the cherry picker whose electric batteries are an unlikely but theoretically possible cause of a stack fire is parked outside of the stack area when not in use.

These arguments against automatically and unthinkingly installing a sprinkler system continue to be persuasive today and the new module in the process of being added also does not contain a sprinkler system. The experience at the University of Cincinnati since the original decision was taken has only reinforced concerns about installing a sprinkler system in such a facility. Several years ago a branch library at UC experienced a malfunction of the library sprinkler, causing it to activate although there was no fire, heat or smoke, resulting in considerable damage to the reference collection, equipment, and furniture. Recently another branch library at UC suffered considerable damage when water pipes were accidentally breached during renovation. Clearly, water damage can be at least as significant a problem as fire.

The last significant feature is that the SWORD depository is designed as a modular, add-on building. The site was identified and building designed so as to accommodate up to three more stack buildings. The logic of this approach was based on both cost and efficiency realizations. Once a stack building was filled, being a very low-use storage facility, it should require very little staff time and attention. The belief was that most of the on-site staff time would be used to process material into the collection. Hence the depository need for staff workspace would change very little, if at all, while the need for stack space (given the steady state collection situations of the three primary SWORD libraries) would continue to grow regularly. In short, depository stack space needs would continue to grow annually while on-site workspace should require little change. Hence a design which separates stack space from work area space and which allows subsequent stack areas to take advantage of the already-constructed staff work area, reducing the costs of constructing the next stack module. While the cost effectiveness of this design is already paying off as the SWORD depository has begun to build its second stack module at a significantly lower cost than the original depository building, the logic of a growth differential between storage and work area has become more problematic.

Contrary to expectation, experience to date indicates that almost half of the on-site staff time on average is taken up with circulation duties—much of it involving article delivery. As the second stack module fills, this could lead to a problem of an undersized work area if circulation needs increase proportionally. Still, as selectors learn to do a better job of identifying ultra low-use materials and particularly as journal back runs are increasingly available electronically, the ratio of time spent by on-site staff in circulation, as opposed to processing, activity should decrease. The jury is still out.

SWORD—
Policies and Procedures

As indicated earlier, the selection and preliminary processing of materials is initiated by the participating libraries within broad categories. For example, by common agreement among the directors, so far only print materials have been shipped to storage. The reason has been twofold: (1) print materials represent our most pressing storage problem; and (2) it is much more efficient for staff to concentrate on only processing one kind of material. No media materials have been sent to storage and only recently have the directors been considering allowing microforms to constitute part of the depository collection.

In terms of processing, staff at the local site check the individual item physically and against the local OPAC record to make sure information is correct and up-to-date and that the item has been correctly marked. While most materials are in good order, it is surprising how many items need corrections of one type or another. Creating an item record is one of the most common tasks required—hardly surprising given that many of these volumes have not circulated in decades. Quantities within shipments and shipment dates from the various libraries are coordinated on an ongoing basis by the depository manager to ensure a steady, rather than erratic, on-site processing flow. Basic decisions about how many volumes each library can ship are determined by the library directors acting in consort and reviewed annually.

At the storage site the books are graded into one of five size categories, since all materials are shelved by size rather than call number order. When the new stack module comes online, it will be possible to implement a more sophisticated grading system using ten size categories. Once graded, the item is then assigned to a bin of similarly sized items. At this point each item is given a new bar code (an additional depository bar code) and its item record is changed to indicate depository status. The bibliographic record is not changed and so still shows the original ownership. In short, the item displays as still a locally owned item but now as in a new location—as if it had been moved to a branch library named depository. The new bar code functions as a new call number associating bibliographic and item information with a precise stacks, that is, bin, location.

Critical to making shelving by size both feasible and cost-effective is special software currently used in three of the five sites. Not only does this software allow the depositories using it to link to their depository partners' OhioLINK OPAC records to indicate the item level location change (and checkout if and when that occurs), but it also puts in order depository items requested for circulation so that the pick list is the most efficient way for staff retrievers to move through the stacks. This preorganized pick list is not a trivial item in saving staff retrieval time given the wide dispersion of the materials and the stately, rather than rapid, ascension required by the cherry picker lift cage to rise 30 feet in the air to retrieve items from top shelves.

An area of considerable, and justifiable, operational paranoia are the data tapes recording the new bar code/call number assigned storage items. It is not considered sufficient that this information exist only in active computer storage and even the processing tapes are backed up twice a day. To lose the record associating the location with the item record would be a disaster when all the materials are shelved by size. If these records were ever lost or scrambled, there would be no way at all to find any given item other than searching through all 1 million items one at a time. In the usual shelving arrangement by classification, the stack order functions as a kind of rough organizational fall back should the OPAC record be lost or destroyed. When books are shelved by size, there is no fall back. Everything depends on having a location record.

Once materials have been relocated to the depository, there are three ways in which patrons may access them. All start with use of the OPAC to determine the item's location and require a request for the on-site staff to retrieve the item. For books, the patron may use the OPAC to directly request delivery of the desired item to his or her local library online 24 hours a day, 7 days a week. During the week items are routinely delivered within 48 hours; over weekends and holidays there is a longer delay since the depository is not staffed then. If large runs of materials (either books or journals) are needed for relatively brief perusal, it is also possible for faculty or students to arrange to go to the depository itself and use the work room there. This was an important option in principle, but it is only moderately exercised in practice. Around five to six faculty a year will actually take the time to drive out to the depository and use the materials there. Without a compelling reason, it appears to be much more convenient to have the materials shipped to one's local library.

The third method is access to individual journal articles. Unfortunately but as is usual in most libraries, the OhioLINK OPAC at both the central and the local level does not provide cataloging for individual journal articles. A journal title is cataloged, but not its articles. A citation to volume, number, and page is required. Sadly, experience has taught us that faculty and students cannot be counted upon to reliably provide correct citations. Consequently, all requests for articles from journals at the depository must first be reviewed by a librarian who verifies the citation. Then the request is forwarded on to the depository where the appropriate journal is retrieved and either photocopied or scanned into a PDF file. In the latter case a URL is sent to the local library which either prints off the article for the patron and informs him or her of its availability or forwards the URL on to the requesting patron to be read or printed off. There is considerable interest in expanding the process of sending URLs directly to patrons, but so far logistical complications do not always make direct receipt of a URL the best delivery method.

A considerable volume of work is handled by fairly few staff. Locally, at the partner libraries, no more than one FTE with some student help suffices to send the materials out. At the depository there is a staff of 5.5 FTE (0.5 of which is janitorial) who also double as retrieval staff. Just less than half of the staff time is spent on retrieval with the remainder used for processing. On average, staff process around 9,000 volumes a month into storage. Since the opening nearly 1 million volumes (996,098 as of March 31, 2000) have been moved to the depository. Present projections indicate that its capacity will be saturated at around 1.1 to 1.2 million volumes—a point which will be reached sometime early in the next academic year. A new stack module has been constructed and began accepting materials in December 2000—a fortuitous transition due as much to luck as to planning and hard work.

SWORD—Budgets

As with all such facilities, there are two main budgets: operating and capital. Operating budgets are submitted, negotiated and approved annually, while capital budgets are submitted as need requires. In FY1999-2000 the SWORD operating budget was $387,000 and was based on the needs associated with operating a single storage module. The principal element in the operating budget is staff salaries but it also includes heating, light, supplies, insurance, security, telecommunications (including rent on a T1 line), maintenance, equipment, and staff development. Historically, these budgets have generally increased annually at about the rate of inflation, approximately 5 percent per year. The FY2000-2001 operating budget jumps to $437,000 (requested but not yet approved), due to the need to operate the new module as well as the original module.

The capital budget for constructing the original module was just under $2.6 million and included all the costs of construction, that is, planning costs, architects' fees, site development, and actual construction. The costs of the new module are slightly less, even with the costs of general inflation due to a later time period and a particularly tight construction market in Ohio—$2.25 million. The savings come largely from the fact that the staff work area and dock constructed with the original module will generally suffice to serve the new module as well.

Problems—Real and Phantom

As the SWORD depository was planned, a number of concerns were anticipated. Some came to pass, some evaporated, and some we chose to ignore.

1. *On-site use of the depository facility.* There was considerable concern from one of the SWORD directors in particular that faculty and students from the universities would want to make extensive on-site use of the storage facility. Although this did not seem as likely to the other directors, it was felt to be important to accommodate such potential use. As has already been mentioned, only very modest use has been made of this option. Having an on-site patron work area proved to be much more helpful in selling the idea of remote storage to faculty than it has proved needed in practice. The value of such a selling point, however, should not be underestimated.

2. *Faculty reluctance to see materials moved to a remote storage site.* This is an issue which has still not completely gone away, particularly in the Humanities where the library is seen as the scholar's laboratory. Of considerable assistance was the state mandate that no new library buildings would be built. Such a state policy helped lend an inevitability to the process of moving materials to a remote storage location. Also helpful were the outstanding storage conditions which the site provided in terms of light, temperature, and humidity control. (Of course, there was also a kind of irony in making this point since our least used and, to a certain extent, least important materials were being stored in environmental conditions which were significantly better than the conditions in many of the local libraries where more highly used and possibly more valuable material was being kept.)

   Additional selling points for the depository involved pointing out that the purchase of JSTOR and other electronic journal back runs made maintaining back print runs of such journals on campus increasingly unnecessary; investing much hard work in making sure that retrievals from the storage facility met the 48-hour turnaround consistently and reliably; and, if push came to shove, allowing faculty to have items returned permanently to the local library if they felt strongly that a mistake had been made. Additionally, ongoing acceptance of remote storage has been enhanced by the success of Ohio-LINK patron-initiated online borrowing. At the University of Cincinnati, for example, over 20 percent of the circulations now involve other OhioLINK libraries. When such high use is being made of other library collections, it is increasingly difficult to get upset about using yet another remote location.

3. *Duplication of stored materials at the storage site.* This is a potential problem at the site level, the state level, and at the national level. At the site level duplication is an issue only when a storage site serves multiple institutions and more than one institution wishes to store copies of the same item. The most likely situation where such duplication occurs is the storage of back runs of a serial such as a common reference annual (e.g. *BIP*, *Encyclopedia of Associations*) or a journal back run (e.g., a JSTOR title). While there are always instances where duplication is desirable, there is a serious question of how many copies are needed for many of these items. This same problem arises on a state-wide level and, as remote storage sites proliferate around the nation, there is even a national issue. In this last case, the matter is further complicated by the existence of CRL and what appropriate role it could and should play in reducing unnecessary storage duplication. Clearly, the question of unnecessary duplication of stored materials is affected by the importance of collection statistics, the reluctance of faculty to see "their" materials withdrawn, and genuine uncertainty as to what constitutes unnecessary duplication in any particular instance.

The problem has not been solved at SWORD nor even in the state of Ohio and certainly not at the national level. For the present it is easier to find the money to build additional storage capacity than to deal with the thorny political question of what constitutes unnecessary duplication and whose materials should be discarded.

4.   *Reversing remote storage decisions.* As the SWORD directors began preparing to move materials to remote storage, there was some concern about how much material it would be necessary to return to local sites. While not a major problem there turned out to be more justification for worry than anticipated due to two main factors. In the first case, no matter how much consultation selectors and local collection development people undertook with faculty, there continued to be faculty who changed their minds about particular materials, who were on sabbatical when the decision for remote storage was made, or who just didn't seem to realize what was happening until after it had happened. Although a very, very small percentage of the total, some material did have to be returned to the local collections. As is often the case in academe, no decision is forever.

The second factor, almost completely unanticipated, was the difficulty in reusing remote storage space freed up by returning material to the local collection. While such spaces are filled with new materials, it is a difficult and time-consuming process to match up large numbers of small spaces which can only accommodate specifically sized materials. Fortunately, with experience and increasing acceptance of the remote storage concept, return of materials to the local collection seems to have become much less of an issue than in the early days.

5.   *Article delivery from remote storage.* From the beginning this was seen both as a critical issue and as an Achilles' heel for the remote storage concept. While books have individual bibliographic and item records in the OPAC so that a patron-initiated request can easily retrieve exactly the intended item, this is not the case for requests for individual articles. Articles require citations and, as noted earlier, even from faculty they have proved to be notoriously error-prone. The solution is library staff mediation at the local institution to check the citations for accuracy. There is also additional staff mediation required at the depository end. Rather than just retrieving an object, performing a quick circulation action of several seconds, and tossing it into a delivery bag, an article must be looked up, photocopied or scanned, and then sent on its way. It is a more time-consuming and complex transaction, especially when delivered electronically.

While there may be a few tweaks and twists still possible to simplify and accelerate delivery of articles from the depository, increasingly the solution seems to lie in making the need for article delivery from print articles very rare. In other words, delivery of print-based journal articles is inherently inefficient and slow, and the real solution is to bypass print articles altogether. To this end, the SWORD directors, as well as many of the other OhioLINK directors, are focusing their energies and resources on increasing access to electronic journals and serials. Already OhioLINK provides almost 3,000 journal titles in fulltext electronic format, including back runs of various lengths, from all the major commercial publishers. And many of the Ohio libraries are supplementing this significant electronic base with such electronic back run approaches as JSTOR, HarpWeek, etc. Ultimately, the value of the print back runs will be simply as backup to electronic versions of the articles and the actual use of print articles to make and delivery copies should be extremely rare.

Conclusion

In many ways remote storage is both the logical conclusion to the huge collection growth of American academic libraries after World War II as well as part of the astonishing digital revolution American libraries are undergoing. While Fremont Rider[1] was wrong about the details of technology and growth rate, he was right about the problem. How does a research library efficiently and cost-effectively store, not just large, but huge, collections? But housing such collections alone is not sufficient; the materials so housed must also be intellectually accessible. Only modern digital technology makes this possible in any broad-based and cost-effective way. Curiously then, for academic libraries, the Ohio remote storage sites joined by OhioLINK automation represent a symbolic connection between the successful growth of the past and the power of a promising digital future.

Notes

1. Fremont Rider, *The Scholar and the Future of the Research Library: A Problem and Its Solution* (New York: Hadham Press, 1944); see also, Fremont Rider, *Compact Book Storage: Some Suggestions Toward a New Methodology for the Shelving of Less Used Research Materials* (New York: Hadham Press, 1949).

5

The Washington Research Library Consortium (WRLC)
Off-Site Storage in a Voluntary Regional Consortium

Lizanne Payne

Origins and Current Status

The Washington Research Library Consortium (WRLC) was established in the late 1980s to support the library resource-sharing programs of seven universities in the Washington, D.C. area: American University, The Catholic University of America, Gallaudet University, George Mason University, The George Washington University, Marymount University, and The University of the District of Columbia. WRLC operates several major programs for the member libraries: a digital library system including a shared library catalog, consortial database licensing, off-site book storage, and an intercampus delivery service to support reciprocal borrowing.

WRLC is a voluntary association among nonaffiliated, mostly private universities, defined by a contractual agreement that specifies the programs to be offered and the members' financial responsibilities. The fact that participation in WRLC is ultimately voluntary (rather than directed by a higher-level government jurisdiction, for instance) affects all aspects of governance, policy-making, and funding models.

WRLC grew out of a long-standing reciprocal borrowing relationship that has existed among the member libraries since the 1960s. Their desire to develop programs of broader scope including a shared library automation system and a shared off-site storage facility led to the establishment of the WRLC not-for-profit corporation in 1987 to implement and operate these programs. The shared library system subsequently began operation in 1990, and the off-site storage program was initiated in spring 1994 upon completion of the multiuse WRLC facility.

The WRLC building, which totals about 33,000 square feet, includes the computing center and consortium staff space as well as the off-site storage facility. The storage section consists of a high-density Harvard-model storage module of almost 12,000 square feet, with a total of 9,900 shelves. A processing area of approximately 6,000 square feet provides room for sorting and accessioning, a staging area for large shipments awaiting processing, catalogers' workstations for projects requiring more substantial data entry, and a small reading room for on-site review of stored items. There is expansion room on the site for an additional 24,000 square feet of high-density storage space, for a total of about 36,000 square feet of storage if fully built out. The original module contains a little over 600,000 items filling over 5,000 shelves. When filled to capacity, this storage module can contain approximately 1.1 million items (volumes and boxes).

Characteristics of
WRLC Storage Operations

A key characteristic of WRLC's storage facility is that it is treated as a single shared collection: stored items from different member libraries are intermixed on the shelves and sometimes even within the same storage tray. Member library materials are not physically segregated into separate shelving areas, nor are libraries allocated a certain number of shelves. This approach works well in the WRLC environment because the member libraries had already been sharing an online catalog for a number of years, so library staff and patrons were already accustomed to the idea of a shared collection.

Inventory control is handled through the shared library catalog system (first NOTIS, now Endeavor Voyager). The majority of library materials transferred to off-site storage are already represented by a bibliographic record in the shared catalog and most even have a bar code label linked to an item-level record. Thus it was not considered necessary to implement a separate stand-alone inventory control system. The WRLC storage facility is treated as another library branch location (the "WRLC Center"), and information about the owning library remains in the bibliographic and holdings record. Accessions staff record the item's assigned tray in an item-level note, and also charge the item to the tray as a kind of pseudo-patron (the trays are pre-assigned to a specific row and shelf, based on size). Because the inventory control information was recorded in standard fields, there was no additional conversion necessary when WRLC migrated from NOTIS to Voyager in 1997.

WRLC staff have developed a variety of reports and database queries to provide data validation and usage reports, including:

♦ a report to compare each item's shelf location and charge information to ensure that the tray numbers recorded there are the same;

♦ Web-accessible reports showing current storage totals by owning library; and

♦ monthly storage activity by owning library to support billing.

Patrons and library staff initiate direct online requests for stored volumes using the shared catalog system (with enhancements developed by WRLC staff). WRLC delivers requested items the next business day (Monday through Friday) using its delivery service, which also transfers interlibrary loan items among the member libraries. However, the majority of storage retrievals (about 75 percent) are for document delivery of articles within bound journals, which are delivered (usually) the same day via ARIEL. WRLC staff are working on a capability to provide requested articles through validated patron access to a secure Web site. WRLC retrieves approximately 3,200 volumes and performs almost 10,000 document deliveries per year (on the current base of about 600,000 items, this is a retrieval rate of approximately 2.2 percent). In practice the retrievals follow the academic year cycle, totaling 75 to 100 items per day during peak times of the semester.

Usage Policies

WRLC's storage usage policies are driven largely by the voluntary nature of WRLC participation and the integrated nature of WRLC programs. The primary goal when the storage program was initiated was to encourage use of the facility and to free campus library space as determined by each institution. The key policies that resulted are:

♦ Use of the storage facility is "first-come, first-served." There is no upper limit or minimum quota for individual member libraries using the off-site storage facility.

♦ Each library may use its own criteria to select materials for WRLC storage. There is no common or mandated set of selection criteria.

♦ There is no prohibition against storing duplicate materials at WRLC (at this time).

♦ Eligible borrowers from any WRLC member institution may use stored library materials belonging to any other WRLC member library (just as they may borrow from the campus collections). Most items are delivered directly to the requesting patron's library, although the depositing library can indicate more restricted uses for certain items or collections.

♦ Libraries that restore stored items to the campus collection are responsible for correcting the shared OPAC record to eliminate the storage location data.

♦ Member libraries may also store uncataloged materials or materials that are not available for use by other WRLC libraries, but the libraries pay extra for such storage. The universities also may store nonlibrary materials on a cost-recovery basis. In other words, preference is given to library materials, but the participating universities may also use the facility for university records or other institutional storage needs.

♦ Libraries that are not members of WRLC may store library materials on a space-available basis. Nonmember materials are not intermixed on shelves with WRLC library materials, and inventory control is maintained using a separate database (but the same software package), not connected to the WRLC libraries' catalog. WRLC currently has off-site storage contracts with four nonmember libraries.

Storage policies are determined by the WRLC library directors with input from standing advisory committees of library staff and WRLC consortium staff. There is no explicit advisory committee especially for off-site storage, rather the policies are discussed within the context of access services, reference, cooperative collection development, and others as appropriate. Policies that might have a substantial financial impact are referred along with the proposed budget to the WRLC Board of Directors (composed primarily of the university presidents).

Operating Costs

Expenditure categories for any book storage operation include:

♦ Fixed operating costs related to the building, equipment, and administration, and

♦ Variable costs resulting from specific operational activities such as accessioning, retrieval and refile, and delivery.

For the off-site storage program, WRLC employs one FTE to supervise operations and retrieve requested items, and one FTE to support a baseline level of accessioning of approximately 1,000 volumes per week. (These staff are part of the total 18 FTE supporting all WRLC programs, primarily the digital library system.) For large accessioning projects, WRLC supplements this staff with contract temporary employees as needed. This is the most efficient way to provide staff for the fairly unpredictable cycle of storage deposits.

Operating costs for the WRLC storage facility total about $400,000 annually. This includes the storage supervisor (1 FTE), other direct costs (such as maintenance of the order picker and photocopying), and indirect costs (the storage program's prorated share of WRLC's overall building operations, information technology, and administration costs). It is important to note again that WRLC's off-site storage service is part of an integrated set of programs provided to the member libraries. While it is possible to identify some expenditures that are incurred specifically for the storage program or for individual member libraries, others are shared with other services. For instance, the storage facility is administered by staff who also oversee other programs; uses the shared library automation system for inventory control; employs the delivery service which also supports the libraries' interlibrary lending activities; and accounts for approximately one-half of the WRLC physical plant and therefore shares building operations expenses with other activities.

The annual per-item storage cost to the WRLC member libraries currently equals approximately $0.66 per item per year (with the facility at about half capacity). Once the storage facility is filled to full capacity, the continuing per-item cost of storage would be reduced to approximately $0.36 per item per year.

Funding Model

All WRLC members share the fixed operating costs of the storage facility through the annual WRLC membership fee (computed by a formula), which entitles members to use the facility for storage of library materials and to request retrieval and delivery of stored items at no additional cost. That is, there is no explicit per-shelf rental fee or retrieval/delivery fee for library materials stored by WRLC members.

The variable costs for activities associated with individual depositing libraries (shipping costs to move materials to the facility in bulk and accessioning costs for handling and inventory control) are paid directly by each library on a cost-recovery basis. Because the quantity and timing of storage deposits are determined by the depositing library, it wouldn't be equitable to share those costs among all members through the member fee formula.

The labor costs have been converted into a per-item accessioning fee (which also includes an estimated per-item share of the supplies required). The fees currently are $0.50 per volume for items already in the shared OPAC, $1.10 if the item record must be added, and $1.75 per box. These are direct cost-recovery fees, because the member libraries are already paying for other related expenses such as administration and the inventory control system through their WRLC membership fees as described above. Nonmember libraries pay contracted rates for shelf rental, accessioning, retrieval and delivery, at a level calculated to recover related indirect costs as well as direct and variable costs.

Future Issues

Now that the WRLC storage facility has been in operation for several years, some of the initial policies are being reviewed in light of the fact that the facility is half full. WRLC has begun to consider the necessity of expanding the facility within the next five years or so. The $4.6 million cost of constructing the original facility was funded by a Graduate Academic Facilities grant from the U.S. Department of Education; the land (3.3 acres) was donated by Prince George's County, Maryland. There is no explicit mechanism in place for funding a building expansion. At the appropriate point in the future, a capital budget will be prepared and a financing plan negotiated among all or some of the members.

In the meantime, of course, WRLC wishes to maximize use of the remaining space. Some of the policies that were instituted to encourage use of the facility within the context of a voluntary consortium are having a noticeable impact on storage capacity. Some of the specific issues are:

♦ Acceptance of duplicates

♦ Proportion of boxes to book volumes

♦ Unlimited storage rights

Duplicates

WRLC has not prohibited duplicates up to now, in order to allow each member library to free up campus library space expeditiously as defined by that library. Before simply prohibiting duplicates, however, the sharing libraries must resolve some related issues so that all members can still reap the benefit of the storage facility. All member libraries, not just the first depositor, must be able to regain shelf space by weeding their local copies with guaranteed access to the stored copy. The WRLC member libraries have begun to look into the implications of instituting a "shared last copy" policy for bound journals, to specify explicit long-term ownership and access rights.

Proportion of Boxes to Book Volumes

WRLC libraries may store archival boxes (such as for special collections) for no rental fee (i.e., covered under the membership fee) as long as the material is made available to other member libraries. (There is an extra accessioning fee for boxes, however.) However, archival boxes result in low-density storage (8 archival boxes to a shelf compared to about 150 volumes to a shelf) and thus use up a disproportionate amount of space in the facility. Within the WRLC facility at the present time, boxes represent about 3 percent of all stored items but use about 35 percent of in-use shelves. WRLC libraries are considering the implications of allowing "free" storage for boxes; the policy may be changed, or reaffirmed—the archival boxes need to be stored somewhere, after all, and the storage facility is more cost-efficient than the main library for this purpose.

Unlimited Storage Rights

Again as part of the policy to encourage use of the facility and to expedite freeing of campus library space, storage at the WRLC facility is offered to member libraries on a first-come, first-served basis. Libraries pay through the formula-based WRLC membership fee for a theoretically unlimited right to space in the facility, and pay direct costs of accessioning and other variable costs. In practice, a small number of libraries have been able to take full advantage of the facility, while others have been less able to exploit it. While the member fee formula is designed to be equitable, the current formula doesn't account for differential storage usage among the members. On the other hand, the existence of the storage facility facilitates the availability of the stored materials even for the nonowning libraries, and thus provides a benefit to them.

WRLC's storage facility has evolved out of its introductory phase into operational maturity, and, like most library storage facilities, it is increasingly perceived as a critical element in the libraries' collection management strategies. It is particularly important in a voluntary consortium like WRLC to revisit from time to time the goals and policies that govern the partnership. The operating policies that have governed usage of the WRLC storage facility may be modified or they may be reaffirmed, but in any case they will be determined through the cooperative processes of a long-term resource-sharing relationship among the member libraries.

6

The Library of Congress

Steven J. Herman

In early calendar 2001, the Library of Congress will occupy its first off-site high-density collections storage facility, specifically designed and built as a collections storage facility. This facility is modular in design and the first building will hold approximately 2 million books. The Library's master plan calls for a complex of 13 storage modules plus a logistics warehouse and a copyright deposit building to be built as needed over a 50-year period to meet the space needs of the Library's collections and other Library activities.[1] The Fort Meade book storage modules will enable the Library to: provide an efficient method to store lesser-used collections; ensure efficient and timely retrieval of requested items; vacate leased collections storage space; and provide an environment to ensure the long-term preservation of the collections stored there. The Library of Congress is also actively developing a separate off-site facility to store its audiovisual collections at a separate location in Culpeper, Virginia. This paper addresses only the Fort Meade facility.

Although this article has been prepared prior to its opening, and some operational details have yet to be resolved, the history and planning the Library experienced in the interim may be of interest to other librarians who are considering off-site storage facilities.

To understand how the Library of Congress is resolving its collections storage problems, it is instructive to understand its role within the Legislative Branch, and the history of space shortages and how they have been resolved.

Each fiscal year, the Library submits a budget to Congress that is reviewed by the Legislative Branch Subcommittees. The Library is overseen by the Joint Committee on the Library, which has responsibility for approving major new policies and initiatives proposed by the Library. The Library also works closely with the Office of the Architect of the Capitol (AOC), which is responsible for the overall infrastructure of the Congress, including the buildings of the Library of Congress. All plans relating to Library buildings, including new construction, require the cooperation of the Congress, the Library, and the AOC.

The Library of Congress celebrated its 200th birthday on April 24, 2000. On that date in 1800, President John Adams approved legislation that appropriated $5,000 to purchase "such books as may be necessary for the use of Congress." The first books, ordered from London, arrived in 1801 and were stored in the U.S. Capitol, the Library's first home. The collection consisted of 740 volumes and three maps.[2]

Today, the Library of Congress is the largest library in the world, with nearly 119 million items on approximately 530 miles of bookshelves. The collections include some 18 million books, 2 million recordings, 12 million photographs, 4 million maps, and 53 million manuscripts. It occupies 2.75 million square feet of space on Capitol Hill in three buildings and an additional 395,000 square feet of space in leased facilities in the District of Columbia, Maryland, Ohio, Pennsylvania, and Virginia.[3] Every year approximately 300,000 items are added to its book collections alone. The nonbook, special format collections, for example, manuscripts, maps, audiovisual material, are also growing rapidly.

The first major storage crisis began in 1870 when, at the urging of Librarian Ainsworth Spofford, Congress amended the Copyright Law and centralized all registration and deposit activities at the Library of Congress. Within a few years the corridors of the U.S. Capitol were filled with books, maps, and works of art. A year later Spofford proposed that a separate building for the Library be built. After much debate and planning over the next 15 years, Congress approved the building, and by the end of 1897, what is now known as the Thomas Jefferson Building opened.[4] Approximate capacity for this new facility is 1.6 million items.

Plans for the new Library of Congress building envisioned that it would be large enough to accommodate acquisitions for the entire 20th century. "The Librarian of Congress a century hence will not find himself cramped in the least," noted *The Washington Star* on July 14, 1894, in the midst of construction of the building.[5] But cramped it became in only 10 years.

In 1907 Bernard Green, Superintendent of the Library Building, noted a "geometrical progression" in the growth of the collections. In 1908 Congress appropriated $320,000 to add additional stack space for books by filling in the southeast courtyard of the Jefferson Building. Approximate additional capacity, is 1.5 million items.

The collections' geometrical progression continued, and in 1925 the first appropriation for construction of a second stack area in the northeast courtyard was approved by Congress. Approximate additional capacity, is 1.7 million items.

Even with this new stack area, Librarian Herbert Putnam warned in 1926 that additional space would be needed within a decade. In June 1930 Congress appropriated $6.5 million for the construction of an annex building, now called the John Adams Building, behind the Jefferson Building.[6] The John Adams Building was completed in 1938 and was designed primarily as a collections storage facility. The approximate capacity of Adams is 11.5 million items.

In 1959 Librarian L. Quincy Mumford noted the need for a third building. During the 1960s the space-shortage problems had become so acute that the Library began to move some of its operations and collections off of Capitol Hill into leased facilities that were never intended to house library materials. The 1969 *Annual Report of the Library of Congress* noted, "The shortage of usable space within the Library's two principal buildings and the fragmentation of activities by the removal of more and more operations to outside locations affected staff operations, Library services, and the storage and preservation of the Library collections and materials."[7] Between the years of 1964 and 1969, the Library leased 11 facilities for its operations and collections. In 1980, the James Madison Memorial Building opened, and space shortages for the collections were relieved, but were far from resolved.

In its FY1989 budget request to Congress, the Library asked for additional space for its collections noting that both the general collections and special collections would approach gridlock in just a few years. Gridlock in this context means that the shelves are filled to capacity.[8] From a collections management perspective, shelf space at 85 percent capacity is defined as functionally full and shelf space at 90 percent equals gridlock. Space needs in the 1980s and early 1990s increased rapidly as the book collections continued to grow by more than 300,000 items annually, the special collections also continued their rapid growth, major renovation/restoration work of the Thomas Jefferson and John Adams buildings impacted on storage space, and the Library established a high-priority arrearage reduction initiative to reduce the backlog of unprocessed materials. A major problem with gridlock is that the Library must resort to shifting collections to make space for new acquisitions. This is both costly and time consuming, and is not an efficient use of staff resources. Constructing a fourth building on Capitol Hill was not an alternative due to the lack of available space. Therefore, a site away from Capitol Hill was explored. To ensure proper planning for an off-site facility was done in a timely manner, a Library-wide Collections Storage Facility Working Project Team was formed consisting of staff involved with collections management, acquisitions, collections development, and public service. This Team addressed issues including material selection, automation support, reader services, logistics and transportation, physical facilities, and inventory control. The team's mission was to identify, plan, and coordinate actions necessary to establish the facility, place it into normal operation, and provide direct and indirect service to readers. It detailed procedures for establishing and operating the facility, and determining the specific requirements for resources of all types. The team also was to perfect the criteria and procedures for selecting materials for movement to the new site. The team was to establish the Facility and coordinate its early operations, and was to be dissolved when it was in full and successful operation. Its management was to be assumed by a designated organization within the Library. After issuing its report, the Collections Storage Facility Working Project Team disbanded and was replaced by a smaller management committee long before the planning was finally completed.

To assist in finding the best storage solutions, Library staff has consulted with librarians and archivists throughout the world and has visited major off-site library collections storage facilities, including the Harvard Depository, Inc., in Southborough, Massachusetts; the California State University in Northridge; as well as the British Library; New York Public Library; National Agricultural Library; and the National Archives complex in College Park, Maryland.

During the early phase, the Project Team established criteria for the new facility that included: a location within an hour of Capitol Hill so that materials could be retrieved and delivered rapidly; proximity to public transportation, on the assumption that a public reading room would be included; capacity of 3 million volumes; design to maximize storage capacity; and HVAC equipment designed to ensure preservation of the collections. The Facility also needed to be designed to meet the Library's fire safety objectives for a collections storage area, and achieve a level of security equal with that of the collections on Capitol Hill. Also needed were loading dock facilities and transportation systems to retrieve and deliver materials to Capitol Hill.

The two most critical decisions needed in the early phase were site selection and facility type selection. From 1989 to 1993, the Library, the Architect of the Capitol, and Congress considered a number of sites. As stated earlier, a key criterion for a site was that it had to be in the Washington metropolitan area in order that materials could be retrieved in a timely manner. The early plans included the possibility of a small reading room for patrons; therefore, the facility needed to be near public transportation.

At the time of the original request, Congress was also considering an off-site storage facility for the Senate, House of Representatives, and other Legislative Branch agencies. As a result, the Library's acute space needs were folded into a Legislative Branch long-term storage strategic plan. A search began to find an area that would be suitable for both. Several locations were considered. In fall 1993, Public Law 103-110 was passed authorizing the U.S. Army to transfer 100 acres located at Fort George G. Meade (Fort Meade) to the Architect of the Capitol for purposes of satisfying long-term storage needs of the Library of Congress and other Legislative Branch agencies. According to the agreement the Library was to use 33 acres. Fort Meade is located approximately 25 miles north of Capitol Hill in Anne Arundel County, Maryland, adjacent to the National Security Agency. The site met the needs of the Library in that it is large enough to accommodate expansion, and would be able to ensure twice-daily deliveries of materials to Capitol Hill. Locating the facility at this site, however, eliminated the possibility of having a public reading room because it is still an active Army defense site.

The Library's goal has always been to maximize the capacity of the storage facility by adopting an efficient collections storage configuration. After exploring a number of options, the Library decided upon the Harvard-style model of the Harvard Depository that serves the Harvard University libraries. This model has been used by a number of other libraries throughout the country. Many of the design features of the Harvard model, including the high-density shelving, high-level environmental controls, and the ability to retrieve materials in a timely manner, met the Library's criteria for its own facility.

Once the model was agreed upon, Library specialists began to analyze the specific needs of the Library of Congress, including the nature of materials to be stored, estimated number of daily additions and retrievals, shelving, boxing of materials, security issues, and technician-level reference services, including photocopying and faxing. For facility design, bidding was conducted by the

Architect of the Capitol and the design work was awarded to the architectural firm of Dewberry & Davis.

The Library adopted a multiphased approach for construction and occupancy at Fort Meade. The scope and size of Phase 1 was determined in large part by budget. In 1993, Congress appropriated $3.2 million for the development of the facility. In August 1995, Congress appropriated an additional $3 million for the construction. Phase I consists of an office, loading dock, mechanical room, vestibule and circulation corridor, along with the 8,000-square-foot collections storage module that is approximately 40 feet high. By use of high-density storage and with top shelves up to 30 feet high, there will be 8,000 square feet to accommodate 2 million books and bound serial publications.

The Fort Meade facility is designed to provide an excellent preservation environment, which will substantially reduce the rate of deterioration of the collections. The Library's Preservation Directorate has played a key role in facility planning, and has actively worked with building consultants. Using calculations provided by the Image Permanence Institute, the new building will operate at 50°F and 35%+/-5% RH, with tight air filtration to minimize the influx and distribution of pollutants and particulates.

The Image Permanence Institute provided data analysis on the life expectancy of collection materials in different temperature and relative humidity conditions,[9] which confirmed the selection of the above conditions. The Fort Meade module is expected to extend the life of collections five to six times over storage in average room conditions. (See Table 1: Preservation at the Library of Congress Fort Meade Off-Site Storage Facility, page 54.)

Another important preservation tool is use of storage boxes for the books. In Module I books will be sorted according to size and stored upright in archival quality lidded boxes that are 18 inches long. Storing materials in boxes will improve handling and minimize the risks of damage if dropped. The box lids will keep out dust particles and deflect water in case of leaks.

To ensure that proper environmental conditions would be incorporated in the design and construction, the firm Garrison/Lull, Inc., was contracted by the Library of Congress to serve as consultants to the architects and construction engineers. The firm issued a report for Fort Meade with specific recommendations on achieving the temperature/humidity criteria for all seasons. It also made recommendations for particulate and gaseous contamination control, lighting, and fire protection.

Some of the design features to ensure a proper storage environment include walls which will be 11 inches thick; an aluminum core vapor barrier; use of a chilled water plant for temperature control; a desiccant dehumidification system; and an air filtration system. Lighting for the module will be provided by high-pressure sodium lights that do not emit ultraviolet radiation or heat. Also all products used in construction had to be approved by the Library's Conservation and Preservation Research and Testing Divisions.

**Table 1. Preservation at the Library of Congress
Fort Meade Off-Site Storage Facility**

In evaluating the proposed temperature and relative humidity conditions, we asked the Image Permanence Institute to do calculations using Preservation Index (PI) and Time Weighted Preservation Index (TWPI) to determine the effect of several different environmental conditions. PI is "an index of environmental quality based on the nominal time for fresh, shorter-lived, organic materials such as color photographic dyes, acidic papers, and acetate film supports to reach significant deterioration." The index is not based on the time to reach the *end* of useable life. "Significant deterioration has been defined as the time it takes to reach 30% color dye loss, time to [reach] 50% loss in MIT fold endurance, or time to reach 0.5 base acidity in acetate film. PI is specifically directed at measuring the effect of storage conditions on inherent chemical reactions of decay—what is normally called natural aging—and does not address other kinds of possible damage such as mold growth or mechanical damage. TWPI represents the overall effect of a changing environment on the decay rate of organic materials and is a kind of "average PI." We looked at several different scenarios:

Type	Winter Condition	Summer Condition	Final TWPI
Static	50°F/35% RH	N/A	254 years
Static	53°F/35% RH	N/A	202 years
Static	55°F/35% RH	N/A	174 years
Cycled	50°F/35% RH	60°F/50% RH	126 years
Cycled	53°F/35% RH	63°F/50% RH	101 years
Cycled	55°F/35% RH	65°F/50% RH	88 years

A five-degree reduction in temperature difference shows an increase in life expectancy of an additional 45%. If one thinks of a typical storage site temperature as being in the low to mid 70's (F) with 40% RH, conditions at 50 degree/35% RH conditions represent approximately a six fold improvement in life expectancy over conditions of the typical building conditions just mentioned.

Source: Excerpt from "Preservation at the Library of Congress Fort Meade Off-Site Storage Facility" Talk by Doris A. Hamburg, *Alternative Archival Facilities Conference*, National Archives and Records Administration, Thursday, March 25, 1999. Quotations and table in text from IPI report, note 9.

While the opportunity for a library to get a major off-site storage facility may be exciting, it is also daunting for those involved in collections management. As the Library began to consider shifting some of its collections to the off-site storage facility, it was important to gain the support of the staff. Even when librarians agree (perhaps reluctantly) that relocating some of the materials is necessary, especially when faced with the alternatives, the first inclination for many is to state "Now let me tell you why my collection should stay here." To gain a consensus, a Materials Selection Working Group consisting of staff representing the different reading rooms of the Library was formed to make recommendations about what class of materials should be transferred. The Library also ceased to use terms such as "remote storage" and "secondary storage " and replaced them with "off-site storage" and "high-density storage." We wanted to ensure that staff understood that the material was remaining in the metropolitan D.C. area to ensure rapid retrieval, and that in no way did we believe that the collections being transferred were of lesser importance than those remaining.

A number of criteria and objectives for materials selection were considered. Among these were: (1) to provide space throughout the targeted stack area and to minimize the need for extensive shifting; (2) to give priority to those areas experiencing the most severe overcrowding; (3) to minimize adverse impact on Congress, scholars, and staff; (4) ideally (although not always practicable), to select blocks of material which are readily identifiable to the requestor in advance of submitting a request; and (5) to select material not subject to great damage during handling and transportation.[10] Selection decisions will combine "automatic" criteria with "intellectual" judgment.

The Library decided that, for the first module, low-use materials would be relocated. Initially, there was debate as to whether entire classes should be transferred or if some of the frequently requested items in the class should remain. However, since the initial discussions, the Library has acquired and implemented a new Integrated Library System (ILS), which permits requestors to identify immediately whether an item is stored on Capitol Hill or off-site. The materials being transferred to the first module include significant portions of classes/subclasses PZ 3+(fiction and juvenile belles letters), PG (Slavic, Baltic, and Albanian literature), RK-RZ (dentistry, dermatology, and therapeutics), S (agriculture), and TN (mining engineering and metallurgy). The African and Middle Eastern Division, Law Library, and Asian Division will also transfer some items from their collections to the first module.

Another daunting aspect for collections management staff is the transfer of materials to the new facility. The Library established an ambitious goal of transferring 4,000 items per day to the new facility. At this rate, the fill period for 2 million books will take approximately 31 months. One important decision that was made was that all processing of materials would be done at the Library before items are transferred. Primary factors entering into this decision included collections security, and the ability to resolve any database linking problems (in the ILS) prior to physical transfer. To accommodate the shift, the Library has built a special processing/loading dock area in the Jefferson Building. At this site, books will be cleaned (using a special vacuum), sorted, bar coded (if not done already), boxed by size, and have their location changed in the ILS, and entered into the warehouse management software.

Transferring materials to the Fort Meade facility is just one aspect for alleviating overcrowding. Much work remains in the general collections storage area to reconfigure the remaining materials. The Library estimates that approximately 16 million volumes as well as the entire collection of microfilm and microfiche will need to be shifted over a three-year period.[11] Four teams consisting of one team leader and five materials handlers will be needed to accomplish this major shift over a three-year period.

The key to tracking the materials at the facility will be a machine-readable Piece Identification Number (PIN) on each item, which will be entered into the item record in the ILS, and then added to a separate warehouse management database, where it will be linked to a Box Identification Number (BIN), and to a Shelf Identification Number (SIN).

At the time this article is being written, the Library has prepared a request for proposal for the procurement of warehouse management database software. The Library recently launched its Integrated Library System (ILS), Endeavor's Voyager. The ILS enhances the collection security, inventory control, and information processing by providing capabilities for identifying and tracking materials from the point of receipt and for sharing bibliographic and inventory information throughout the Library. The plan calls for the warehouse tracking software to interface with the ILS. This will enable a requestor to enter a request in the ILS, and have the request automatically transfer to the warehouse management system, with no staff intervention.

To assist and advise on the transfer of materials as well as with shelving design, fire sprinkler, and box designs, the Library contracted with Reese Dill of Dill and Company to serve as materials handling consultant. Mr. Dill did all of the materials handling design work for Harvard and numerous other library storage systems throughout the nation. Specifically, he has been contracted to advise the Library on activities related to the processing, transport, and transfer of items to Fort Meade as well as the delivery and return between Fort Meade and Capitol Hill; and processing and handling of materials at Fort Meade.

At the facility, the boxes will be placed two deep on industrial shelving that is 36 inches deep. The boxes will be fabricated in five different widths, each width with two different heights. They will be arranged by height on shelves that are placed as close together as possible to minimize the amount of unused air space between the top of the box and shelf above it. The boxes will be loaded onto book trucks specially designed to be raised by a forklift.

A warehouse employee filling a request for a book will maneuver the forklift, called an "order picker," that will be able to reach as high as 30 feet and retrieve the box containing the book. Once the book is removed and the tracking software is updated, the box will be returned.

Costs

Cost figures at this time have not been finalized. Estimates for the construction, staffing, and relocation of the materials are as follows:

♦ Phase I (consists of Storage Module I as well as an office module, loading docks): $4.7 million

♦ Mechanical rooms, vestibule and circulation operating costs (staff on Capitol Hill and at facility): $750,000 annually

The Library plans to hire permanent staff, relying on student assistants to the maximum extent practical to support collections transfer and maintenance activities. Initially, Module I will have five employees assigned to Fort Meade (a foreman, two warehousemen, a driver, and a library technician). In addition 17 staff members will support this program on Capitol Hill.

As the first module is being constructed, final design plans are underway for the second module, which will contain both books and paper-based special collections materials, for example, manuscripts, sheet music, and maps. Module II is scheduled for completion in 2003.

In the late 1980s, the Library considered leasing additional space on an interim basis to solve the immediate storage problems until a permanent facility could be found. However, this was not done. The use of leased facilities has been both costly and, in some instances, harmful to the collections. Warehouses constructed for leasing were not designed to store collections. As a result, the Library had to retrofit the buildings with capital improvements such as upgrading the HVAC system, providing special shelving, and enhancing security. These expenses added substantially to the base lease costs.

Designing and constructing a high-density, off-storage facility is a major operation. There are costs involved in design, construction, preparation, and processing of materials, and actual transfer. Once the facility opens, there will be operational costs at the site in addition to costs of shifting materials within the main Library buildings.

While realizing this long-needed off-site facility has taken quite some time, the Library's conviction that our criteria needed to be met has resulted in a facility of the proper size, the potential for long-term expansion, a state-of-the art preservation environment, and a configuration to maximize storage space. It has indeed been time well spent.

Notes

1.   Library of Congress, *The Gazette: A Weekly Newspaper for Library Staff*, November 12, 1999.

2.   Library of Congress Web site: www.loc.gov.

3. Library of Congress, *Collections Storage Plan*, 1992.

4. John Y. Cole, "The Main Building of the Library of Congress: A Chronology, 1871–1965," *The Quarterly Journal of the Library of Congress* 29, no. 4 (October 1972): 267–70.

5. Helene-Anne Hilker, "Monument to Civilization," *The Quarterly Journal of the Library of Congress* 29, no. 4 (October 1972): 261.

6. Cole, "The Main Building of the Library of Congress," 270.

7. *Annual of the Librarian of Congress*, 1969, 71.

8. Gridlock causes additional costs. Libraries may resort to major collection shifts to apply relief. These shifts are labor-intensive, costly, and result in materials being unavailable during the shift.

9. James Reilly and Douglas Nishimura, Image Permanence Institute, *Analysis of Environmental Data Scenarios Regarding Fort Meade Off-site Storage Facility, Using Time Weighted Preservation Index Methodology*, Report to the Library of Congress, July 1996.

10. Steven J. Herman, Chief, Collections Management Division, to Michael Shelley, Chair, Space Planning Committee, memorandum, June 7, 1989, "Secondary Storage Facility Overview Document."

11. "Management Decision Package," *Shifting Jefferson and Adams Collections*, prepared by Steven J. Herman, Chief, Collections Management Division, June 22, 1999.

7

Design and Construction Process
An Architect's Perspective

Bruce M. Scott

As architect for the first Harvard depository module, built in 1985, my task was to design a facility to house lesser-used books at the lowest possible per book cost. These books were to be stored in environmental conditions that would extend the books' useful life, in addition to obviating the need to construct additional on-campus stacks. Implementing the goal into an efficient, functional structure was a challenge then, and trying to improve the execution of the concept continues to be a learning experience for this same architect after designing nine projects following the initial Harvard model.

Transforming the concept into reality was, and continues to be, a collaborative effort involving many participants. Central to the transformation was the layout of racks and shelves, designed by Reese Dill, an industrial engineer who designs high-density, high-efficiency warehouses for industrial users. His design called for books to be stored in cardboard trays by size in shelving units 30 feet high. The trays would be shelved and retrieved by specially modified forklift trucks operated by trained personnel. Because the collection was predicted to have a very low retrieval rate (typically 2 percent to 5 percent of stored items retrieved per year), storing trays two deep on each shelf was economical. The tradeoff of having half of the trays "stuck" behind another tray was the very high density of books that could be stored within a small building.

This chapter, written from an architect's perspective, aims to describe the essential design and construction steps followed to create a high-density shelving facility, and the rationale behind fundamental decisions concerning site selection, module size, fire protection, the building envelope, and the location of mechanical equipment. Discussion of major project management issues from the bidding and contract negotiation, through selection of a contractor or construction manager, contracts, schedules, and costs will conclude the chapter.

Planning

The construction process begins with the appointment by the library or the institution of a project manager. The project manager organizes contracts with consultants and contractors, establishes schedules, provides central communications, manages the work of all the consultants, and represents the library on issues of construction and design to the consultants. If the library staff does not include facilities planning and management specialists, the project manager may be someone on staff at the institution, or may be selected from among a number of firms supplying such services. Regardless, it is the responsibility of the library to inform the project manager about the goals and requirements for the building.

The client (the library or institution) and project manager normally make up a list of consultants whom they would like to interview for the project. Typically, consultants who have had experience with similar projects are interviewed. Planning begins with projections of the needed size of the building and includes diagrams and master plan drawings to describe space needs and functions. Projections made for the growth of a depository facility are by definition estimates. The demand for storage is often underestimated. Thus, all the facility's components: storage functions, processing functions, shipping and receiving and if possible, unforeseen functions should have room to expand. A master plan diagram should include growth swaths which will remain open-ended for unknown amounts of building growth. The diagram can be overlaid on potential sites to determine how well they meet total projected building needs.

Site Selection

If the total present and future storage requirement for a facility is less than 12 million volumes, the following criteria can be utilized for the most economic development of space. Table 1 lists criteria that might suggest conditions necessary in the selection of a physical building site.

Table 1. Site Selection Criteria

♦ 400 ft x 400 ft mostly flat area for building, loading, and parking

♦ 2000 pounds per square foot minimum soil-bearing capacity

♦ Elevation above 500-year flood plain (100-year flood plain minimum)

♦ 1200 kilovolt-ampere (kVa) power (the amount of power to run four modules)

♦ natural gas

♦ minimum 8-inch water main for fire protection

♦ public sewer or percolation test for septic system

After the architect has done a sketch which indicates that the site fulfills the criteria for the building, he or she normally obtains a zoning ordinance from the municipality and determines if the proposed maximum development can fit within use restrictions, set-backs, floor area ratio, open space requirements, and other conditions specified in the ordinance. Most available sites in urbanized areas require some special permits and/or reviews. Sites that require a zoning variance may be worth considering if there is sufficient time to go through the process.

Some jurisdictions require extensive and time-consuming reviews and approvals by multiple boards and agencies. The time required to obtain permits and the potential for being rejected needs to be analyzed by the client and architect. If public hearings or variances will be required, and the client is not familiar with the jurisdiction's practices, an attorney who is familiar with the process should be engaged to evaluate the potential for a successful result. As the project manager constructs the project's schedule, adequate time for such reviews and approvals must be incorporated.

Unless the institution owns a suitable site, the time required to locate and secure a site can be the most drawn-out phase of development. Often months elapse between the time potential sites are located and a suitable one is acquired. The owners' site selection person can send site maps of potential sites to the architect and/or storage system designer. They can overlay the site with possible buildings and vehicle circulation schemes to determine if a site is worth further action.

Schematic Design

As the site is being selected, the architect will begin the schematic design process. The architect takes the program and layout produced by the storage rack system designer and adds the offices, rest rooms, and mechanical rooms necessary to operate a complete building. The architect coordinates the design and drawings for the site design, working with structural, mechanical, rack design, and electrical engineers. The sequence of installing the elements in a high-density book storage building and the size of some of the elements require special design considerations. If the architect anticipates the unusual aspects of this building type and designs for them, significant extra costs and/or delays can be avoided. Coordination of the rack system, storage module heating, ventilation, and air-conditioning (HVAC) system, and sprinklers require special attention as the systems interlock in a constricted space. The plans will be reviewed and refined with the client until the relationship of the functional facilities and the approximate building area is agreed upon.

Code Issues

A meeting should be scheduled early in the schematic process with the municipal and/or state officials who must approve the proposed plan. If photographs of existing depositories can be obtained, they will greatly help code officials understand the concept of a high-density book storage facility. The architect will explain the design of the building and cite the portions of the building codes that he or she believes govern the components of the design. It is particularly important that agreement on the design of the fire protection systems be reached before detailed design proceeds.

Module Size

Typically, systems are designed with four to six aisles. A four-aisle module has a capacity of approximately 1.6 million volumes. A six-aisle module has a capacity of approximately 2.4 million volumes. If not limited by fire insurance restrictions, six-aisle storage modules are more cost-effective for HVAC and structural design. Building codes typically permit unlimited area, single-story sprinkled storage buildings. Desiccant dehumidifiers come in standard sizes. HVAC costs for a five-aisle module are the same as a six-aisle module because the same desiccant dryer is needed for both. With this insight, a six-aisle module was built at Yale University in 1998 to maximize space supported by the investment in the desiccant dehumidifier.

Fire Protection*

The underwriter who will insure the building should be contacted during the schematic design phase. The design requirements specified by the insurer can have significant cost and design implications. Every insurance company has a specific amount of its money, called capacity, that it can expose on any given risk or location. For exposures that exceed their capacity (often in the hundreds of millions for large property insurance companies), the insurance company will arrange for other insurance companies to share both the risk and the premium. To the insured, this means fewer insurance company options, higher insurance premiums, and a less stable insurance program in terms of both pricing and conditions. For the insurance company, it means that they pass along a portion of their profit to these "reinsurance" companies that share the risk. Consequently, it is in the best interest of both the insured and the insurance company to limit the maximum foreseeable loss (MFL), from a single catastrophic fire to less than $200,000,000. Such a loss could occur if a sprinkler system was not installed, turned off, or inoperable. The odds of an average commercial facility having a fire in any given year is about 1:100. In an unprotected storage facility, it is likely that the fire will continue to spread until it becomes catastrophic. The odds of an MFL event in a sprinkled building, however, are approximately 1:15000. At some point though, even with a defined and limited MFL, the total amount of value exposed at a location can also cause problems with regard to available capacity, flexibility, and cost. Even though the chance that a tornado or airplane will hit the facility is much lower than the chance of an "MFL Event," it is still possible. Care should be taken not to put too many eggs in one basket no matter how well protected the facility is.

Each aisle of a 200-foot-long depository will typically store 400,000 volumes. Librarians will need to work with the risk management officers at their institutions to establish an acceptable maximum foreseeable loss level. Table 2, page 64, provides a sample valuation analysis.

To prevent fire jumping from one storage module to the next, maximum foreseeable loss (MFL) walls have been introduced between modules. These are different from standard firewalls; they are specially designed so that they will remain an effective fire barrier even when the adjacent building structure collapses during an uncontrolled fire. Each module has an independent three-hour rated structural wall. The wall of an adjoining module is spaced at least eight inches away to accommodate building structural component expansion during a fire. No pipes or ducts are permitted to penetrate the MFL walls or cross from one module to the next. Power, water, and gas services either come underground to each module or from the accessory processing building. Double three-hour rated doors are utilized between modules.

---

*The author would like to extend his thanks to Thomas A Gaitley, CBCP, Vice President, Marsh Risk Consulting, for his review and suggestions for this section.

Table 2. Sample Valuation Analysis

Books Valued at $50 per Volume			
Facility Size	4 Aisle	5 Aisle	6 Aisle
Volumes Shelved	1.6 million	2 million	2.4 million
Collection Valuation	$80 million	$100 million	$120 million

Books Valued at $100 per Volume			
Facility Size	4 Aisle	5 Aisle	6 Aisle
Volumes Shelved	1.6 million	2 million	2.4 million
Collection Valuation	$160 million	$200 million	$240 million

By 1990 the efficacy of freeze-dry recovery of wet books had been proven. Wet books can be recovered. Charred books are not recoverable. All but three depository buildings built since then have included sprinkler protection. Wet systems deploy more quickly and open fewer heads than dry or pre-action systems to control a fire. Risk advisors and most fire marshals prefer the simplicity of wet systems. Each head turns on individually in response to temperature above 165°F. According to FMGlobal, a large insurance, research, and testing organization (a.k.a Factory Mutual), 85 percent of all fires are controlled by the operation of only a few sprinkler heads. The remaining 15 percent are typically controlled by the number of sprinklers specified during the original design, provided that the storage arrangements are unchanged. The individual heads are protected by wire cages. To my knowledge, to date, no sprinkler has accidentally opened in any occupied depository facility.

High-bay storage building fire protection systems are specified by the National Fire Protection Association publication NFPA 230.[1] However, this publication does not address the unusual density of stored materials in book storage facilities. As of early 2000, fire code officials, and insurance underwriters have generally accepted four layers of sprinklers within the flue space between aisles plus a full ceiling system and vertical metal barriers to limit horizontal fire spread in the shelves. When a full-scale fire test is funded, or as a result of an actual fire, these standards may change. The future standard of NFPA 909, "Standard for the Protection of Cultural Resources Including Museums, Libraries, Places of Worship, and Historic Properties," may specifically address the unique protection requirements for book depositories.

Pre-action systems employ a system of smoke detectors or heat detectors to open valves and fill the pipes only when smoke or heat has been detected by the system. Fear of water and sprinkler leaks makes pre-action systems attractive to some librarians. The response time of pre-action systems is similar to wet systems (since the pipes are filled when a detector is activated and prior to the actuation of a sprinkler head), but these systems are inherently more complicated and less reliable. Unlike wet systems, which are mechanical, pre-action systems rely upon both electrical and mechanical systems to operate.

Dry systems are similar to pre-action systems except the water is kept out of the sprinkler pipes by air pressure rather than by an electrically operated valve. When a sprinkler head is activated, the air escapes, dropping the air pressure in the system, and allowing water to flow into the pipes. Since this takes time, the fire will be larger when the water arrives than it would be for a wet system. Thus, risk advisors, insurance companies, and fire marshals prefer wet systems to either pre-action or dry systems.

A gas suppression system is a possibility, but usually only as supplementary protection to sprinkler systems. With such a system, heat or smoke is detected by detectors within the module, a valve is opened and the entire module is "flooded" with carbon dioxide (CO_2) gas, which is colorless and odorless. The gas dilutes the oxygen within the module to a level that will not support combustion. The concentration of CO_2 is maintained for at least half an hour once the system has deployed. Especially with books, which smolder, once the oxygen level goes back up when the fire department arrives and opens the doors, the fire can and often does rekindle. A large refrigerated tank of liquid CO_2 is maintained on site. Gas suppression systems create significant life safety issues for employees who might be in the module at the time of an incident. Oxygen masks must be provided on each lift truck and for any person who might be overcome when the oxygen is diluted in the space. This is particularly acute if an employee is 30 feet up on the order picker. Specialized personnel training is also needed. All suppression systems must be tested at least once a year by the fire department. The cost of the gas for the annual test is more than $5,000.

The Building Envelope

Two important structural features requiring attention in designing high-density library storage facilities are the building envelope and the location of heat and ventilating equipment. Structural engineers and cost estimates determined that a concrete block bearing wall structure will provide a fire resistive structure at the lowest capital cost. However, single wythe (one thickness of block or brick) masonry walls are known to leak. The usual method of avoiding wall leaks is to construct double wythe walls—an inner wall to structurally hold up the roof and an outer decorative wythe of brick to act as the first line of defense against water driven through the wall by wind and rain. A cavity between the two wythes allows the water that is driven through to run down the inside of the outer wall and be drained by weep holes to the exterior. The cost premium of a double wythe wall is significant. As constructed at Harvard and Yale, a high-quality water shedding paint to "seal" the exterior from driven water penetration is applied to the exterior of the single wythe concrete block walls. The HVAC systems for depository buildings pressurize the interior of the structure. Pressurized structures are less susceptible to leaks than those that are not positively pressurized. As far as I know, to date (September 2000), no leaks have been experienced in masonry walls of high-density shelving facilities from wind-driven rainwater penetration.

Load bearing pre-cast concrete wall panels can be lower to or equal in cost to concrete block and save construction time. The panels can be cast with insulation within the panel, eliminating the need for installation or insulating liner panels on site. A separate vapor barrier that bridges the joints between pre-cast panels should be installed to provide a vapor tight envelope.

Insulated metal panel walls and/or ceilings can be less costly and faster to install than heavy concrete assemblies. However, they are not designed to provide fire resistance. If the facility is to grow and provide separation between modules that will be acceptable to the insurance risk advisors, metal walls may not be suitable.

An insulation value of not less than R22 (a standard measure of heat loss/gain through the wall) and a vapor barrier with a perm rating (a standard measure of moisture transfer through the barrier) of not greater than 0.033 for walls and ceilings are appropriate for the temperature and humidity conditions to be maintained within the module.

Early designs built up the wall system with steel studs, fiberglass batt insulation, lapped and sealed vapor barrier membranes, and gypsum boards to prevent damage to the vapor barrier. The joint between the wall system and roof decking is a potential source of air leaks and condensation, as it is difficult to design and install a joint that will work in the many different conditions along the joint.

Depository buildings operating at 50°F/35%RH (relative humidity) create high vapor pressure differences between outside and inside space. Moisture vapor moves from the humid side toward the drier side. In depository buildings this moisture drive reverses direction frequently. The potential of water condensing within the insulation is significant. An unbroken vapor barrier in the walls and ceiling structures is essential. "Minor" air leaks in the joints between wall and roof or wall and floor can produce "leaks" due to moisture drive on hot, humid days in summer if care is not exercised in detailing those joints. Failure to understand the dynamics of moisture drive is the most common cause of trouble in walls and roofs.

Steel joists have been utilized to free span between the structural walls. Steel decking is welded to the top of the joists. Five inches of closed cell foam insulation typically is laid on top, then weather sealed with a rubber EPDM (Ethylene Propylene Diene Monomer) roofing membrane ballasted against wind uplift by 12 pounds per square foot of No. 3 river-washed gravel. The heavy ballast is specified to prevent hot embers from dropping on the ballast and igniting the roofing membrane and insulation. No roof drains are placed over the stored collections.

Location of
Heat and Ventilating Equipment

Equipment is typically positioned on the rooftop or in mechanical mezzanines. Placement of equipment in mechanical mezzanines is gaining popularity among newly constructed library storage facilities. To reduce duct and fan sizes, engineers like to locate HVAC units at the middle of the conditioned space. If a mechanical room is created on the roof, this location can work well. The first depository at Harvard University was built without a mechanical room with commercial rooftop units at the middle of the roof. Commercial rooftop units tend to have service doors that fit poorly after a year or so of opening and closing by maintenance personnel. Rainwater is sucked in through the loose fitting doors and drips on the stored collections.

Alternatively, creating a mechanical mezzanine above the cross-aisle efficiently utilizes otherwise dead space for HVAC equipment. The space above the main cross-aisle needs only to be high enough for the lift truck to operate and for unloading of tractor trailers during construction. Thus the HVAC equipment can be located within the building above the cross-aisle without building greater volume to house it. If HVAC equipment within the mezzanine develops a leak, the drip would occur over the cross-aisle, not on the collection. The mechanical mezzanine is separated from the storage module with a two-hour-rated demising wall.

Temperature and Humidity
Settings

By 1993, the Image Permanence Institute had developed the Time Weighted Preservation Index. The predicted life of collections stored in a library stack at 68°F/50%RH is 44 years. The introduction of desiccant dehumidification can dry the air to a 27°F dew point, increasing predicted book life to 244 years at 50°F/35%RH. In general, low temperatures in the storage modules increase book life more than low humidity. However, lower temperatures add significant capital and operating costs. Desiccant dehumidification increases capital cost by approximately $100,000, and operating costs by about $10,000 per year per module. Collections that do not require higher preservation conditions can be maintained at 60°F/50%RH with standard refrigerative HVAC equipment at the lowest capital and operating costs. Materials stored in such conditions will have a predicted book life of 75 years.

Recently constructed modules recirculate the air through carbon filters within the space every 30 minutes and bring in sufficient fresh air to flush the module every 8.5 hours.

Central Mechanical Rooms
vs. Individual Systems

Institutions that have mechanical engineers on staff and in-house maintenance personnel may prefer to design the HVAC system with a central plant
rather than multiple individual units. The rationale for a central plant is outlined
in Table 3.

Table 3. Evaluation of Using a Central Plant

Advantages

- ◆ Centrifugal chillers are more reliable than multiple small reciprocating
  compressors.

- ◆ Large central, chilled water plants with water-cooled towers produce
  chilled water cheaper than other types of refrigerative equipment.

- ◆ It is easier for maintenance personnel to check on and maintain a unit
  within a central plant.

- ◆ Chilled water from a central plant provides more accurate temperature
  control than direct expansion cooling.

Disadvantages

- ◆ Piping, power, pumps, and chillers often need to be oversized to provide
  capacity for future expansion, thus capital costs are higher.

- ◆ A larger amount of space must be built up front for a central plant with
  room for expansion.

- ◆ The complexity of central plants increases maintenance contract costs.

- ◆ Running pipes from one module to the next becomes difficult with MFL
  walls that discourage the passage of piping between modules.

- ◆ Owners often must have skilled operating personnel on staff to run central plants.

In order to centralize the responsibility for creating a reliable storage module system, some owners and designers have chosen to specify a single supplier
for the complete HVAC system and insulated wall panel system for each module. Foam insulated panels with metal surfaces on both sides and interlocking

joining details are installed by the supplier inside the masonry structural walls. These panels are usually three inches thick to provide an R22 rating. Making an airtight seal between the floor and the panels and between the panels and the roof deck becomes the responsibility of the supplier. Experience shows that personnel who are accustomed to installing insulating metal panels in cold storage and freezer rooms understand the need to seal the joints better than installers who do not specialize in cold room installations.

Design Development and Construction Documents

Once schematic design drawings have been reviewed with and approved by the client, the project moves into a phase of design development. Preliminary elevations, sections, structural systems, and exterior materials are investigated during this phase. Elevation drawings show how the building will look from the outside. Section plans describe the height of structure and ceilings and show how the racks fit within the building. Structural drawings show the locations of columns, beams, and structural walls.

Construction document drawings are further refinements of the design drawings and give dimensions and details to provide a contractor sufficient information to construct the building. A specification book is prepared to list acceptable products and describe proper installation requirements. The specification book normally specifies the type of AIA (American Institute of Architects) contract which will be used between owner and contractor, that is, lump sum, or construction management with a guaranteed maximum price, or cost plus a fee. A bid form is included with any add or deduct alternates which the owner wishes to consider. Some clients may require contractors to meet Equal Employment Opportunity hiring standards and/or to pay prevailing wages as set by the Department of Labor. All of these requirements are specified in the general conditions of the contract or the modifications to the general conditions.

The construction documents are listed in the contract for construction to describe the work that the contractor agrees to build for the contract sum. The contractor may request a change order for any work not specified in the drawings and specifications. The contractor will prepare a schedule of values, which breaks the work into categories in accordance with the CSI (Construction Specification Institute) format. This document becomes the basis for each monthly payment for work completed.

Bidding and Contract Negotiation

Once the working drawings and specifications are complete and approved by the client, the project is put to bid. The architect answers questions from bidders regarding the intent of the design. He or she will provide written answers to questions posed during the bidding period. When the bids are received, the architect may tally them on behalf of the client to help the client understand if the contractor's proposal is complete and which builder is most appropriate to build the project.

Design-Build Approach

Library storage facilities are "back of the house" support facilities, usually constructed on lower-cost land away from the center of the institution. As such, the goal is often to get the building designed and built at the lowest cost. It is possible to write a detailed program and performance specification, then ask several trusted general contractors to package the design and construction in one "design-build" contract. The efficacy of this approach depends on the completeness and clarity of the performance specification.

The client is relieved of having to assemble a design team and manage the process. The contractor hires the architects and engineers believed to be best qualified for the project. Duke University is building a depository with this process. When this project is completed, it will be instructive to compare total costs for design-build versus conventionally designed projects.

Contracts for Construction

Institutional owners often have ongoing relationships with a number of trusted contractors. Full construction documents and specifications can be given to a list of pre-selected contractors and the construction award given to the lowest-qualified contractor. Alternatively, the owner can select a firm to become construction manager (CM) of the project at an early stage. By having the CM on board early, the CM can provide valuable estimating advice and help the architect and owner sort out alternative construction details which best suit the local market. If a construction manager form of contract is selected, the award is based on the fee charged for the construction management and the amount of overhead to be charged to the job.

Book storage facilities are often built when institutions are desperate to move books from their existing facilities. Delays in completing the storage facility will have domino effects throughout the institution. The temptation to insert "liquidated damages" (fines for being late) clauses, coupled with "bonus" provisions for early completion, seem to be great ideas. Such clauses would appear to protect the interest of the user-owner. In practice, liquidated damages for late completion are very difficult to collect, whereas, contractors very often complete jobs early if there are bonuses for doing so. However, experience shows that the existence of bonus clauses often leads to rushed, shoddy construction. It is preferable to choose a contractor who is trusted and work realistically with him or her to achieve the completion date goals without penalties or bonuses.

Awarding a separate contract with a rack installer for the installation of the rack system has proved to be beneficial. Installation of the rack system takes several months during which the general contractor often has little work to do on the job. The specialists who install rack systems are far more productive than workers hired locally and often work longer days and weekends if permitted to do so. General contractors usually have little or no experience with rack installation. Owners may wish to have only one entity responsible for the entire project. However, in practice, the installation of the racks is separate enough from the normal construction trade work proceeding on site, that it is better to allow the installer to work directly for the owner under the observation of a rack designer and specifier, such as Reese Dill.

Construction

The general contractor's subcontractors produce shop drawings of the products they will be supplying. The shop drawings must be reviewed and approved by the architect. The architect is expected to see that the individual pieces are coordinated so they will fit together properly. It is during the shop drawing approval stage and construction observation stage that an architect who has specific experience with this type of building can bring expertise to the project that may not be covered by the drawings or specifications.

The storage module can usually be ready for installation of racks in eight months after construction begins. Sixteen weeks should be allowed for installation of the rack system and shelves. Projections should assume not less than one year for on-site completion after receipt of permits. See Table 4 for general minimum/likely estimates of the time for key phases of the project.

Table 4. Construction Schedule Range

Project Phase	Minimum Duration	Likely Duration
Permits	4 weeks	10 weeks
Site Preparation	2 weeks	6 weeks
Building Construction	34 weeks	40 weeks
Rack Installation	12 weeks	16 weeks
Start to Finish Total	52 weeks	72 weeks

The design and construction of shelving facilities over the past 15 years has and continues to evolve. Tested solutions have emerged for many of the problems of creating an affordable way to provide an excellent environment for the storage of low-use library materials. While overall costs have increased, primarily as a result of using desiccant dehumidification and fire protection sprinklers, the benefits for preservation have also risen. Construction costs for the first Harvard Depository, including shelving, was $1,249,000 in 1985. Escalated to 2000 pricing, the cost for that building and shelving would equal $0.96 per book.[2] The predicted book life provided in such an earlier design without desiccant dehumidification and without sprinklers is 75 years. High preservation standard facilities built in 2000 equal between $1.47 per book for basic designs (Yale) to $1.84 per book for designs with premium exteriors and larger processing areas (Columbia/NYPL/Princeton Consortium). These high preservation standard facilities with desiccant dehumidification and sprinkler protection provide a predicted book life of 244 years.

Choices exist today in how to design and construct an off-site storage facility. The knowledge gained from trying alternatives provides libraries the necessary information to judge the value gained for each local situation in investing in different options and design features.

Notes

1.   National Fire Protection Association, *NFPA 230: Fire Protection of Storage*, 1999 edition (Quincy, MA: National Fire Protection Association, 1999). http://www.nfpa.org/

2.   Assumes an average of 190 books per shelf. Costs listed for 2000 have been escalated by utilizing the Historical Cost Indexes and factored to the average location using the City Cost Indexes published in R. S. Means, 58th edition.

8

What to Build

Ron Lane and Reese Dill

Behind the Bricks

In the next few pages, we will examine the impact of your situation and the decisions you will make on what you will build. Although some basic level of aesthetics is desired for the sake of the soul, we assume that efficient and effective use of resources is the objective. It is important to strike a balance between the volume of space necessary to house the collections, desired preservation requirements, technological realities, and the funding required to provide them. "Vaulted ceilings, soaring windows, a stunning serendipity of wood and stone, steel and glass all reflecting the absolute epitome of architectural splendor" is unlikely to describe what you will build.

Let us begin with a review of some of the underlying concepts of why you should be building a **H**igh **D**ensity **B**ook **S**helving **S**ystem rather than expanding the library. In 1984, Harvard University pioneered the development of the HDBSS to relieve intense pressure on its library system. The task force charged with solving the space problem combined advances in bar code and computer technology with truly innovative application of new techniques to the shelving venue. The resultant system revolutionized the way in which books, as well as other types of media, are shelved. As of this writing, there are 18 operating facilities utilizing some, many, or all of the following concepts that evolved from the initial Harvard Depository design. (See Appendix: "Harvard Model" Facilities.)

Efficiency

There are six basic concepts of HDBSS shelving efficiency in the "Harvard" model, an understanding of which might prove helpful.

1. *Using Bar Codes and a Computerized Locator System*
    Bar code labeling and computerized locator systems provide virtually perfect item and location tracking. Separating "book data" from "item data" through association of bar codes with the bibliographic item records on the one hand and locations on the other provides the flexibility to shelve without regard for content.

2. *Sorting by size*
    Sorting and shelving by size eliminates the unused vertical space found on a typical library shelf. It is an approach made possible by using a locator system different from call number order and results in greater vertical storage density.

3. *Containerizing like-size items*
    Containerizing like-size items provides the opportunity to use shelves deeper than 9 inches by allowing the books to be shelved perpendicular to the aisle rather than parallel. This results in greater down-aisle lateral density.

4. *Lateral modularity of tray lengths and widths with shelf dimensions*
    Standardized tray sizes in combination with properly dimensioned shelves will accommodate exact multiples of each size of container without wasted space, thereby contributing to shelf density.

5. *Vertical modularity of shelves with tray/book heights*
    A properly designed shelving system will accommodate shelf spacing which minimizes the amount of unused space by providing compatible combinations of shelving heights throughout the entire vertical rise.

6. *A high-rise system serviced via equipment*
    Thirty-foot-high stacks serviced by standard man-aboard "order picker" industrial trucks contribute to increased cube utilization and offer significant efficiency and ergonomic advantages over segments of shelving serviced from the floor.

Acting in concert, these six basic concepts provide better than a 3.5 to 1 advantage over a typical library shelf configuration. Figure 1, Vertical Density Comparison, and Figure 2, Lateral Density Comparison (page 76), attempt to illustrate some of these HDBSS efficiencies.

TYPICAL LIBRARY SHELF
12 IN. LONG X 14 IN. HIGH X 9 IN. DEEP
APPROXIMATELY 24% UNUSED SPACE

TYPICAL LIBRARY SHELF LINEAR FOOT
EFFICIENCY RATING = 76%
EFFICIENCY FACTOR = 1

TYPICAL HDBSS SHELF
12 IN. LONG X 14 IN. HIGH X 36 IN. DEEP
APPROXIMATELY 7% UNUSED SPACE

TYPICAL HDBSS SHELF LINEAR FOOT
EFFICIENCY RATING = 93%
EFFICIENCY FACTOR = 1.22

The collection represented by the percentages in the illustration consists of over two million volumes, ninety-five percent of which fit on shelves 14 inches high or less. Distribution approximates 15% on 14 inch shelves, 60% on 12 inch shelves, 20% on 10 inch shelves, and 5% on 9 inch or smaller shelves. By multiplying these percentages by the 12 inch width of shelf used for illustration we can obtain an average distribution by height analagous to that depicted. By subtracting the appropriate number of square inches not occupied by books and dividing by the total number of square inches available we are able to determine the percentage of unused space. An average of one inch, or half the 2 inch differential in shelf heights, has been included in the unused space calculations for both the library and HDBSS shelves. In the case of the 9 inch and smaller category, a 3 inch differential has been used to also account for 7 inch & 5 inch sizes included in this category. These calculations are represented by the algebraic equation below.

D = DISTRIBUTION %
C = DISTRIBUTION CATAGORY SHELF HEIGHT
U = AVG UNUSED SPACE / CATEGORY

H = TYPICAL SHELF HEIGHT
W = TYPICAL SHELF WIDTH
A = SQUARE INCHES OF TYPICAL SHELF FACE ($H*W$)

UNUSED SHELF SPACE = $[DC_1*(H-(C_1-U_1))+DC_2*(H-(C_2-U_2))+DC_3*(H-(C_3-U_3))+DC_4*(H-C_4-U_4))]*W/A$

UNUSED SHELF SPACE = $[0.15*(14-(14-1))+0.60*(14-(12-1))+0.20*(14-(10-1))+0.05*(14-(9-3))]*12/168 = .24$

UNUSED SHELF SPACE = $[1.00*(14-(14-1))]*12/168 = .07$

With unused space representing 24% of the library shelf illustrated, it's efficiency rating equals 76%. Similarly, with unused space representing 7% of the HDBSS shelf illustrated, it's efficiency rating equals 93%. By dividing the efficiency rating of the HDBSS by the efficiency rating of the library shelf, we can see that the HDBSS shelf has a relative advantage in vertical density of 22% (1.22 to 1).

A further vertical density advantage of 20% (1.20 TO 1) is obtained by full utilization of the 30 feet of high-rise shelving in a HDBSS (see Figure 6) as opposed to a comparable 30 feet diminished by 6 feet (four 18" floors) of steel grating as would be the case in a comparable minimally floored library configuration.

Figure 1. Vertical Density Comparison

TYPICAL LIBRARY AISLE
9 IN. OF SHELF - 42 IN. OF AISLE - 9 IN OF SHELF
2 LINEAR FEET OF BOOKS / LINEAR FOOT OF AISLE

| 9 | 42 | 9 |
| 60 |

TYPICAL HDBSS AISLE
36 IN. OF SHELF - 54 IN. OF AISLE - 36 IN OF SHELF
8 LINEAR FEET OF BOOKS / LINEAR FOOT OF AISLE

| 36 | 54 | 36 |
| 126 |

14

FOOTPRINT = AISLE WIDTH * AISLE DEPTH / SQUARE FOOT

LIBRARY $\dfrac{60W \times 12D}{12W \times 12D}$
FOOTPRINT

FOOTPRINT = 5 SQUARE FEET

2 LINEAR FEET / 5 SQUARE FEET

EFFICIENCY RATING = .40

EFFICIENCY FACTOR = 1

HDBSS $\dfrac{126W \times 12D}{12W \times 12D}$
FOOTPRINT

FOOTPRINT = 10.5 SQUARE FEET

8 LINEAR FEET / 10.5 SQUARE FEET

EFFICIENCY RATING = .76

EFFICIENCY FACTOR = 1.91

The diagram above compares the square foot efficiency of 1 linear foot of a library aisle to that of 1 linear foot of a HDBSS aisle. One linear foot of library aisle equals 5 square feet. Represented with-in that footprint are 2 linear feet of 9" wide shelves, 1 foot on either side of the aisle. This results in 2 linear feet of books per 5 square feet of space, or an efficiency rating of 40%. Similarly, the footprint for 1 linear foot of HDBSS aisle equals 10.5 square feet encompassing 8 linear feet of 9" wide shelf equivalents, 4 on each side of the aisle, for an efficiency rating of 76%. By dividing the efficiency rating of the HDBSS aisle foot by the efficiency rating of the library aisle foot, we see that the HDBSS has a relative advantage of 91% (1.91 to 1).

An additional HDBSS lateral advantage of 20% (1.20 to 1) is acheived by the fact that a library shelf is "full" at 80% to allow for call number category additions.

A further lateral density advantage of 7% (1.07 to 1) is obtained by full utilization of a typical 165 feet of HDBSS aisle length uninterupted by an assumed four 3 foot cross aisles (one every 42 feet) in an equivalent length of library aisle.

The cumulative advantage of the HDBSS as outlined in Figures 1 & 2 and referred to in the text is calculated as follows:

S = HDBSS SHELF VERTICAL DENSITY ADVANTAGE
F = HDBSS FACE VERTICAL DENSITY ADVANTAGE

L = HDBSS SQUARE FOOT DENSITY ADVANTAGE
R = RESHELVING "FULL" DENSITY ADVANTAGE
A = HDBSS AISLE LENGTH DENSITY ADVANTAGE

COMBINED HDBSS DENSITY ADVANTAGE = S*F*L*R*A

= 1.22*1.20*1.91*1.20*1.07 = 3.59 to 1

Figure 2. Lateral Density Comparison

Preservation

Evolution in environmental and fire protection technologies has led to new opportunities for protecting collections in a HDBSS. The combination of highly insulated construction, near-perfect vapor barriers, and mechanical systems utilizing desiccant wheels currently allows a temperature and humidity controlled environment not previously possible in large spaces. For example, a combination of 50 degrees and relative humidity of 35 percent is readily, even economically, obtained in a HDBSS. It is a combination virtually impossible to achieve in a library where books must share the environment with people. Similarly, new fire protection standards and the incorporation of cost-effective in-rack sprinkler designs have enhanced fire protection for the cooler, drier, more densely packed collections in a HDBSS.

Cost

The true advantage of the HDBSS, however, is perhaps most readily appreciated from a different perspective. A HDBSS six-aisle facility can store 225,000 linear feet of books (roughly equivalent to 2.6 million volumes of 9" x 10.5" x 1.2" size) in an environment that is ideal for long-term preservation. The shelving portion of such a building would approximate 14,000 square feet. Given the shelving density advantage of the HDBSS of 3.5 to 1 demonstrated above, it would require roughly 50,000 square feet of generally more expensive library construction to house the same number of books. Additionally, the substantially greater number of shelves and uprights required (62,000), even at a lower per-item cost, would be a significant dollar differential in favor of the HDBSS.

The cost per book to accommodate substantial additions to collections in a library depends on many factors. Regardless of specific square foot construction costs in a particular area, however, or of particular shelving contract prices, or of relative labor costs, building a HDBSS will provide an overall cost advantage of three to six times over expanding the library.

So, a HDBSS is multiple times more efficient in use of space than a library, provides absolute precision as to location (no lost books), and produces a *significantly* lower capital cost per book shelved. It provides a near-perfect preservation environment, and is substantially more secure than an open-stacks operation. Definitely food for thought.

Form and Function Forever

Before determining how big a facility you will need, let us take a moment to consider the underlying philosophy of your decision:

1. You are choosing to focus on the most effective use of space in the library.

    Implications of this decision include making an objective assessment of what should remain in the library versus what should be sent to the HDBSS. Generally, one of the primary objectives is to achieve/maintain 80 percent stack utilization in the library; it follows that the books retained should be the most active volumes in the collection. Another major justification for building a HDBSS is the conversion of stack space to more direct patron use, or for other critical library functions that did not exist when the original library was designed.

2. You are choosing to preserve the shelved collections "forever."

    A major implication of this decision is that if the collections must last forever, the building must last forever. Such a statement obviously bears on siting, materials, and building design itself to withstand that which has reduced castles to rubble. You must consider floods and earthquakes as well as wind, rain, sleet, and snow loads in your calculations. Consider local codes to be a minimum. Also required will be focused thought as to how future upgrades or replacements will occur with regard to both the structure and the environment. For example, you do not want a design that will require exposure of the collections in order to replace the roof, nor do you want to employ a location scheme that would complicate moving the media. The best preservation environment for the material to be shelved and how to achieve it economically will require expert advice. Your choice of consultants and/or architects will be very important. You are not building a shopping mall that will be torn down in 30 years.

3. You are choosing to minimize the capital cost per book shelved.

    The HDBSS is designed to offer the lowest possible cost alternative for dense shelving of books. There is often a desire, however, to explore use of an Automated Storage and Retrieval System. When all costs are considered for a given shelving requirement, the capital investment in ASRS retrievers, special aisle hardware, high tolerance racks, and metal trays is substantially higher than for the HDBSS. Unless you are building adjacent to the library and can tie an ASRS into the library's closed-stack circulation function, it is unlikely you will find such a system to be cost-effective. There are currently two ASRSs used for shelving books. One of these is at California State

University at Northridge and the other is at Eastern Michigan University. Both of these ASRSs are located on the campuses and service the libraries directly.

How Big Is "Just Right"?

The impetus to build a HDBSS is generally a critical overcrowding in the library coupled with a reluctant realization that expensive expansion of the library is not a viable option. By the time this conclusion is reached, 95 percent to 110 percent stack capacity levels are usually creating major reshelving workloads. There may also be other pressing demands, such as those mentioned above, or for major library renovations. Once the decision has been made to build a HDBSS, whatever the reason, you are faced with determining the size best suited to your needs.

First, you must determine the type and volume of material you will have to move to achieve your objectives. As stated above, this is usually 80 percent stack capacity in the library, plus the amount of books that may have to be removed to make space available for other library uses. This is referred to as the "initial load-in."

Second, you must determine the time frame over which a move of this magnitude is feasible from both a sending and receiving point of view. It may be necessary to spread the initial load-in over several years.

Third, you must estimate the ongoing volume of material to be sent annually. Acquisitions will certainly continue despite the finite amount of stack space. After the initial load-in, the ongoing level of accessions into a HDBSS is usually equal to the total acquisitions by the participating libraries.

Once these data are assembled, you will be able to determine the magnitude of the accession processing operation and the number of shelves required to house the collections. This will, in turn, determine the size of both the shelving and processing sections of the building. It will also help you choose the most cost-effective building size. Because of the design of the shelving systems, most HDBSS have between four and six aisles. Systems of this size can be housed in simple buildings where the walls support the roof and internal columns are not required. In general, the larger six-aisle systems have HVAC costs that are somewhat less on a cost per book shelved than smaller facilities. Properly configured, a six-aisle HDBSS can most efficiently deliver the desired preservation environment for less than 1.5 times the cost of a four-aisle unit. Your "fill" rate versus the carrying cost of the financing and operating a full utility load for a partially filled facility will be a major factor in determining the optimum size for your facility.

Figure 3, Sample Transfer Requirements Worksheet (page 80), Figure 4, Sample Collection Conversion Worksheet (page 81), and Figure 5, Sample HDBSS Shelving Capacity Worksheet (page 82), illustrate the mechanics of this focusing process.

(Text continues on page 83.)

CATEGORY / SPECIFIC YEAR	100% STACK CAPACITY	# ITEMS ON-HAND	% CURRENT	% GOAL	REQUIRED REDUCTION	# ANNUAL ACQUISITIONS	# TRNSFRS YEAR 1 FYxx	% EO YEAR 1	# TRNSFRS YEAR 2 FYxx	% EO YEAR 2	# TRNSFRS YEAR 3 FYxx	% EO YEAR 3	# TRNSFRS YEAR 4 FYxx	% EO YEAR 4	# TRNSFRS YEAR 5 FYxx	% EO YEAR 5
BOOKS																
BEGIN YEAR LIBRARY STACK LEVEL (ALL)	2,200,000	2,000,000	91%	80%	240,000	120,000	2,000,000		1,865,000		1,805,000		1,760,000		1,760,000	
RESEARCH LIBRARY	1,000,000	1,000,000	100%	80%	200,000	25,000	150,000	88%	76,000	83%	50,000	80%	25,000	80%	25,000	80%
SCIENCE LIBRARY	250,000	200,000	80%	80%	0	50,000	50,000	80%	50,000	80%	50,000	80%	50,000	80%	50,000	80%
BUSINESS SCHOOL	200,000	100,000	50%	80%	(60,000)	20,000		60%		70%		80%	20,000	80%	20,000	80%
SCHOOL OF EDUCATION	150,000	100,000	67%	80%	(20,000)	10,000		73%		80%	10,000	80%	10,000	80%	10,000	80%
LAW SCHOOL	300,000	300,000	100%	80%	60,000	5,000	25,000	93%	25,000	87%	25,000	80%	5,000	80%	5,000	80%
MEDICAL SCHOOL	150,000	150,000	100%	80%	30,000	5,000	15,000	93%	15,000	87%	15,000	80%	5,000	80%	5,000	80%
SCHOOL OF THEOLOGY	150,000	150,000	100%	80%	30,000	5,000	15,000	93%	15,000	87%	15,000	80%	5,000	80%	5,000	80%
TOTAL BOOKS (ALL)	2,200,000	2,000,000	91%	80%	240,000	120,000	255,000	85%	180,000	82%	165,000	80%	120,000	80%	120,000	80%
END OF YEAR LIBRARY STACK LEVEL (ALL)	2,200,000	2,000,000	91%	80%	240,000	120,000	1,865,000	85%	1,805,000	82%	1,760,000	80%	1,760,000	80%	1,760,000	80%
OTHER THAN BOOKS																
BEGIN YEAR OTHER THAN BOOKS STACK LEVEL (ALL)	270,000	233,000	86%	80%	17,000	15,500	233,000		229,500		226,000		222,500		219,000	
LEGAL SIZE DOCUMENT BOXES	0	2,000		0%	2,000	0	2,000	80%		80%		80%		80%		80%
MICROFILM	80,000	60,000	75%	80%	(4,000)	10,000	6,000	80%	10,000	80%	10,000	80%	10,000	80%	10,000	80%
LETTER SIZED DOCUMENT BOXES	30,000	26,000	93%	80%	2,000	3,000	5,000	88%	3,000	86%	3,000	84%	3,000	82%	3,000	80%
UNIVERSITY RECORDS BOXES	150,000	135,000	90%	80%	15,000	2,000	5,000	95%	5,000	90%	5,000	85%	5,000	80%	5,000	80%
OTHER SIZE BOXES	10,000	10,000	100%	80%	2,000	500	1,000		1,000		1,000		1,000		500	
TOTAL OTHER THAN BOOKS (ALL)	270,000	233,000	86%	80%	17,000	15,500	19,000	85%	19,000	84%	19,000	82%	19,000	81%	18,500	80%
END OF YEAR OTHER THAN BOOKS STACK LEVEL (ALL)	270,000	233,000	86%	81%	17,000	15,500	229,500	84%	226,000	82%	222,500	81%	219,000	80%	216,000	80%

A worksheet such as Figure 3 helps determine HOW MUCH of WHAT must be transferred in order to meet established goals WHEN. The "Category" column lists the various types of material and/or their location. Completing the "Capacity", "Items on Hand", and "Goal" columns allows calculation of the "Current Capacity" percentages and "Required Item Reduction" columns. Filling in the "Annual Acquisitions" column completes the data input necessary to commence determining the initial load-in. By assigning the number of annual transfers to be sent from each entity each year, a determination can be made as to when the goal will be achieved. In the example above, stack capacity for books is 2,200,000 volumes and the number of volumes on hand is 2,000,000 or 91% of capacity. A goal of achieving 80% of capacity has been established meaning that a reduction of 240,000 volumes is necessary. Annual acquisitions of 120,000 must also be taken into account in the calculations. The example shows 255,000 books being transferred in the first year, 180,000 in the second year, and 165,000 in the third year. At that point, the 80% goal will have been achieved and on-going transfers will be equal to annual acquisitions. Following the same process for the "Other Than Books" category, the initial load in of 17,000 items plus 15,500 items per year of new acquisitions will be completed in the fifth year, following which on-going transfers will equal annual acquisitions in this category also.

Figure 3. Sample Transfer Requirements Worksheet

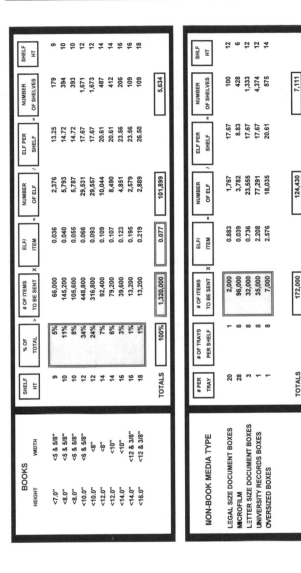

| BOOKS | | SHELF HT | % OF TOTAL > | # OF ITEMS TO BE SENT X | ELF/ ITEM = | NUMBER OF ELF / | ELF PER SHELF = | NUMBER OF SHELVES | SHELF HT |
HEIGHT	WIDTH								
<7.0"	<5 & 5/8"	9	5%	66,000	0.036	2,376	13.25	179	9
<8.0"	<5 & 5/8"	10	11%	145,200	0.040	5,793	14.72	394	10
<8.0"	<6 & 5/8"	10	8%	105,600	0.055	5,787	14.72	393	10
<10.0"	<6 & 5/8"	12	34%	448,800	0.066	29,531	17.67	1,671	12
<10.0"	<8"	12	24%	316,800	0.093	29,557	17.67	1,673	12
<12.0"	<8"	14	7%	92,400	0.109	10,044	20.61	487	14
<12.0"	<10"	14	6%	79,200	0.107	8,490	20.61	412	14
<14.0"	<10"	16	3%	39,600	0.123	4,851	23.56	206	16
<14.0"	<12 & 3/8"	16	1%	13,200	0.195	2,579	23.56	109	16
<16.0"	<12 & 3/8"	18	1%	13,200	0.219	2,889	26.50	109	18
TOTALS			100%	1,320,000	0.077	101,899		5,634	

NON-BOOK MEDIA TYPE	# PER TRAY	# OF TRAYS PER SHELF	# OF ITEMS TO BE SENT X	ELF/ ITEM =	NUMBER OF ELF /	ELF PER SHELF =	NUMBER OF SHELVES	SHLF HT
LEGAL SIZE DOCUMENT BOXES	20	1	2,000	0.883	1,767	17.67	100	12
MICROFILM	28	8	96,000	0.039	3,782	8.83	428	6
LETTER SIZE DOCUMENT BOXES	3	8	32,000	0.736	23,555	17.67	1,333	12
UNIVERSITY RECORDS BOXES	1	8	35,000	2.208	77,291	17.67	4,374	12
OVERSIZED BOXES	1	8	7,000	2.576	18,035	20.61	875	14
TOTALS			172,000		124,430		7,111	

Figure 4 illustrates the methodology for converting library linear feet to HDBSS Equivalent Linear Feet. The basis for the distribution and ELF / Item figures used in this illustration is the same collection referenced in Figure 1. Determining the number of ELF in the collections being sent (refer to Figure 3) allows ar accurate estimate of the number and heights of shelving to be installed, as well as when additional HDBSS space will be required (See Figure 5). Simply fill in the appropriate numbers and/or percentages in the shaded double-outlined boxes and multiply or divide as indicated in the heading. For example, books that are less than 10 inches high and less than 6 and 5/8 inches wide fit on 12 inch shelves and represent 34% of the 1,320,000 volumes to be sent in the first 10 years; at .066 ELF / volume they will occupy 29,531 ELF which divided by 17.67 ELF per 12 inch shelf will require 1,671 twelve inch shelves to be set for these 448,800 books. Similarly, it will take 428 six inch shelves to house the 96,000 microfilm projected for transfer. (Using the 10 year accumulation figures of 226,329 ELF allowed a determination of shelf heights and numbers for a 225,000 ELF 6 aisle unit.)

Figure 4. Sample Collection Conversion Worksheet

CATEGORY / SPECIFIC YEAR	# TRANSFERS YEAR 1 FYxx	% EO YEAR 1	# TRANSFERS YEAR 2 FYxx	% EO YEAR 2	# TRANSFERS YEAR 3 FYxx	% EO YEAR 3	# TRANSFERS YEAR 4 FYxx	% EO YEAR 4	# TRANSFERS YEAR 5 FYxx	% EO YEAR 5	# TRANSFERS YEAR 6 FYxx	% EO YEAR 6	# TRANSFERS YEAR 7 FYxx	% EO YEAR 7
BEGIN YEAR HDBSS BOOKS	0		255,000		435,000		600,000		720,000		840,000		840,000	
BOOKS ADDED	255,000		180,000		165,000		120,000		120,000		120,000		120,000	
END YEAR HDBSS ITEMS - BOOKS	255,000		435,000		600,000		720,000		840,000		840,000		960,000	
0.077 OOKS / ELF FROM FIGURE 5 > END YEAR HDBSS BOOKS ELF ADDED	19,635		13,860		12,705		9,240		9,240		9,240		9,240	
END YEAR HDBSS - BOOKS CUMULATIVE ELF ADDED	19,635		33,495		46,200		55,440		64,680		73,920		83,160	
BEGIN YEAR HDBSS	0		19,000		38,000		57,000		76,000		94,500		110,000	
OTHER THAN BOOKS ADDED														
LEGAL SIZE DOCUMENT BOXES	2,000		10,000		10,000		10,000		10,000		10,000		10,000	
MICROFILM	6,000		3,000		3,000		3,000		3,000		3,000		3,000	
LETTER SIZE DOCUMENT BOXES	5,000		5,000		5,000		5,000		5,000		2,000		2,000	
UNIVERSITY RECORDS BOXES	5,000		5,000		1,000		1,000		500		500		500	
OTHER SIZE BOXES	1,000		1,000											
OTHER THAN BOOKS ADDED	19,000		19,000		19,000		19,000		18,500		15,500		15,500	
END YEAR HDBSS ITEMS - OTHER THAN BOOKS	19,000		38,000		57,000		76,000		94,500		110,000		125,500	
FIGURE 5 ITEMS / ELF #s > END YEAR HDBSS - OTHER ELF ADDED	19,301		16,220		16,220		16,220		14,932		8,307		8,307	
END YEAR HDBSS - OTHER CUMULATIVE ELF ADDED	19,301		35,522		51,742		67,962		82,894		91,201		99,508	
END YEAR HDBSS - TOTAL ELF ADDED	38,936		30,080		28,925		25,460		24,172		17,547		17,547	
END YEAR HDBSS - TOTAL CUMULATIVE ELF ADDED	38,936	>	69,017	>	97,942	>	123,402	>	147,574	>	165,121	>	182,668	
150,000 ELF CAPACITY IN 4 AISLE MODULE - END YEAR ELF REMAINING >	111,064	74%	80,983	54%	52,058	35%	26,598	18%	2,426	2%		27%		
225,000 ELF CAPACITY IN 8 AISLE MODULE - END YEAR ELF REMAINING >	186,064	83%	155,983	69%	127,058	56%	101,598	45%	77,426	34%	59,879	27%	42,332	19%

A worksheet such as Figure 5 allows you to estimate the number of Equivalent Linear Feet being accessioned into the HDBSS each year, as well as projecting the time frame in which you can expect the HDBSS to be full. In the example presented, the number of books added each year has been carried forward from Figure 3 and multiplied by the average number of ELF / Item from Figure 4 to obtain the requisite number of HDBSS accession ELF being added each year. The 255,000 books being sent in year 1 is multiplied by .077 average ELF / Book to yield 19,635 Equivalent Linear Feet of HDBSS accessions in the first year. Similarly, each of the Other Than Books items is multiplied by its ELF / Item factor to yield a total of 19,301 Equivalent Linear Feet of HDBSS accessions in the first year. These steps are repeated for each year and cumulative totals are tracked to determine when an addition to the HDBSS will be required. In the illustration above, at the beginning of year 4 for a 4 aisle module, or the beginning of year 8 for a 6 aisle module.

Figure 5. Sample HDBSS Shelving Capacity Worksheet

One of These and Two of Those

Accession Levels
A worksheet such as Figure 3 allows you to determine your transfer and initial load-in levels vis-à-vis capacity in your library stacks. The scenario depicted shows an initial load-in spread over three years for the libraries and five years for the records. Once you have determined how much of what you intend to send when, you must determine the quantities of all tray sizes and shelf heights that will be required to accommodate said material. To do this you must "size" the collections by estimating either the percentage or the number of each size category represented.

Shelf Heights
A worksheet such as Figure 4 allows you to calculate the total number of shelves of various heights you should have the shelving company erect during construction, as well as the number of trays of each type you will need. Use a projected accession total that will approximate the total Equivalent Linear Feet of a HDBSS unit. The number of trays is a function of how many trays of a particular type fit on each size shelf.

Equivalent Linear Feet
By using the number of items to be transferred from Figure 4 and the average ELF/Item data from Figure 4 in a worksheet such as Figure 5, you will be able to estimate when you will need to build the next HDBSS module. In the illustration, construction of the next module will be required in year 3 for delivery in year 4 in the four-aisle version; year 7 for delivery in year 8 for the six-aisle version. Remember that construction takes a year and you should ensure the availability of the new unit well before you run out of space in the old. In addition, time needs to be allowed for planning and approvals prior to construction.

Please Pack Separately

Now that you have estimated how many of each size shelf is required, you need to determine their distribution throughout the system. These decisions are driven more by operational than by strictly shelving considerations, and address issues such as the following.

If you have a need for collection separation requirements, you may wish to consider segregating them by section or aisle. This will facilitate circulation as well as overcoming concerns about the mixing of specific collections.

If you can identify large active collections beforehand, you might wish to segregate them as well, again in order to facilitate circulation (it's quicker to retrieve six items in one aisle than six items in six aisles).

It's a good idea to shelve boxes and lighter material in the bottom shelf levels in order to limit awkward handling from a stooped or kneeling position. You should employ this concept at least to the 60-inch level.

Figure 6, Shelving Planograph, illustrates an HDBSS aisle face. You should provide the shelving installer with one of these for each aisle face based upon your analysis of where you expect to put each collection. Each of these could be different depending upon the collections you anticipate receiving and whether or not you have a need to shelve them by collection, activity level, etc.

The Operating Room

The fiscally conservative people who control the purse strings are generally reluctant to hear about the administrative and processing space required to support the more clearly understood need for shelving. But hear about it they must; the books won't just magically appear on the shelves. You must provide adequately for the activity side of the shelving coin, *but*, you should make every effort to ensure that the administrative/processing space requested is as closely aligned with your expected activity levels as your shelf space has been aligned with your shelving needs. Solid workflow planning and media handling expertise should drive this analysis. Some of the basic considerations in determining the size of this "administrative/processing" space are:

Fixed Space

Fixed space will be required regardless of activity levels, and includes:

♦ A truck dock (preferably with a dock leveler) to facilitate bulk moves and delivery of palletized book trays, which will be especially prevalent in the first year. The truck dock will also serve as the electric man-aboard charging area;

♦ A van dock (preferably garage) to accommodate vehicles with lower decks than can be serviced from the truck dock. A van is probably the type of vehicle you will use for delivery to the participating libraries;

♦ A staging area of sufficient size to stage at least 22 pallets of material (a trailer truck load) until it can be moved through the processing area, plus an additional space sufficient to store associated internal operations and transportation related material;

♦ If required, a media cleaning station and staging space as appropriate to deal with expected levels of accessions;

♦ Closeted space for telecommunications and security equipment;

♦ If required, a "reading room" and/or patron work room/area for on-site review of material;

♦ Office space as appropriate, with an eye to future needs as well as present;

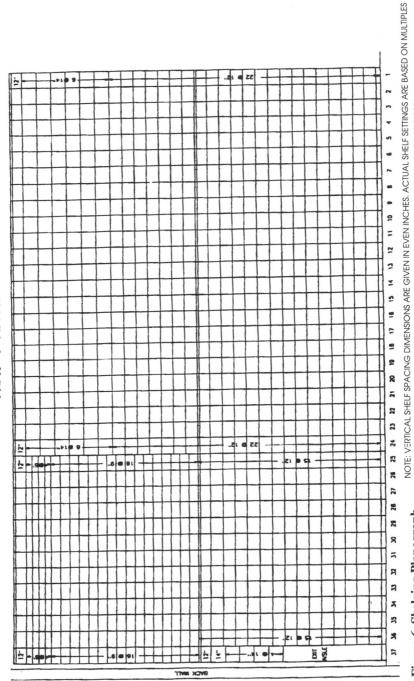

Figure 6. Shelving Planograph

♦ A lunch room and staff lounge space of appropriate size;

♦ Lavatory facilities in accordance with code;

♦ Space for custodial equipment, supplies, etc., to include a "slop" sink;

♦ A parking area sufficient to support the operation.

Variable Space

Your need for variable space will depend upon your anticipated accession and circulation forecasts, as well as any other activities you may intend to perform in the facility. Included will be space for:

♦ The assembly and stacking of a day's supply of book trays;

♦ Sorting stations and a staging area of sufficient size to deal with a day's worth of accession book size sorting;

♦ Database data entry workstations and a staging area of sufficient size to support a day's worth of data entry and verification;

♦ A staging area of sufficient size to accommodate a day's worth of processed accessions before their placement onto the shelves;

♦ A circulation desk and sufficient area to stage a day's worth of retrievals and a day's worth of refiles.

When All Is Said and Done

In the foregoing pages, we have tried to give you a brief exposure as to why and how big to build a High Density Book Shelving System to fit your needs. Although it represents a major departure from conventional library book shelving, a HDBSS provides the best opportunity to achieve efficient and cost-effective shelving of your collections. It also provides the opportunity for what should be in everyone's best interest: the long-term preservation of the media. High density book shelving systems are a wise use of scholars' dollars.

Appendix:
"Harvard Model" Facilities

Currently Operating (April 2001)

1. Bowling Green State University
2. Cornell University
3. Duke University
4. Harvard University
5. Johns Hopkins University
6. Miami University of Ohio
7. Northeast Ohio Library Consortium
8. Ohio State University
9. Ohio University
10. University of Minnesota
11. University of Missouri
12. University of Pennsylvania
13. University of South Carolina
14. University of Texas
15. University of Virginia
16. Virginia Polytechnics Institute and State University
17. Washington Research Library Consortium
18. West Virginia University
19. Yale University

In Design or Construction

1. Columbia University, Princeton University, and the New York Public Library Consortium
2. Indiana University
3. Library of Congress

9

The Preservation Environment

Paul Conway

The perpetuation of society as we are accustomed to conceive or idealize it is dependent to a very large extent on the preservation en masse of our accumulated group memories and consciousness stored in the form of the printed and otherwise recorded word or symbol.[1]

A preservation environment is the most cost-effective collection management tool that librarians and archivists have for extending the collective life expectancy of their vast scholarly resources. The preservation environment built in a modern library shelving facility embodies a conscious commitment to preservation and distinguishes such a building from a book warehouse, a book attic, or a typical full-service library. The concept of a "preservation environment" is a complex one that has emerged over nearly a century of concern over deteriorating library collections, several key conceptual breakthroughs in the past 40 years, and focused research in materials science. This chapter reviews how the idea of the library building as a preservation facility has changed over time, how materials science has contributed to the definition of a preservation environment, and how architects, engineers, and librarians designed the Yale University Library Shelving Facility to maximize the building's preservation value. The chapter concludes by identifying one lingering preservation issue that requires further research.

The Library Building as a Preservation Tool

The principal preservation goal in building a high-efficiency, high-density library shelving facility is to extend the useful life of the paper-based and film-based materials held there in comparison to a typically air-conditioned (or, worse, unconditioned) library shelving space. Library collections consist of different types of objects with widely varying rates of deterioration. Books, manuscripts, maps, photographs, films, and magnetic tapes will all last longer when kept in a preservation environment. The concept of "environment" encompasses common factors such as temperature, relative humidity (RH), light, and pollution as well as vibration, exposure to animal pests, insects, bacterial and fungus, and other more exotic agents of destruction. The preservation environment includes security and protection from fire and water damage. A preservation environment is lower in temperature, drier and more stable; is darker; is better sealed; has air freer of particulate matter (dust and dirt) and gaseous contamination; and is more secure than typical library buildings.

Deterioration is in the nature of things, and yet the attempt to cheat death is a part of our human nature. Some 30 years ago, Edwin Williams summed up in one sentence the challenge and the responsibility of library preservation. "Everything in library collections is deteriorating today, was deteriorating yesterday, and will continue to deteriorate tomorrow although we ought to retard the process."[2] This challenge has been with us for some time and it has been common knowledge for at least 175 years that the materials we use to record textual and visual information in published and unpublished form are fugitive and fragile. The problem for libraries and archives, however, is that awareness of a problem and the identification of causes and remedies—most pointedly in the value of the preservation environment—is a relatively recent phenomenon.

Both basic science and actual experience agree that temperature and relative humidity are the primary rate-controlling factors in chemical decay, mechanical damage, and bio-deterioration. All organic materials in collections deteriorate because of chemical reactions that speed up or slow down in response to environmental conditions. Two decades of rigorous laboratory testing have established predictive models of deterioration for materials commonly found in libraries, archives, and museums. These models, which are like maps that relate storage temperature, storage RH, and time-required-for-a-given-amount-and-kind-of-deterioration, show just how long even inherently unstable materials can last under the right storage conditions. They also show the converse—that the wrong environment can doom collections to very short lifetimes.

In the past five years, in particular, corroborative evidence from several laboratories working independently gives library managers new confidence in specifying environmental set points for shelving facilities. These set points are generally 10° cooler and up to 20 percentage points drier than specifications promulgated as recently as 10 years ago. We have a lot to learn about chemical and physical deterioration inside containers (such as a box, bag, or the book itself). We also need to understand more fully the impact of "microenvironments," such as the narrow air spaces surrounding shelved materials. Scientific testing of adhesives and other materials used to construct modern books also leaves too much room for interpretation.

Awareness of Preservation Problems and Solutions

Library materials are by and large organic in character. Deterioration of organic materials—paper, leather, and glue—is a fact of life; as inevitable as the sunrise but nowhere near as predictable. Paper is an amazing substance—strong and flexible when new, friendly to readers, and capable of holding in fixed form printed and handwritten words and images produced with nearly innumerable tools and techniques. Paper and the publishing revolution go hand in hand. Unfortunately, modern machine-made paper and the preservation challenges in libraries and archives are also inextricably linked.

People have been aware for millennia that the materials we use to record facts and ideas deteriorate to the point where they cannot be used for their intended purposes. The *New Testament* (Matt. 6:19) admonishes its readers: "Do not store up for yourselves treasure on earth, where it grows rusty and moth-eaten, and thieves break in to steal it." Book and paper historians report on age-old stories of prohibitions on the use of paper in deeds and manuscripts because of fears it was far more perishable than vellum (Grove, 1964). As early as 1823, alarms sounded in the Western press about the poor quality of writing and printing papers. By the early years of the 20th century, concern for the fragility of modern, machine-made papers reached a state of such frenzy that a search for stable copying methods began in earnest. This search culminated in the development of early standards for paper manufacture and the pursuit of archival microfilm, which remains the preservation strategy of choice when deterioration has undermined the physical integrity of books and papers (Higginbotham, 1990).

Beginning early in the decade of the 1960s, pieces of the preservation puzzle began to fall into place. The puzzle's image portrays the crucial role of environmental forces in exacerbating the deterioration process whose origins are clearly founded in the manufacture of paper, film, and other organic media. And yet the scale of the preservation challenge in research libraries, government cultural institutions, and archival repositories throughout the world, when combined with the significant costs of treatment and copying solutions, preclude addressing comprehensively preservation needs on an item-by-item basis. The recognition of this fact in the latter half of the 20th century has led to consistent and successful efforts to find a collection-based approach to preservation that stands half a chance of buying time for systematic preservation treatment if not solving the preservation problem altogether.

Materials Science and the Scientific Method

A preservation environment has comprehensive impact. All library materials shelved in a preservation environment benefit from increased life expectancy. This is true regardless of the quality of the materials when first manufactured or the condition of the materials when they are placed in the preservation environment. The specification of a preservation environment is based on contemporary understanding of materials science.

Paper and other organic materials deteriorate for a variety of reasons, some of which are related to the source of the material or the way it was manufactured and some of which are related to the way the material is stored or handled. At its most comprehensive, scientific research in materials science considers chemical factors (light, temperature, humidity), biologically induced degradation, and physically induced loss of strength that comes from handling and use. Path breaking materials science and the power of trial and error have fine-tuned the specifics of a preservation environment. The following are the major elements at play in a high-density, high-efficiency shelving facility.

> **Elements of an Ideal Environment**
>
> a) Pollutant-free air
> b) Total darkness
> c) Constant temperature
> d) Constant relative humidity
> e) Vibration-free structure and protection against shock and sound waves
> f) Absence of all organisms (including humans)
> g) A site on high land and a fireproof structure
> h) Elaborate emergency back-up control systems
> I) Cooperation of the Almighty
>
> *Source:* Duncan Cameron, "Environmental Control: A theoretical Solution," *Museum News* 46 (May 1968): 17.

Damage from Light

Among the suite of agents that cause deterioration, sunlight accounts for the most widespread destruction of materials outdoors. Sunlight, or solar radiation, and certain sources of artificial light are important in photochemical and photosensitized reactions because they are the sources of the radiant energy that make the reactions possible. Short wavelength radiation, especially ultraviolet rays, are far more damaging to library materials than either visible light or the longer wavelengths of infrared rays, radio waves and the radiation from high-voltage power lines. Light damage is cumulative; the amount of damage depends upon wavelength and the length and intensity of exposure. Brief exposure under relatively high intensity can be just as damaging as extended exposure to low intensity. Chemical reactions initiated by exposure to light continue even after the light source is removed and materials are put into dark storage (Ritzenthaler, 1993).

Indoors, damage from light is most troublesome on external surfaces such as the spine bindings of books and containers for archives and manuscripts collections. Light speeds up the oxidation of paper and therefore its chemical breakdown. Photo-oxidation of cellulose is accelerated by the presence of pollutants such as sulfur dioxide and nitrogen dioxide. Light is also a bleaching agent; it can cause some papers to whiten and can cause colored papers and inks to fade. Upon exposure to light, lignin reacts with other compounds in paper, causing lignin-containing paper to darken. Newspapers left outdoors for even a day or two provide graphic evidence of this effect.

Researchers discovered the negative consequences of light on library materials well before they zeroed in on other, even more damaging external sources of damage. Technical reports published in 1936 and 1941 pinpointed the damaging power of short wavelength radiation, especially ultraviolet (UV) radiation. Research by the National Bureau of Standards culminated in the extraordinary measures taken by the National Archives to protect the Declaration of Independence while on public display (Calmes, 1988).

By the late 1950s, architects of library buildings began to emphasize the need to build stack spaces without windows and to equip them with light fixtures that filter UV light. The first truly modern library storage facility, designed by Paul Banks and built as an extension to Chicago's Newberry Library, was a windowless cube with a darkened interior lit only to retrieve volumes. The latest thinking on lighting in shelving spaces that will not be browsed by the general public emphasizes limited duration lighting, low-intensity light sufficient to retrieve items, and the use of lighting systems that emit little or no ultraviolet rays. High-pressure sodium lamps, for example, cast a yellow light, but can be used where color rendering is not important. Sodium lights are highly efficient, are low in heat generation and operating costs, and relight quickly after being shut off (Lull & Merk, 1982).

Temperature and Humidity
in Theory and Practice

Temperature and relative humidity are inextricably linked in a preservation environment. One of the best ways to grasp the significance of this linkage is by way of the "Isoperm Theory," developed by Don Sebera of the Library of Congress and refined for film and other organic materials by James Reilly of the Image Permanence Institute. The Isoperm Theory is based on a simple idea: the rate of deterioration of water-absorbing materials such as paper is influenced strongly (perhaps even controlled) by the temperature and relative humidity of its surrounding environment. Paper and other organic materials commonly found in libraries, archives, and museums will lose strength with increased temperature and moisture content. Conversely, lowering either or both temperature and moisture content reduces the rate of chemical deterioration and so increases life expectancy. The Isoperm Theory combines and quantifies the preservation effects of temperature and relative humidity and presents the results in a comprehensible graphical form.

An isoperm is a graphical plot of the influence of temperature and relative humidity equilibrium on paper permanence. Underlying the theory is the assumption that temperature and relative humidity act together to speed up or slow down chemical deterioration to more or less the same degree in most organic materials. Figure 1 is a graph of isoperms from Sebera's seminal publication. The predictive power of the graph derives from varying one of the set points (temperature or relative humidity) while leaving the other set point constant. For example, by starting with environmental conditions at 68 degrees temperature and 50 percent relative humidity and then lowering the humidity level to 30 percent, the life expectancy of a collection is increased by a factor of two beyond what it would be if stored at the higher humidity setting. By raising the temperature from 68 to 80 degrees, the life expectancy of the collection decreases by a factor of three. Varying both set points simultaneously can have an even more dramatic impact on collection life expectancy.

Definition of an Isoperm

A line of constant permanence (isopermanence). Consider a paper at equilibrium with some initial considerations of temperature and relative humidity that determine its rate of deterioration and permanence. Now let us increase the relative humidity to a higher value; if the temperature is unchanged, the rate of deterioration will increase. However, if we reduce the temperature by exactly the right amount, the resulting temperature induced rate decrease will exactly compensate for the relative humidity induced increase so the overall deterioration rate (and permanence) is unchanged from that at the initial environmental conditions. We can make another change in relative humidity (or temperature), and another temperature (or relative humidity) can be found that will exactly compensate for the new relative humidity (or temperature) induced permanence change. These paired values, when plotted on a graph of T and %RH as axes, generate a line.

Source: Donald K. Sebera, *Isoperms: An Environmental Management Tool* (Washington, D.C.: Commission on Preservation and Access, 1994), 4.

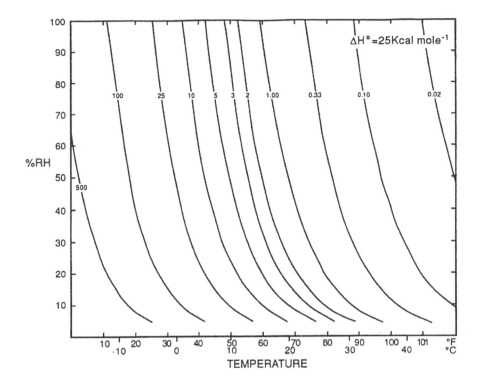

Figure 1. Isoperm Diagram Showing Percent Relative Humidity Versus Temperature

For some, the most confusing aspect of Sebera's Isoperm Theory is that his method is a view of the relative rather than the absolute rate of deterioration—the measure of the relative change in the deterioration rate resulting from the change in environmental conditions. It is the deterioration rate **ratio** that the preservation manager can control through changes in the temperature and percent relative humidity of the collection shelving areas. It is not possible to change nonenvironmental factors such as paper fiber type, fiber length, degree of heating of the pulp, the character of sizing agents, and the like, all of which influence the absolute rate of deterioration of a given paper.

To illustrate, suppose a certain decrease in temperature and/or relative humidity results in the initial deterioration rate, r_1, dropping to a new lower rate, r_2, such that the r_2/r_1 ratio = 0.5. This ratio carries the implication that all papers subjected to this change in environmental conditions will have their rates of deterioration cut in half. The rate reduction would be the same twofold value irrespective if a paper was short or long-lived. A paper which, for example, reached a given state of embrittlement in 45 years under the initial set of conditions would, because its rate of deterioration was halved, attained the same state of brittleness in 90 years under the new conditions. Similarly, a paper with a 200 year life expectancy would see its permanence extended to 400 years.[3]

Under the direction of James Reilly, the Image Permanence Institute at the Rochester Institute of Technology extended the research underlying the Isoperm Theory to predict the preservation value of shelving situations that experience seasonal variation in temperature and/or relative humidity. He derived a time-weighted measure of the impact of environmental fluctuation on collection life. Reilly and his colleagues, with the support of the National Endowment for the Humanities, summarized the measure in a report published in 1995 by the Commission on Preservation and Access. The following is a description of the measure taken from the report.

The Preservation Index (PI) is a means of expressing how ambient temperature and RH affect the chemical decay rate of collections. PI has units of years and gives a general idea of how long it would take for vulnerable organic materials such as poor-quality paper to become noticeably deteriorated, assuming that the temperature and RH did not change from the time of measurement onward. PI helps us to quantify how good or bad the environmental conditions are at that moment for chemical deterioration of the collections. The "years of life" aspect of IP values was chosen deliberately to reflect the behavior of relatively short-lived materials. PI is *not* meant as a predictor of the useful life of any particular object. It is simply a convenient measure of the effect of current environmental conditions on the overall life expectancy of the collection, using shorter-lived materials as a yardstick.[4]

The research of the Image Permanence Institute, when combined with the recent research at the Smithsonian Institution argues strongly for consistent set points within reasonable limits, erring on the side of cooler and drier as much of the time as possible. The Smithsonian research, controversial because of its suggestion that significant seasonal cycling has no negative impact on the mechanical properties of library materials, nevertheless does not undermine the value of a cool, dry environment for slowing or stopping deterioration from chemical reactions (Erhardt & Mecklenburg, 1995).

Pollution and Particulates

Airborne contamination takes two forms: gaseous pollution and particulate matter. The damage from gaseous pollution is not well understood. Mechanisms for controlling pollution inside a shelving facility are prone to uncertainties. Wessel (1970) reported at great length on the variety of pollutants and their possible effects on library collections without reaching meaningful or practical conclusions. In the intervening 30 years, little consensus has been found on the maximum allowable levels of atmospheric pollution in a preservation environment. The obvious conclusions that levels should be (a) as low as possible (or affordable) and (b) well below the recommendations of the Environmental Protection Agency for outdoor air quality are not particularly helpful for establishing design parameters.

The report of the National Research Council (1986) cautioned against the hasty establishment of indoor pollution levels based on suspended molecules in a mass of air. "Unless a more sophisticated definition of particulate air quality is adopted than one based solely on total aerosol mass concentration, there is a danger that ventilation systems will be designed that will lower mass loadings without achieving a proportionate reduction in damage potential." Nevertheless, when pressed for specific recommendations to guide the design and construction of a new building for the National Archives and Records Administration, the group relied on expert opinion rather than scientific evidence of pollution damage. The resulting recommendations of less than 0.4 parts per billion (ppb) for sulfur dioxide, less than 1.0 ppb for ozone, and "best available technology" for nitrogen dioxide exceed by a large degree the detection limits of continuous monitoring equipment.

William Lull and Paul Banks (1995) and William Wilson (1995) recognize the inherent uncertainty of pollution control and recommend maximum levels that, while well below EPA recommendations, are within the range of common detection devices. Lull and Banks describe succinctly the complexity of the gaseous pollution challenge. "The gaseous contamination may come from pollution in outdoor air, from contamination by off-gassing from the building's construction or cleaning materials, from building occupants, or from the collection itself." The theory, which is not yet subjected to rigorous scientific analysis, is that collections have lower tolerance than human occupants of a given space because the human body is living and can effect repairs to itself, while collections have no such self-renewing mechanism.

The level of particulate matter in the air may not appear to be a pressing preservation problem, in the sense that particulates may not be a direct cause of deterioration. Nevertheless, once a collection of library materials shelved in a high-density shelving facility becomes dirty, it is virtually impossible to clean. The spaces between materials shelved by size and the shelves themselves typically averages one inch or less. The sheer volume of materials housed in a room with shelving systems stretching 35 feet in the air precludes moving collections for general maintenance. Additionally, infestations of insects, rodents, and biological agents such as mold spores are extraordinarily challenging to halt in a high-density facility. The most prudent preservation strategy is to prevent infestations from the start. Without a doubt, extraordinary attention to cleanliness of the facility (through rigorous custodial activity) and to cleanliness of the collections (through cleaning routines applied uniformly) is a vital preservation concern.

Preservation at the Yale University Library Shelving Facility

The Yale University Library Shelving Facility (LSF) was completed in November 1998 following a two-year process that encompassed programmatic planning, physical and operational design, and construction. The LSF consists of an 8,000-square-foot processing area and a single shelving module of 12,500 square feet (inside dimensions). The module is outfitted with a single tier shelving system arrayed in six aisles. The capacity of the module is approximately 2.3 million volumes. The site of the facility is large enough to accommodate six shelving modules and should provide for collection growth over the next 50 years.

Although a number of libraries and museums have installed cold rooms for the storage of archival films, at the present time, the LSF is the coldest and driest building designed for the shelving of general library collections. The decision on environmental set points was not an easy one. Making it involved balancing a number of assumptions about what types of materials would and would not be shelved in the facility over its life, circulation rates from the facility, and costs of construction and operations.

Yale's decision about life expectancy was informed by the state of research on environmental control, but influenced most directly by the research findings of the Image Permanence Institute. Working with IPI data (Figure 2), the LSF planning committee identified the PI values for five combinations of temperature and relative humidity that satisfied combinations of criteria.

						Temperature (°F)							
		32	37	42	47	52	57	62	67	72	77	82	87	92
	5	2634	1731	1147	767	516	350	240	165	114	80	56	40	28
	10	2234	1473	979	656	443	302	207	143	99	70	49	35	25
	15	1897	1255	837	562	381	260	179	124	86	61	43	30	22
	20	1613	1070	716	482	328	224	155	107	75	53	37	27	19
	25	1373	914	613	414	282	194	134	93	65	46	33	23	17
	30	1170	781	525	356	243	168	116	81	57	40	29	21	15
	35	998	668	451	307	210	145	101	71	50	35	25	18	13
	40	852	572	387	264	182	126	88	62	43	31	22	16	12
	45	729	491	333	228	157	109	76	54	38	27	19	14	10
% RH	50	624	421	287	197	136	95	66	47	33	24	17	12	9
	55	535	362	247	170	118	82	58	41	29	21	15	11	8
	60	459	312	213	147	102	72	51	36	26	18	13	10	7
	65	394	269	184	128	89	62	44	31	22	16	12	9	6
	70	339	232	160	111	77	54	39	28	20	14	10	8	6
	75	292	200	138	96	67	48	34	24	17	13	9	7	5
	80	251	173	120	84	59	42	30	21	15	11	8	6	4
	85	217	150	104	73	51	36	26	19	14	10	7	5	4
	90	187	130	90	63	45	32	23	16	12	9	6	5	3
	95	162	112	79	55	39	28	20	15	11	8	6	4	3
							PI Values, in Years							

Figure 2. Preservation Index (PI) Values (showing predicted lifetime, in years, of short-lived organic materials at various combinations of temperature and relative humidity conditions)

The planning committee then asked consulting engineers to estimate the impact of these combinations on the cost of building and maintaining the preservation environments. The five combinations investigated, the reasoning behind the choices, and utility cost estimates in 1997 dollars, included:

1. 68°/40%RH (PI=58 years)
   Conditions in newly renovated Sterling Memorial Library
   No special dehumidification system required
   Lowest RH without special equipment
   Readers and library materials together
   Est. $1,724 per month electric costs

2. 60°/30%RH (PI=131 years)
    Emphasis on RH; compromise on temperature
    Less concern for transitions to and from the LSF
    Est. $2,708 per month electric costs

3. 50°/40%RH (PI=217 years)
    Emphasis on cool temperature, compromise on RH
    Appropriate for art, rare books, natural history collections
    Est. $3,998 per month electric costs

4. 50°/30%RH (PI=275 years)
    Coolest conditions for nonspecialized clothing for staff
    Overengineered for relative humidity control
    Appropriate for paper, film, and tape that does not circulate
    Est. $3,998 per month electric costs

5. 45°/40%RH (PI=300 years)
    Push limits on human working conditions
    Emphasis on temperature; compromise on RH
    Explore limits on operating costs
    Est. $8,152 per month electric costs

The decision to establish set points of 50°F and 30%RH was based on these assumptions, which were developed after much discussion and debate in the planning committee.

♦ The LSF is not intended to serve as a shelving space for art objects or natural history collections. Research suggests that these types of materials, not commonly found in quantity in research libraries, benefit from humidity levels that are higher than optimum for paper- and film-based library collections.

♦ A key planning assumption for the LSF is that annual circulation rates will not exceed 3 percent of the contents. For example, if the LSF contained an average of 500,000 items in a given year, that no more than 15,000 items would be retrieved by patrons. The assumption of low use allowed the Yale planners to de-emphasize the need for and the cost of special procedures that mitigate the adjustment of materials to higher temperatures and different humidity levels that exist outside the LSF during transportation and use of the materials.

♦ A key design assumption was that the environmental control system should be overengineered. A control system designed and built to hold cooler and drier conditions than are typical in shelving facilities today would permit future adjustments downward or upward as new scientific understanding emerges on the impact of environments on library collections. Over the past decade, the science has pointed clearly toward cooler and drier. Yale wanted to build the capacity from the outset to adjust conditions as needed or recommended.

♦ The cost assessment undertaken during the design phase demonstrated that there was no difference in either construction or operating costs of an environmental system overengineered to produce relative humidity set points below those in the typical library shelving facility.

Ultimately, the decision on temperature and relative humidity set points turned on the desire of the planning group to maximize the useful life of the collections shelved there, while making it possible for staff to operate in the shelving module without special clothing and equipment.

The Harris Box

The preservation environment in the Library Shelving Facility is a turnkey system designed, constructed, and installed by Harris Environmental Systems, Inc. under terms of a sole-source contract.[5] Harris Systems is one of the country's oldest and largest manufacturers of specialized environments. In business since 1939, the company has concentrated for the past 40 years on environmental rooms, clean rooms, dry rooms, cycling test chambers, and archival storage vaults. Harris builds its rooms in a factory and then installs the rooms and associated equipment on site using its own mechanics and carpenters. Since 1995, the company has installed more than 1,000 environmental rooms. Recent library and museum customers include The Art Institute of Chicago, J. Paul Getty Center, the Smithsonian Institution, Kansas State Historical Society, and the Harvard University Depository.

The Harris system is essentially a giant refrigerator built to fit a cinder block and concrete box 197 feet deep, 69 feet wide, and 38 feet high (outside dimensions). The walls and ceiling of the single room are lined with 3-inch-thick, metal-clad, polyurethane insulated panels. The wall and ceiling panels have an insulation value of R23.8 at +30°F. Under the wall panels is a double-layer, high-density, polyethylene vapor barrier with a perm rating of 0.045. Under the shelving module's concrete slab is a flexible sandwich of high-density polyethylene and aluminum with a perm rating of 0.0142.

The daily-use doors into the shelving module (as opposed to the emergency exits) are single leaf, horizontal sliding, and power operated. The doors are insulated with an R-value of 28 at 40°F and are equipped with reinforced polyester gaskets all around.

Temperature and Relative Humidity

The shelving module holds a temperature of 50°F ±2°. Humidity levels in the module are maintained at 30%RH ±2%. Both the temperature and relative humidity levels are held constant at all times of the day and night, every day of the year. The Harris system is engineered with the potential for seasonal variation of both temperature and humidity levels. Yale has chosen to keep both levels flat until research findings settle the issue of the costs and benefits for collections of seasonal variation.

Potential heat gain in the module is an issue. The design of the mechanical systems assumes that access doors will be opened no more than 10 times per day and that only two people will be working in the module at a given time. The system exchanges air in the shelving module at the rate of 2.2 times per hour (12,000 cubic feet per minute). Make-up air from outside the module is limited to 10 percent of the total air exchanged.

The principal cooling device is an air-cooled condensing unit with a 78-ton capacity. Manufactured by Technical Systems (a RAE Corporation), the system features redundant independent refrigerant circuits for increased reliability (Figure 3). Effectively adding humidification to an air stream without creating wetness in the system is critical to maintaining a healthy environment, free of conditions that foster mold growth. Humidification, when needed, is provided by an electric steam system manufactured by DRI Steam Humidification Co. The systems capacity is 12 lbs/1.4 gal/5.4 kg.

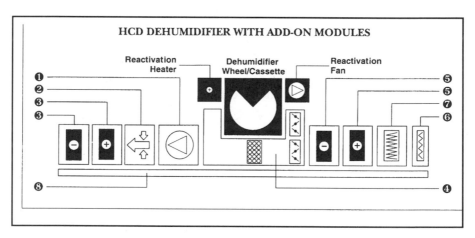

Figure 3. Schematic Diagram of Typical Mechanical System of a Preservation Environment. (1) Process Air Blower Plenum; (2) Mixing Plenum; (3) Post-Heat/Cool Coil Plenum; (4) Pre-Heat/Cool Coil Plenum; (5) Face and Bypass Plenum; (6) Filter Plenum, 30%; (7) Filter Plenum, High Efficiency; (8) Skid

Courtesy Cargocaire Division—Munters Corporation.

The particular combination of constant temperature and relative humidity that Yale has chosen to hold in the shelving module cannot be accomplished without the assistance of a desiccant dehumidification system. The Cargocaire desiccant system features a large rotating wheel filled with a lithium chloride desiccant, which is a nontoxic and nonmetallic compound. Dehumidification is accomplished by forcing cooled air through the wheel across the desiccant materials. As the wheel rotates, natural gas–heated air flows over the moisture-laden desiccant to release water, which is drained away, and restores its drying properties. The system can remove up to approximately 50 pounds of water per hour.

Temperature and relative humidity values in the shelving module are detected and transmitted to a central control panel. The sensors are mounted on the walls of the shelving module. They detect room temperature with an accuracy of ±0.5°F. The sensors detect humidity levels with an accuracy of ±1%RH. Linearized output signals are provided for transmission over a length of cable. The sensors are low-maintenance models and need calibration once every two years.

Continuous recording of temperature and relative humidity readings is provided on a 10-inch circular chart. Digital data from sensing devices is translated to analog traces by two disposable fiber-tip ink pens. Stepper motors controlled by a microprocessor drive the chart and the pen to help insure precise, maintenance-free operation. Since the speed of the chart is configurable, users can record environmental readings with variable levels of granularity. At Yale, one chart records a single week of continuously plotted temperature and humidity readings.

Air Filtration

The air handling unit for the shelving module contains a four-stage filtration system. The four stages include a pre-filter for large particulate matter, a rigid filter for fine particulates, and two chemical filters that have the adsorptive properties of activated carbon combined with the chemisorptive properties of chemically treated media. One of these filters is designed to control diesel exhaust drawn into fresh air intakes and to trap gasses released from compounds used in the building construction, such as adhesives, sealants, and paint. This filter system absorbs toluene, formaldehyde, nitrogen dioxide, and ozone. The second carbon filter is designed for airborne pollution from outside air and compounds released during the process of organic deterioration. The filter is highly effective against sulfur dioxide, nitrogen dioxide, high molecular weight volatile organic compounds, chlorine, ozone, and many other oxidizable materials.

Harris engineered the Yale filtration system to function at 95 percent efficiency for particulate pollution. The system has the capacity to reduce levels of sulfur dioxide, nitrogen dioxide, ozone, and other gaseous pollutants to less than 10 parts/billion/volume. The actual level of particulate and gaseous pollution in the LSF depends in large measure on the quality of the outside air and the long-term maintenance of the filtration system. Harris recommends annual air quality measurements as part of the system's maintenance contract. The LSF is too new to determine the overall effectiveness of the pollution filtration system.

Lighting

The lights in the shelving module are 250 watt sodium vapor bulbs suspended in a heavy-gauge aluminum reflector designed to provide a long and narrow distribution of the light. Two parallel internal panels reflect the light at high angles to provide high vertical illumination on the stacks. Two additional panels provide uniform illumination up and down the aisle. Each light (spaced at 30 feet) casts approximately 11 foot candles along the stacks and at the floor level. Lighting is free of UV rays. Lights in the shelving module are off when the building is not in use.

Fire Protection

The entire Library Shelving Facility, including the shelving module, is equipped with a wet-pipe sprinkler system conforming to the standards of the National Fire Protection Association (Artim, 1999). A wet-pipe system has automatic sprinklers attached to a piping system containing water and connected to a water supply so that water discharges immediately from sprinklers when they are opened by fire. All sprinkler heads are UL-listed Quick Response Commercial heads designed for ordinary hazard application. Piping for the sprinkler system extends into the shelving system in two horizontal tiers at 15 and 25 feet above the floor. Sprinkler heads are located approximately at eight-foot intervals and heads are staggered on the two tiers so that every shelving segment has one sprinkler head associated with it.

Extending Preservation Through Care and Handling

The Yale University Library Shelving Facility, by the mere existence of its environmental conditions, is a state-of-the-art preservation program. The ways in which materials are chosen, prepared, and handled as part of the transfer process from campus collections to the off-campus LSF extend the preservation value of the facility. The processing of library materials from their campus libraries to the LSF is guided by one overarching goal: do no harm. In practice, the accomplishment of this goal requires that the entire processing system—from the point of pulling an item from a shelf in a campus library to placing the item in the shelving module—ensures the transfer of materials as quickly and efficiently as possible without damaging items or exacerbating damage that may already have occurred due to age or past use. It is important to reiterate that the goal of inserting preservation sensibilities into the processing procedure is to make sure that items are transferred without damage, rather than to facilitate collection care or other preservation activities, either now or later.

The premise of low use drives much of the preservation planning at the LSF. As a general rule, less than 3 percent of the total collection can be expected to circulate in a given calendar year. This rule is derived from decades of cumulative experience of the Harvard Depository and a dozen other high-density facilities. The low-use premise stands in stark contrast to typical circulation rates in full-service research library collections, which may range from 15 percent per year to well over 100 percent per year. The low-use premise shifts the focus of care and handling procedures from those governing active use to those governing transfer to the facility initially.

Beyond the past and expected use of the collections transferred to a high-density shelving facility, preservation procedures must be informed by the overall condition of collections slated for transfer. A study conducted at Yale while planning the LSF suggested that no more than 11 percent of Yale's collections would require special preservation handling during the transfer process. A study undertaken at the University of Kansas for completely different reasons supports the findings of the Yale study (Baird, 1997). This relatively low rate of fragility may come as a surprise to preservation administrators more commonly accustomed to the daily routine of broken and brittle materials circulated by readers. Procedures for handling materials that need be handled only one time under controlled circumstances may be more forgiving than general care and handling procedures for general circulating collections used repeatedly by the general public.

Transfer Risk of Low-Use Materials: A Survey

In planning the transfer of library materials from their current locations to the new Library Shelving Facility, one of the factors considered was the physical condition of the material to be moved. Differing opinions among selectors suggested that from 35% to 50% of all material might need extra care before safe transportation is possible. The path breaking and highly influential Yale condition survey from 1986 suggested that 40% of the Library's collection was in brittle condition. Decades of seasonal changes between humid summers and the hot, dry steam heating of winter, combined with fossil fuel pollutants from New Haven's industrial past produced brittle books with imprint dates as early as 1800, fifty years earlier than the acknowledged beginning of the "brittle books era." Given the possible fragile condition of much of the collection, it was conceivable that significant damage could be caused by the handling and processing required to meet the expected 2,500 volume per day production quota. Also, if the level of fragility in the transfer collections was as high as suspected, it would be virtually impossible to provide item-level conservation treatment to transferred items and still achieve the daily transfer quota. The purpose of the survey was to gain information about the transferability of material and determine the preservation impact of filling the LSF with low-use but possibly badly deteriorated library.

(Continued)

The preservation aspects of the LSF processing system are based on the following assumptions:

♦ Selectors or their delegates (including, perhaps, Preservation Department, Access Services, or LSF staff) retain responsibility for identifying items needing special handling.

♦ All flags, printouts, and other objects placed in items during the transfer process that have any chance of remaining with the item on the LSF shelf will be constructed of archival quality paper.

♦ Processing efficiencies derive from batch processing, wherever possible.

♦ Efficient processing routines mitigate preservation concerns in many domains.

♦ The proportion of materials transferred to LSF that will require special handling of any kind will not exceed 10 percent overall.

In the course of planning the processing routines for Yale's LSF, the Preservation Department derived a set of rules and guidelines built around six transfer principles. See the appendix for details on the implementation of the transfer principles at Yale.

The principal study question was "What percentage of the total material within selected subject domains would need to be excluded from transfer to the LSF due to its present condition?" To answer this question, Preservation Librarian David Walls examined the physical condition of six hundred volumes from six subject areas of the collection. Additional data on imprint date, last circulation date, and whether the item had a barcode were also collected. Large serial sets were skipped to increase the variety of material surveyed. Items were examined in call number order as they stood on the shelves. Data were recorded in a spreadsheet designed to calculate simple percentages for each class surveyed.

The findings of the survey suggest that the vast majority of the low-use material scheduled for transfer to the LSF could be safely sent without causing further damage. About 11% of the material will need to be handled with extra care to ensure safe transfer. This activity could be targeted at the point of selection during the move, barely slowing the daily transfer rate, if at all. While some pamphlets were found to be adequately housed for safe transport, all of the material disqualified from immediate transport, 7%, consisted of brittle pamphlets or pamphlets housed in brittle or non-supportive enclosures. These pamphlets may be divided into three readily recognizable categories: brittle pamphlets housed in brittle or soft covers; brittle pamphlets housed in envelopes; and pamphlets housed in oversized boxes. In the survey no formats other than pamphlets were identified as being at risk during transport.

(Continued)

Transfer Principle No. 1: Every item transferred to LSF must have a container that is intact or secured.

Transfer Principle No. 2: Every container transferred to LSF must have a bar code associated with it, unless the container can't or shouldn't accept a bar code.

Transfer Principle No. 3: Specially designed tubs should be used to transfer containers from the campus library to the LSF.

Transfer Principle No. 4: Dual processing streams separate containers needing special care from those that can be processed routinely.

Transfer Principle No. 5: Information about the condition of an item transferred to LSF is best retained in the LSF inventory database, rather than in the online catalog.

Transfer Principle No. 6: Every container will be cleaned at LSF prior to processing and shelving, even if it appears to be clean.

It is important to recognize that the condition survey addressed only whether an item is physically capable of being sent to the LSF with a reasonable degree of safety. A brittle volume with a history of low use demands little intervention as long as it is housed within an appropriate environment. If this same volume were suddenly added to a course reading list, for example, immediate intervention would be required to preserve its integrity.

Source: David Walls, "A Condition Survey of Six Subject Classes of Low-Use Material," unpublished study report, Yale University Library, October 1997.

Cleaning Items Prior to Shelving

The Yale University Library Shelving Facility is the first library building of its kind to incorporate into the design of the building and into the processing workflow the systematic cleaning on site of all items shelved there. Four arguments drove the cleaning plan.

♦ Most items transferred from campus libraries exhibit some level of visible dirt and grime.

♦ Dirt is a carrier of and a breeding ground for mold spores and can be an important source of acidic and corrosive compounds that exacerbate the deterioration of library materials.

♦ Once lodged in the shelving module, dirt and dust is almost impossible to remove, due to the low rate of air exchange and the high-density shelving system.

♦ Most libraries from which materials are transferred do not have sufficient space to clean items systematically and efficiently.

Yale's planning team inspected existing library shelving facilities during the early design phases. In the process the team convinced itself that particulate matter (from paper and cellulose, as well as from brake pads of order-picker equipment operated in the shelving module) should be minimized by cleaning all accessioned items and through rigorous building and equipment maintenance.

The final design of the cleaning facility was completed while the building was under construction. Consultations with Yale's Office of Health and Safety as well as creative brainstorming by an ad hoc planning group clarified key design issues, such as efficient processing, ergonomics, and the preservation handling of library materials. Personnel from the construction management team mocked up a prototype cleaning apparatus, which was tested using representative examples from the library stacks. Additionally, the planning group received valuable advice on mechanical system design from Professor Peter Kindlmann of Yale's Electrical Engineering Department. The net result of this work was a clarification of the goals of the cleaning program and an outline of the specific requirements for the layout of the cleaning room, the design of the cleaning system, and the capabilities of auxiliary equipment and supplies.

The following is an outline of the capabilities of the cleaning facility as built at Yale.

Room Capability

♦ Four identically outfitted workstations

♦ Continuous work surface along one wall

♦ Redundant vacuum systems; one per cleaning station

♦ Negative pressure in the HVAC system associated with the cleaning room to improve the overall cleanliness of the LSF

♦ Cleaning process and equipment stations combined to accommodate at least 2,000 items per day, every day

♦ Vacuum machinery located outside the work area to minimize noise, heat, and dust inside the work area

♦ Cleaning room exclusively dedicated to the cleaning of library materials.

Cleaning Station Design (specifications for each station)

Work Surface

♦ Continuous, smooth surface

♦ Nonstatic

♦ 36 inches in height

♦ 36 inches in depth

♦ 68 to 72 inches of surface allocated to each station

Vacuum System

♦ Remote location, yet easily serviced and emptied

♦ Outside venting to eliminate need for HEPA filters

♦ Capability to support brush-on-hose cleaning and fixed cleaning head

♦ Left- and right-handed hose attachment flush with surface

♦ Cleaning head assembly mounted flush with surface

♦ Ability to switch from hose to head cleaning with little difficulty

♦ Produces 200 to 500 cfm at cleaning surface with capability to adjust and monitor airflow

♦ Special catch filter in clear plastic housing that prevents pieces from particularly fragile items from being drawn into the vacuum.

Cleaning Head Assembly

♦ Modular design (component parts, removable, interchangeable)

♦ Simultaneous brushing and surface vacuum

♦ Bristle assembly is removable for easy replacement

♦ Assembly can accommodate bristles of different material (natural or synthetic) and length

Auxiliary Equipment and Supplies

A certain level of harmonious design and selection of carts and other equipment is needed to support the efficiency of the overall cleaning process.

Carts

♦ Function fluidly with tubs chosen for transfer

♦ Position top rim of tub of materials to be cleaned at 36 inches, preferably through some sort of adjustment mechanism

♦ Top of carts should be smooth and without lips, flanges, or handles to facilitate the movement of oversize materials

Chairs

♦ Seating at processing workstations is not used in many shelving facilities for accessioning work. Following an ergonomic review of the Library Shelving Facility, the operations manager decided that all cleaning operations would be undertaken while standing

Health and Safety Equipment

♦ Cushioned pads for standing at cleaning station

♦ Appropriate dust masks and aspirators for special circumstances

♦ Task lighting at each cleaning station (if appropriate)

Continuing Controversy

In spite of an emerging consensus on the components of a preservation environment, forged from almost two decades of experience with high-density shelving facilities, at least one major technical issue remains unresolved. This has to do with the need for rigorous temperature and humidity set points throughout the year and the related concern over the possible negative impact on library materials when they are moved out of the shelving facility temporarily to be used.

Researchers at the Smithsonian Institution have focused attention on the issue of seasonal cycling (Erhardt and Mecklenburg, 1995). The heart of the matter is the cost of maintaining the preservation environment in the facility once it is built. The argument of the Smithsonian researchers is that materials can withstand seasonal variation without physical damage and that allowing seasonal variation in temperature and relative humidity set points can save many dollars in utility costs. The Smithsonian research focuses on mechanical damage to materials based on extreme changes in temperature and humidity over varying time frames. Their work is not necessarily concerned with chemical damage that occurs when temperature and/or humidity levels climb even for short periods of time. Only rigorous scientific inquiry and rigorous investigation of the assumptions outlined in the Smithsonian Institution research will resolve the controversy. The present state-of-the-art argues that stable temperature and humidity levels are the foundation of a true preservation environment. Just because library collections can withstand temperature changes without mechanical damage does not mean they should be put at risk of chemical damage through cycling.

The concern about the impact of physical stresses when library materials move from cool-dry conditions of a shelving facility to the warm-humid conditions of a reading room on a summer day derives from the Smithsonian research findings. No systematic research has been carried out on this issue. Yet informal commentary exchanged among facilities designers and operational staff suggests that there is little need for concern when paper is the principal medium being shelved. For film, however, a period of acclimatization is needed between the transfer from a preservation environment to a normally conditioned (or unconditioned) environment. The LSF handles this by transporting films in picnic coolers and recommending a 24-hour adjustment before films are viewed.

Conclusion

Yale University's Library Shelving Facility, along with nearly all such facilities built within the last 10 years, is a first line of defense against the deterioration of library materials. There may always be room to improve upon the basic model. And yet, these facilities go a long way toward satisfying the core criteria of an effective preservation program articulated by Gordon Williams some 35 years ago.

> A preservation program must preserve all books of significant value; it must preserve the maximum amount of information carried by the original books; it must provide for the longest period of preservation practicable with present technology and compatible with the other requirements; it must provide for the continuous and ready availability of the preserved materials to anyone who needs them; and it must avoid unnecessary duplication of effort and expense.[6]

Notes

1.   Guy Petherbridge, ed., *Conservation of Library and Archive Materials and the Graphic Arts* (London: Butterworths, 1987), 10.

2.   Edwin E. Williams, "Deterioration of Library Collections Today," in *Deterioration and Preservation of Library Materials*, ed. Howard W. Winger and Richard Daniel Smith (Chicago: University of Chicago Press, 1970), 3.

3.   Donald K. Sebera, *Isoperms: An Environmental Management Tool* (Washington, D.C.: Commission on Preservation and Access, 1994), 4.

4.   James M. Reilly, Douglas W. Nishimura, and Edward Zinn, *New Tools for Preservation: Assessing Long-Term Environmental Effects on Library and Archives Collections* (Washington, D.C.: Commission on Preservation and Access, 1995), 4.

5.   Harris Environmental Systems, 11 Connector Road, Andover, MA 01810, (978) 470-8600; Web site: http://www.harris-env.com

6.   Gordon Williams, "The Preservation of Deteriorating Books," *Library Journal* 91 (January 1, 1966): 51–56, and (January 15, 1966): 189–94.

Appendix: Transfer Principles

Transfer Principle No. 1: *Every item transferred to LSF must have a container that is intact or secured.*

Examples of containers include:

♦ binding

♦ slip case

♦ phase box

♦ Paige box (for archival records)

♦ document case or envelop (for loose pamphlets or archival materials)

♦ microfilm box

At the point of selection from the shelf, each item should be inspected quickly for the integrity of the container—with one question in mind: can this item be transferred to LSF and processed without damaging it? If the answer is "YES," pull it. If the answer is "NO," the selector or delegate must decide to secure it for transfer or leave it on the shelf. Visual signs of condition that may indicate a container is NOT OK to send as is include:

♦ One or both covers/boards loose or falling off

♦ Spine loose, separated from boards/covers

♦ Many pages loose, leaf loose

♦ Pages crumbling from very advanced brittleness

♦ Leather, vellum, etc. bindings are rotting, rubbing off, crumbling

♦ Leather, vellum etc. bindings are cracked, splitting in solid pieces

♦ Spills, stickiness obvious anywhere on container

♦ Pest (worms, etc.) obvious to eye

♦ Container appears wet/damp, verified by touch

♦ Container has been seriously mutilated/is torn, cut in some way

♦ Heavy smell of mildew

The manager of the LSF will return an item to a sending library that cannot be handled routinely or processed to the LSF shelf without causing damage to the item.

Transfer Principle No. 2: *Every container transferred to LSF must have a bar code associated with it, unless the container **can't** or **shouldn't** accept a bar code.*

♦ A container **can't** accept a bar code because of its **physical condition** (e.g., rotting leather, very soiled surface, very rough or mottled surface, etc.)

♦ A container **shouldn't** accept a bar code because of its **artifactual value** (e.g., rare, valuable, or decorated bindings; rare or unique item; highly valuable item, etc.)

When in doubt, a bar code should be placed on the surface of the container. The Processing Group recommends that containers that cannot or should not be affixed with a bar code should be wrapped or placed in an acid-free envelope with the bar code attached to the wrapper or envelope.

Transfer Principle No. 3: *Specially designed tubs should be used to transfer containers from the campus library to the LSF.*

The risk of damage to items transferred on book trucks is simply too great. Damage will likely occur when trucks spill or are jostled during transfer to and from the van, to and from the home library loading areas, and while in transit. Over-packed book trucks will damage an item as it is loaded on or taken from the truck. The risk of damage from book-truck transfer far exceeds the risk of damage from transfer in and out of tubs, particularly if a subset of tubs can be identified and marked "Fragile—Handle with Care." Tubs are cheaper, more durable, and more flexible to transport than book trucks.

The following are some of the specifications for transfer tubs:

♦ Distinctive from other library portables for quick identification
♦ Dimensions: 23" x 15.5" x 8.5" (l x w x d)
♦ Maximum 50 lbs. capacity when full
♦ Snap-down lid with channel drainage for water resistance
♦ Stackable when full up to five high
♦ Nested when empty
♦ Constructed of high density polyethylene
♦ Sides labeled for easy sorting (as needed)

Transfer Principle No. 4: *Dual processing streams separate containers needing special care from those that can be processed routinely.*

Since no more than 10 percent of the containers (more likely 5 percent) received at LSF will require special handling of any sort, the overall efficiency of the LSF program depends upon the routine and efficient processing of containers that do not need special handling. Those that do should be processed as a batch as time permits during a given week, rather than integrating preservation handling procedures into the normal workflow. Wrapping for preservation handling can and should be handled centrally at the LSF, especially if fragile containers arrive in specially marked tubs. A wrapping workstation must have the capacity to provide for the wrapping, bagging, enveloping, and/or securing of fragile containers and the attachment of bar codes where necessary and appropriate.

Transfer Principle No. 5: *Information about the condition of an item transferred to LSF is best retained in the LSF inventory database, rather than in the online catalog.*

Condition information will facilitate safe retrieval and transfer from LSF to the campus library. Additionally, a record of poor condition is an investment improving the possibility that fragile items shelved at the LSF can be retrieved in the future specifically for batch preservation processing. The LSF inventory database must provide a data field in which preservation condition or value codes will be entered; up to five codes identify specific conditions. Parallel processing of preservation items will greatly facilitate the consistent and efficient entry of condition/value codes.

Transfer Principle No. 6: *Every container will be cleaned at LSF prior to processing and shelving, even if it appears to be clean.*

Thorough cleaning of every container is essential to the long-term cleanliness of the LSF shelving environment. Only in exceptional circumstances, and with the prior approval of the LSF manager, are containers to be processed without cleaning. Items inside containers (e.g., pamphlet in envelope, book in a box, fully wrapped periodical volume) need not be cleaned separately if the container is new. Items wrapped by the home library prior to transfer will require surface cleaning only.

References

Artim, Nick. "An Introduction to Fire Detection, Alarm, and Automatic Fire Sprinklers." In *Preservation of Library & Archival Materials: A Manual.* Andover, MA: Northeast Document Conservation Center, 1999.

Baird, Brian J., Jana Krentz, and Brad Schaffner. "Findings from the Condition Surveys Conducted by the University of Kansas Libraries." *College & Research Libraries* 58 (1997): 115–26.

Banks, Paul N. "Environmental Standards for Storage of Books and Manuscripts." *Library Journal* 99 (1974): 339–43.

Banks, Paul N. "Environment and Building Design." In *Preservation Issues and Planning*, edited by Paul N. Banks and Roberta Pilette, 114–44. Chicago: American Library Association, 2000.

Barrow, William J. *Deterioration of Book Stock: Causes and Remedies: Two Studies on the Permanence of Book Paper.* Richmond: Virginia State Library, 1959.

Blades, William. *The Enemies of Books.* 3rd ed. London: Trubner & Co., 1881.

Calmes, Alan R. "Documenting Changes in the Physical Condition of the U.S. Declaration of Independence, Constitution, and Bill of Rights: The Charters Monitoring System." *Government Publications Review* 15 (1988): 439–49.

Calmes, Alan R., Ralph Schofer, and Keith R. Eberhardt. "Theory and Practice of Paper Preservation for Archives." *Restaurator* 9 (1988): 96–111.

Cameron, Duncan. "Environmental Control: A Theoretical Solution." *Museum News* 46 (May 1968): 17–21.

Erhardt, David, and Marion Mecklenburg. "Relative Humidity Re-examined." *Preventive Conservation: Practice, Theory and Research.* Preprints of the Contributions to the Ottawa Congress, September 12–16, 1994. London: International Institute for Conservation of Historic and Artistic Works. 1995.

Fortson, Judith. *Disaster Planning and Recovery: A How-To-Do-It-Manual for Librarians and Archivists.* New York: Neal Schuman, 1992.

Gertz, Janet, et al. "Preservation Analysis and the Brittle Book Problem in College Libraries: The Identification of Research-Level Collections and Their Implications." *College & Research Libraries* 54 (1993): 227–39.

Grimes, William. "A Cool Oasis for Frazzled Films." *New York Times*, June 22, 1996, 9.

Grove, Lee E. "Paper Deterioration—An Old Story." *College & Research Libraries* 25 (1964): 365–74.

Gwinn, Nancy E. "Politics and Practical Realities: Environmental Issues for the Library Administrator." In *Advances in Preservation and Access*, vol. 1, edited by Barbra Buckner Higginbotham and Mary E. Jackson, 135–46. Westport, CT: Meckler, 1992.

Harmon, James. *Integrated Pest Management in Museum, Library, and Archival Facilities: A Step by Step Approach for the Design, Development, Implementation, and Maintenance of an Integrated Pest Management Program.* Indianapolis: Harmon Preservation Pest Management, 1993.

Higginbotham, Barbra Buckner. *Our Past Preserved: A History of American Library Preservation, 1876-1910.* Boston: G. K. Hall, 1990.

Kadoya, Takashi. "On the Degradation of Paper and Printed Matter." In *Research Libraries: Yesterday, Today, and Tomorrow*, edited by William J. Welsh, 334–53. Kanazawa Institute of Technology, 1993.

Lull, William P., with Paul N. Banks. *Conservation Environment Guidelines for Libraries and Archives.* Albany: State Library of New York, 1991; republished Ottawa: Canadian Council of Archives, 1995.

Lull, William P., and Linda E. Merk. "Lighting for Storage of Museum Collections: Developing a System for Safekeeping of Light-Sensitive Materials." *Technology and Conservation* 7 (1982): 20–25.

McCormick-Goodhart, Mark H. "The Allowable Temperature and Relative Humidity Range for the Safe Use and Storage of Photographic Materials." *Journal of the Society of Archivists* 17 (1996): 7–21.

McCormick-Goodhart, Mark H., and Marion F. Mecklenburg. "Cold Storage Environments for Photographic Materials." *I.S.& T. Final Program and Advance Printing of Paper Summaries,* I.S.& T. 46th Annual Conference, 277–80. Springfield, VA: Society for Imaging Science and Technology, 1993.

Merrill-Oldham, Jan, and Jutta Reed-Scott. *Library Storage Facilities, Management, and Services.* SPEC Kit 242. Washington, DC: Association of Research Libraries, 1999.

Metcalf, Keyes D. "The Design of Book Stacks and the Preservation of Books." *Restaurator* 1 (1969): 115–25.

Metcalf, Keyes D. *Planning Academic and Research Library Buildings*. New York: McGraw Hill, 1965.

Morris, John. "Protecting the Library from Fire." *Library Trends* 33 (1984): 49–56.

Murray, John. "On the Bad Composition of Modern Paper." *Gentleman's Magazine* 93 (July 1823): 21–22.

National Bureau of Standards. *Air Quality Criteria for Storage of Paper-Based Archival Records*. NBSIR 83-2795. Gaithersburg, MD: National Bureau of Standards, 1983.

National Research Council. *Preservation of Historical Records*. Washington, DC: National Academy Press, 1986.

Ogden, Barclay. "Preservation Selection and Treatment Options." In *Meeting the Preservation Challenge*, edited by Jan Merrill-Oldham, 38–42. Washington, DC: Association of Research Libraries, 1988.

Patkus, Beth Lindblom. *Monitoring Temperature and Relative Humidity*. Technical Leaflet, no. 2.2. Andover, MA: Northeast Document Conservation Center, 1999.

Petherbridge, Guy, ed. *Conservation of Library and Archive Materials and the Graphic Arts*. London: Butterworths, 1987.

Price, Lois Olcott. *Managing a Mold Invasion: Guidelines for Disaster Response*. Technical Series, no. 1. Philadelphia: Conservation Center for Art and Historic Artifacts, 1996.

Reilly, James M. *IPI Storage Guide for Acetate Film*. Rochester, NY: Image Permanence Institute, 1993.

Reilly, James M., Douglas W. Nishimura, and Edward Zinn. *New Tools for Preservation: Assessing Long-Term Environmental Effects on Library and Archives Collections*. Washington, DC: Commission on Preservation and Access, 1995.

Ritzenthaler, Mary Lynn. *Preserving Archives and Manuscripts*. Chicago: Society of American Archivists, 1993.

Schunk, Russell J. "Stack Problems and Care." *Library Trends* 4 (1956): 283–90.

Sebera, Donald K. *Isoperms: An Environmental Management Tool*. Washington, DC: Commission on Preservation and Access, 1994.

Shahani, Chandru J. *Accelerated Aging of Paper: Can It Really Foretell the Permanence of Paper?* Preservation Research and Testing Series, no. 9503. Washington, DC: Library of Congress, 1995.

Smith, Richard D. "New Approaches to Preservation." In *Deterioration and Preservation of Library Materials,* edited by Howard W. Winger and Richard Daniel Smith, 139–71. Chicago: University of Chicago Press, 1970.

Thomson, Garry. *The Museum Environment.* London: Butterworths, 1986.

Van Bogart, John W. C. *Magnetic Tape Storage and Handling: A Guide for Libraries and Archives.* Washington, DC: Commission on Preservation and Access, 1995.

Walch, Victoria Irons. "Checklist of Standards Applicable to the Preservation of Archives and Manuscripts." *American Archivist* 53 (1990): 324–38.

Walker, Gay, et al. "The Yale Survey: A Large-Scale Survey of Book Deterioration in the Yale University Library." *College & Research Libraries* 46 (1985): 111–32.

Wessel, Carl J. "Environmental Factors Affecting the Permanence of Library Materials." In *Deterioration and Preservation of Library Materials*, edited by Howard W. Winger and Richard Daniel Smith, 39–84. Chicago: University of Chicago Press, 1970.

Wessel, Carl J. "Deterioration of Library Materials." In *Encyclopedia of Library and Information Science*, vol. 7. New York: Marcel Dekker, 1972.

Williams, Edwin E. "Deterioration of Library Collections Today." In *Deterioration and Preservation of Library Materials,* edited by Howard W. Winger and Richard Daniel Smith, 3–17. Chicago: University of Chicago Press, 1970.

Williams, Gordon. "The Preservation of Deteriorating Books." *Library Journal* 91 (January 1, 1966): 51–56 and (January 15, 1966): 189–94.

Wilson, William K. *Environmental Guidelines for the Storage of Paper Records.* NISO Technical Report, no. 1. NISO-TR01-1995. Bethesda, MD: National Information Standards Organization, 1995.

V. Material Selection Issues: Case Studies

10

A Harvard Experience

Kenneth E. Carpenter and Jeffrey L. Horrell

Off-site storage is now so commonly a part of library operations that American scholars find it an expected—and accepted—element in their lives. Twenty, and even 10 years ago that was not the case. The construction of off-site facilities was strenuously fought. Opposition was particularly strong at Harvard. Every library engaging in off-site storage needs to communicate openly and sensitively with its users, but the fact that Harvard was one of the pioneers in off-site storage led to the need for special efforts to gain faculty support. This essay details those, in part because the story may still be informative to librarians, even if they face less intense opposition.

This essay will also cover the criteria used in the early years of off-site storage from Widener. (The term *Widener* includes Pusey Library, a building connected to Widener and forming essentially an extension of Widener.) Then, the essay will bring the account up-to-date and will conclude with additional observations, some of them having to do with the process of ongoing selection for storage.

Exploring Options for the Space Crisis

It had been clear from the early 1980s that Widener was running out of space, but there was no agreement on a solution. Clearly, some sort of new facility was needed, but even with a new facility there was no agreement on what to house in it: entire classes, books before a certain date, books in certain languages, new books, old books? Practicality entered into this, for there were not yet machine-readable records for the retrospective holdings. Neither librarians nor faculty could agree among themselves or with each other. A faculty "Priorities Committee" even advocated storing all new books as they came in.

One possible solution was to build a new library in Harvard Yard or its vicinity, perhaps across from Widener on Massachusetts Avenue, with a connection by tunnel or bridge. Another site was on land nearby that was the site of a Gulf Station. (It was ultimately torn down and the Inn at Harvard built there.) Some faculty members very much urged this solution, some vociferously. A faculty member who did not favor this solution was historian Oscar Handlin, who was at that time Director of the University Library. He felt that a nearby library would be problematic by so increasing the time to get from one part of the library complex to another that the difficulty of use would be heightened.

Another possible solution was storage—in the vicinity—for little-used materials, but with the possibility of browsing them. Some advocated unused subway tunnels for this purpose. Some, who had heard of the New England Deposit Library in Allston, across the river from Cambridge, favored expanding this building. (It was inexpensive construction from the era of World War II that was totally without climate control.)

The other possibility, on which Oscar Handlin acted, was construction of an off-site storage library that could be expanded, that would provide adequate climatic conditions, and that would be inexpensive to operate. Virtually without support from either librarians of the various Harvard faculties or faculty colleagues, Handlin arranged for a module to be designed and managed by Iron Mountain. Browsability was not a feature of this facility, for it was determined that efficient storage and retrieval was incompatible with shelving on which books could be browsed. Indeed, provision was not made for readers at all. It was anticipated that a desired volume would be returned to the Harvard library that had stored it.

Proving the Harvard Depository

The Harvard Depository (HD) did not in itself solve the problem of what to store there, nor did it mean that all concerned parties accepted the desirability of storage off-site. Other libraries could not be pointed to as having demonstrated that off-site storage of this sort worked. Consequently, the other options continued to surface, and the efficacy of the new facility had to be proved—in two ways. One was by efficient service. The other was by housing materials that it could generally be agreed were appropriate for off-site storage.

Service was efficient from the start. To be sure, one had to go to the circulation desk of the owning library in order to request a book, but the library's users were accustomed to going to other libraries. In fact, all but the newest members of the Harvard community were able to recall when it had been necessary to go to a library in order to check its subject catalog on cards. The initiation of the request was not under the control of HD, but HD did get the books within a day of the request. Once-a-day delivery, five days a week, has become the accepted standard at Harvard.

There was, however, another service aspect that could not be dealt with solely by empirical evidence. This was the fear that books were being lost at HD. To be sure, some books have been lost, most of them no doubt by improper bar coding from the sending library. But in addition books are for some period of time in transit and in process. To the reader, those books are "lost." It was not easy to demonstrate that the lost books were only a small percentage, for, after all, only a small percentage of the books had been requested in the first place. Even less easily responded to, largely because it was rarely expressed directly, was a fear that the library was in fact destroying many books, not storing them—that storage was a euphemism for weeding. This fear was, of course, not entirely susceptible of being dealt with by simply saying that it was groundless.

Facing Faculty Fears

The other way of demonstrating that the Harvard Depository was the best solution to the space problem was to send out the books that would not be missed. Again, the issue involved fears. If selection for storage were done in a highly public way, it could turn the whole matter into a *cause célèbre* that would only heighten fears. In fact, a methodology that backfired was initially chosen. Called the "dotting project," it was carried out by casual workers who put dots on books in the Library of Congress classification (it had been adopted in 1976, and the records were machine-readable). They were instructed to put dots on all books published before a certain date that had not circulated within a given number of years, but not to dot and hence to exclude from consideration for storage all serials and multivolume sets. Users of the library were then expected to remove dots from books that they felt should not go to HD. In actual practice, the proposal worked in the sense that users were generally responsible and only in a few cases removed all dots or dotted all of the books of a category.

The process was, however, so widely publicized that it aroused great fears and left unanswered the question of how storage would be dealt with in the future. To say this is not to criticize the project, for these books were the only ones that had machine-readable records. They had to be the targeted volumes, and the methodology seemed entirely fair. Faculty did not, however, want to go through the process again.

The faculty did not want to select the books for storage, but they also felt that librarians would not select the right books to go to HD. It was at this point that I (Kenneth E. Carpenter) volunteered to select books for storage and to do so in consultation with the faculty, with the aim of thereby improving selection as well as fostering faculty approval of the HD solution. (I find the next section of this essay is more readable in the first person.) I was conscious of the fears of all sorts, and I felt that the faculty would never be happy with a solution that called for a global policy of selection. Any such policy would always be liable to sound arguments against it, and perhaps worst of all, to a sense by some faculty that their interests were being discriminated against, that they were victims of librarians who did not understand the importance of their field.

I was asked by Richard DeGennaro to prepare a report to the faculty. The human tendency to avoid a negative reaction by not communicating what you were going to do was not an option for the library and for me—and by good luck, a senior faculty member who was a vociferous opponent of storage was also willing, even eager, to talk. He and I lunched frequently, and we went over several versions of my report to the faculty. From him I learned what were the rumors, misunderstandings, and fears of the faculty. Just to give one example, I found that the Harvard Depository, a state-of-art building, was confused with the New England Deposit Library, where the books baked in summer and truly were lost.

Those lunches also gave me an opportunity to hear expressions of the sense of loss that storage represented. Books are the tools of the scholar. Any delay at all in running down a footnote, for example, is a loss, for the process of scholarship is not linear. One book may lead to a different path, even into new directions, and a route not taken one day may not be in one's consciousness the next. Thus, I learned: Put the best possible face on storage, explain the methodology for storing and retrieving books and the speed with which this will be done, the good climate control in the storage facility (which will increase the life of the paper), the safeguards against losing books, etc. But do not go too far. Acknowledge the loss, for off-site storage does mean loss. In expressing awareness of this, far from losing faculty support, I furthered consciousness of the unpleasant reality that books had outrun space on campus, that the problem was not of the library's creation, and that it had to be faced.

Written communication to the faculty was not enough. Though it was crucial, I also set out to discuss the details of storage with various faculty members. My approach was to set up a meeting for about 11 A.M. and for the meeting, often to be followed by lunch, to take place in the stacks. The day or days before I would go through the relevant classification. (Harvard's Old Widener classification is primarily by cultural area, so that it was easy to find the material that would, for instance, interest the professor of modern German history.) I would prepare myself thoroughly with a knowledge of what was there, and I would have questions that would transform the discussion from the general to the specific: "How about these books on the Franco-Prussian War?" "Note the run of editions of Carlyle's life of Frederick the Great."

It was never difficult to demonstrate that there were materials that could go to HD with relatively little loss. Although I never used the term *useless* to refer to a book, I always gently substituted *store* for every use of *get rid of* that the faculty member might make. There are no useless books, and none were being gotten rid of—or almost none. I did reject some books present in multiple copies. Whereas the faculty member would see concretely that there were books that could go to HD, I also learned about faculty interests. For example, source material had to be kept. Local materials had to be kept. The histories of the past, even of the relatively recent past, could go to HD, for they represented primarily scholarship of an earlier era that had accomplished its purpose of moving along historical analysis and understanding. They were not the "live" books for today's historians, but the antiquarian local history was.

The meeting in the stacks was generally followed by further discussion over lunch, for real exchange had begun to take place. After many meetings, I entered my notes of the faculty member's concerns into a computer and sent the person a copy. They felt heard, and, in fact, one person replied: "You made me sound more intelligent than I thought I had been."

How time-consuming, one might say. The reality was that I did not need to do this with very many faculty members, for I made an important discovery. It came about because I began to hear things that I had told one person coming back to me in recognizable form by another. The discovery was that the faculty talk to each other—a lot. Once a few faculty had decided that I understood their concerns and could be relied on to try to decide intelligently, it was no longer necessary to have meeting after meeting. The meetings that I did have served, it turned out, another purpose besides storage. There were lots of questions about what was happening in Widener, and the meetings presented an opportunity to explain various matters; for example, that computerization was overdue in Widener and that among other things it was increasing staff productivity, or that the removal of Harvard's Union Catalog was necessary to retrospective conversion of the catalog. Thus, discussion about storage helped to increase dialog with the faculty.

Besides HD itself and the details of selection, faculty members had at that time two major concerns. One was whether the quantity selected to go to HD would be a given percentage. The other was fairness, and this did not apply only to those working in the smaller language areas. Would, for example, more be stored from German history than from French? Both of these concerns were related, and the answer addressed both of them. There was no percentage, and there would, in fact, be differences in the quantity selected, but that those differences would not represent personal prejudices. Instead, there would be no fixed quantity and there would be differences, for two reasons. One was the nature of the literature in a given area and, related to that, the nature of the collection.

Two examples made this clear. More could go from French history than from German history, because France, long a unified country, had more editions of given works and more multivolume histories of the country than did Germany, where the literature was much more local history, given that Germany had been unified only late in the nineteenth century. Those local histories did not go through multiple editions. It was also possible to point out that the literature being most heavily selected was English literature. This was because there were numerous instances of multiple editions. Even if most of the editions of a given work, a novel by Dickens, for example, had circulated at some point, not all had to be in the stacks. The natural tendency for a library in the English-speaking world to accumulate multiple editions of English-language works had been heightened by the presence of many collections donated to the library by individuals. These tended to include numerous translations, which were naturally infrequently read or consulted. (To mention the storage of English literature was to allay the rumor, which was circulating at least as far away as Princeton, that Widener was going to house solely an English-language collection.)

Some of those consulted wanted to have lists produced for them to review. This was tried, but my experience was that it did not work, and the degree to which it did not work was in inverse relationship to the amount of concern over storage evinced by a particular scholar. Put differently, the more that a scholar was unhappy about storage, the more that scholar would indicate not knowing whether a book should go and the higher the frequency of suggestions to consult someone else. Lists gave promise of consuming enormous quantities of time for little return, and the problem was exacerbated if the list consisted only of books of a given category, such as books before a certain date or books that had not circulated for a given period. Such a list did not show what else was on the shelves, so it gave a false picture.

There were three responses to this. One was frankly to discuss the problem of time with faculty. They readily understood it. Another way, used in one instance, was to show that decisions are made in a context, by presenting a list of about a hundred books from a particular call number range with indications of the decision on each one. Context, it was explained, also included the physical condition of books. The advantage of working from the shelves is that the books in very poor condition could be selected for HD, which was particularly a factor employed when there were multiple editions of a work. Context, it could be noted, also involves those elements that scholars are now generally calling the paratext, that is, those elements outside the text itself that convey information about the book's intended readership and mode of readership. For example, a quick examination of a book might show its small format and its intended use as a schoolbook. Or, perhaps a given book could go to HD because it was primarily an example of fine printing. Or, perhaps a book would be kept because it represented a genre that was popular in nineteenth-century America.

Another response was to point out that books can be returned to the stacks, though at the same time indicating that this should rarely be done, because of the labor and expense involved. In fact, in only a handful of cases was a book that I had sent out to HD returned to the stacks at the request of a faculty member, but speaking of this possibility was a way of avowing that mistakes would be made.

Another fear of the faculty was that the amount of use as represented by circulation stamps (use is inevitably a criteron employed in selection) would be misemployed. They knew very well that books are not only borrowed and read; books are also consulted. It can readily be understood that there are two kinds of use, borrowing a book for reading at another location, and consulting a book onsite, but the faculty commonly used the term *browsing*.

The term *browsing* does encompass the process of going into the stacks simply to explore. In fact, one faculty member occasionally just goes to an unfamiliar section of the stacks and randomly removes a book from the shelves. The term can also mean looking at the books shelved to either side of a book identified through a catalog search, and scholars can readily point to cases of useful books identified through that process. Provision in the OPAC for call-number browsing, that is, being able to go back and forth from a given number, can alleviate the loss resulting from not being able to go directly to the shelves.

"Browsing" does, though, have another meaning, referring to the consultation that takes place in the stacks. The scholar might look in a volume of letters for ones from a particular individual. Or, the scholar might go through local histories in the search for information on, say, the existence of musical groups. Or, a scholar might look through the printed matriculation lists of a number of European universities in an effort to trace an individual. Or, if the collection of anthologies of American literature is very strong, as it is in Widener, a scholar might wish to consult a large number in the course of pursuing an hypothesis on an aspect of the kinds of poetry included. This kind of use—looking in many places for information that may not be found there—is at the heart of the research process. And, every scholar knows that he or she will do less of that if the books are less readily available. Moreover, the books that one uses for such purposes may not be the ones that are charged out and taken away to be read.

It was clear, then, that circulation statistics alone could not adequately determine what should be in the stacks. A more nuanced approach was needed.

Selection of Monographs for the Harvard Depository

Electronic records are essential for efficient processing for storage and for efficient retrieval, and it was the start of retrospective conversion of the Widener catalog that made possible the selection of individual items. Thanks to Carol Ishimoto, then Head of the Cataloging Services Department, retrospective conversion of the catalog proceeded in the fashion most useful to storage, in that the cards for certain classes were removed for first processing. These classes were those in which there are large numbers of alphabetical sequences, namely, the classes devoted to various national literatures. Thus, as soon as the records for all authors whose names began with the letter C had been converted, the volumes corresponding to those records could be considered for storage.

These electronic records made it possible to begin by selecting from various parts of the stacks and, most importantly, to begin with the three best types of materials to store. One was early books. It was decided, in consultation with the faculty, that the year 1821 could be taken as a satisfactory point to make the emergence of modern scholarship and the transformation of printing technology. All books before that date, with the exception of reference works of current usefulness, it was agreed, would appropriately be sent to HD. It was further decided that these books would generally be retrieved to the Houghton Library's reading room, on the grounds that they would most likely be used in connection with other research in Houghton. Since it was estimated that there were at least 100,000 pre-1821 books in Widener, despite earlier extensive transfers to Houghton, storage of these books was a good way to send to HD significant quantities, while also enhancing security and preservation.

Beginning with literature also made it possible to store large numbers of duplicate copies. To be sure, some few duplicates were discarded; most were sent to HD. Beginning with literature also made it possible to store large numbers of copies of books available in multiple editions. Duplicates and especially works available in multiple editions were available in profusion in Widener. It is part of being a great library that all printings or editions of a text are kept—but all need not be available in the stacks, even if at some point all had been charged out. These books were easy to identify simply by walking down the aisles of stacks. Users preferred not to borrow books in leather bindings, but, given a choice, took the book in library binding. In general, it is safe to store the earlier edition, but the classics are the exception.

Translations were generally stored, except those done by prominent individuals. Even translations in English were often stored, if the original language is widely read (French), or if the translation was made for political purposes (as in the Soviet Union).

If there is a Collected Works or Collected Verse, separately published editions were stored, unless heavy use suggests otherwise. Editions for schools and students were stored. Editions on poor paper were stored, as were those in fragile bindings, with many books in original bindings being stored so as to preserve them.

Such practices have made it possible to store several hundred thousand books from Widener. (Statistics could be gathered for storage by class, by date, or by language; it is not possible, however, to determine how many are copies of multiple editions or other such categories.) Obviously, more had to go to HD. The initial policy, adopted primarily for the literatures of smaller language areas, such as Danish, Icelandic, Bulgarian, etc., was to draw up lists of major authors, either by going to full-scale histories of the literature or to encyclopedias. The idea was that all authors not cited could be stored. On further consideration, this methodology was deemed to be lacking. It would have the effect of reinforcing the canon, and it would prevent the exploration that browsing in a great library makes possible.

A new policy was adopted. It called for representing on the shelves all authors now in the collection, but for sending to storage some works of more prominent authors, unless they are used. In selecting which to keep, retained in Widener were works in different genres, autobiographical works, and collections of letters. This approach was not adopted in the expectation that masterpieces would thereby be discovered. It was hoped, though, that this practice would result in scholars and students discovering other authors worth reading and studying.

Eventually, as retrospective conversion progressed, it was possible to store more from the nonliterary classes, using the most basic of criteria. Thus, in addition to duplicates, there were stored some copies of unneeded multiple printings or editions, pre-1821 publications, and translations. Likewise, in the case of works for school instruction, and throughout all classes there were large numbers of books that were basically textbooks, even if the title did not so designate them.

Conversations with historians led to storage of all but the most recent general histories, except for a few classics. By and large older histories covering a broad span or a significant era are no longer commonly read. The works of earlier generations of historians advanced historical studies, but they are now useful for the history of scholarship and are not otherwise generally useful.

Widener is an international collection, but some types of foreign-language works were candidates for storage. One is foreign-language works on a topic very well covered in English, for example, the Gulf War; experience showed that these were rarely borrowed, apparently because of the large number of English-language works. Similar are works in a language other than the language of the culture being described. Thus, a Russian work on French history could be stored, unless it were about French-Russian relations or a historical figure who was active in both cultures. Or, perhaps it was an exception, such as a Russian work about Voltaire's library, which had been acquired by Catherine the Great. Also stored were foreign-language works that had obviously been intended for a more popular audience in the country of origin; these are often identified by a lack of footnotes.

Books were not stored just because of being in a foreign language, but Russian books and those in East European languages were heavily selected for HD. The reason is that so much of the output was propagandistic. Of a couple of shelves of books on Russian agriculture, for example, few were solid scholarly works.

Books on some subjects were commonly sent to HD, as, for instance, British constitutional history, which is rarely a subject of scholarly inquiry. Similar are works on a particular event that attracted attention at the time but that is now little studied. An example would be the Crimean War, particularly the siege of Sebastopol.

Each class presented particular opportunities for storing material whose utility would diminish only slightly by being off-site. Thus, in Church History most sermons were sent to HD, keeping only those on some social issue, for instance, slavery, or sermons that related to women's studies, that is, those on the duties of women, or sermons by particularly prominent individuals, particularly locally prominent ones. Doctrinal works or those on administrative structures receive little use and were stored, save for those on the papacy, which are heavily consulted. (It should be noted that it was often obvious from the dates recording charges whether the book had been used by one reader or several.)

In a field such as Linguistics it is easy to select older and specialized grammars for storage. However, even dictionaries tend to require the assistance of a specialist, and whenever possible, appropriate individuals were hired to review such areas of the stacks.

Widener's holdings of subjects such as Economics and Political Science contained a particularly large number of textbooks or very general statements, but, in addition, it was kept in mind that most economics works age quickly. Only the most important theoretical works of prominent economics needed to be kept in Widener. Some types of works of economic history were also prime candidates, some because they are on topics little studied, some because they have limited scope, and some because they have highly descriptive titles that make it easy to identify and retrieve them. In some cases, a book fit all three of these categories, such as a French work on the finances of Romania in the 1920s.

A subject such as economics presents, however, tempting opportunities that should, in fact, be passed over. They are tempting because they come in the form of a large set, and because the information they contain, statistical data, seems arcane to almost all librarians. Yet, the large set, and particularly the set of statistics, is likely only to be consulted. It is particularly frustrating to have to recall—and deal with upon receipt—large numbers of volumes that are only going to be examined for a particular piece of information. A run of directories is a similar kind of publication. So, too, often are the publications of local historical societies, particularly those in Britain, which sometimes consist basically of names. In selecting for storage, it can be useful to make it a rule to be very cautious about storing what you do not understand, particularly if it is a series of information.

It can be generalized that such series fit into the category of documentary source material. Although the printed form of the information may be superseded through digitization, the data will never be superseded. And, above all, it is the original source material that scholars want at hand: the economist, the statistics; the historian, the printed versions of original documents and lists of names of various sorts; and all scholars in the humanities, the letters, the autobiographies, the work of highly diverse content—all of which permit exploration, the discovery of new leads, the testing of hypotheses.

Selection of Serials for Storage

Serials present special issues, not the least of the reasons being that they are commonly thought to be basically identical. In the research library, the common model is the *PMLA* or the *Journal of American History*. But a moment's reflection reveals that there are different types of serials, just as there are of monographs. There are those that appear only annually and those that appear more frequently. Some that appear annually may have contents that resemble the regular learned society periodical, but many annuals are annual reports of organizations, annual statistics, directories, annual membership lists, and so on. Then, there are the serials published by and for members of an organization, which may be annual but also of more frequent publication. Some serials are designed to persuade and have a particularly timely content, as those issued by political groups. Some give the news and appear weekly; some are of general content, such as *The New Yorker*. Then, there is the traditional scholarly serial. It has individually authored essays, but many of the above types do not have authored articles at all.

Of course, the above typology of the serial is only suggestive, with the aim of making clear the point that serials differ so greatly as to require when deciding on storage the kind of review that one would make of monographs. Serials also require that decisions be made about the unit stored and retrieved. Users of some of the many types of annual volumes generally need to consult a number of volumes rather than a volume for one year. This led to the decision to provide for storing some serials in cartons and for making the carton the unit of retrieval. The traditional scholarly serial, in contrast, is commonly wanted in order to read or consult a single article, and each volume is the unit of retrieval.

News and general interest periodicals have generally been stored, with only the last five years or so kept in Widener, the exception being earlier illustrated periodicals, particularly of the nineteenth century. They need to be seen in order to determine their utility.

Practices also different with respect to scholarly periodicals, depending on the field. In Classics the scholarly literature retains its usefulness to a greater extent than in other humanistic disciplines, and only periodicals published before 1875 were selected to go to HD. In English, in contrast, periodicals issued before 1930, except for the major ones, went to HD. This is both because the articles in those periodicals tend to have become incorporated into the literature to such a degree that scholars do not go back to the originals and because new critical approaches and interests make them outdated.

In Economics the date was moved up so that only the last ten years were kept, with only the major journals being retained earlier than that. Moreover, storage was the default position with respect to social science periodicals from communist countries.

The Stacks Renovation and HD-Push

Storage entered into a new phase with the decision to renovate the stacks of Widener Library, the first major work on the stacks since the opening of the building in 1915. The project will protect and preserve the collection for generations to come, and, as well, facilitate their use; for there will be a new climate-control system, fire detection and suppression systems, improved lighting and security, new carrels and network connections, and two new reading rooms. The new and enhanced infrastructure of the stacks will, however, reduce shelving capacity by about 10 percent. Moreover, on the lowest level of the stacks, the bottom shelves will be removed in order to limit the potential for water damage, flooding from underground streams being an almost yearly occurrence in Widener if there is a prolonged rain.

Since the stacks were full, there also being a great deal of compact shelving in Pusey, it was imperative to reduce the collection on-site below its current capacity of 3.2 million volumes. The enhanced infrastructure was one reason. Another was to provide some space for growth, without frequent shifting of the collections, for that is hard on the books as well as harmful to ease of access. Yet another was the fact that it is important to Harvard faculty and students as well as to the broader scholarly community that the collections remain fully accessible during the course of the renovation. This was especially important for undergraduates, given that no part of the collection could be inaccessible for six weeks—the length of time for work on each stack section—without seriously interfering with the research and writing of term papers or honors theses. A plan was devised whereby each portion of the stacks will be moved to another stack section during renovation, with all of the books being accessible except during the actual move. For this to work, additional storage was also required, and it was crucial that the books in a given area be reduced by the required number.

The books also had to be sent to storage in a timely fashion, for a construction schedule had been developed. In fall 1998 the project HD-Push was conceived, in order to select and process for storage approximately 500,000 volumes from the Widener Collection. The project was planned by library staff, with input from the members of the Faculty of Arts and Sciences Library Committee, particularly its Subcommittee on Collections. It involved three crucial elements. The first, as noted, was to determine the quantity to be stored from each section of the stacks. This was carried out by library staff, in particular, Ronald Tesler, Head of the Stacks Division. The second was to select the material to be stored. The Widener bibliographers, who had for years been identifying new materials to be housed at the Depository, became involved as well in selecting retrospective titles for transfer. Through the bibliographers, a number of faculty were also involved in reviewing lists.

The third element was larger-scale processing of materials for storage. There had long been a small Transfer Team, but it was greatly expanded under the direction of Marilyn Wood, Librarian for Information and Document Delivery Services in Widener Library. Staff had to be hired, trained, and supervised—during two shifts. The larger scale also meant changes in every aspect of processing, from cleaning the books, to making sure there were enough book trucks, to enhanced record-keeping (by class), to space for temporary housing, and to arranging for processing on the part of Depository staff.

The criteria for selection, as well as the methodology used, has varied, depending on the selector and the discipline. Low use (no circulation within the past 25 years, the date when electronic record-keeping began) was a factor considered. Age was another, in that identification of all pre-1821 material was accelerated. Periodicals that had ceased to be published were major candidates for storage, as were older runs of some periodicals. The methodology varied. Some selectors worked primarily from lists of noncirculating items; others used lists as an initial point of departure and then went into the stacks. Yet others, either themselves or their staff, went directly into the stacks. This made it possible to select materials of particular fragility. Such items were given a "noncirculating" status so that when recalled to Widener they would not leave the newly created controlled reading room. Selectors shared lists with interested faculty members and modified the criteria in response. Selectors also took into consideration the current teaching curriculum, the developing electronic collections, and changes affecting scholarship, particularly from an interdisicplinary perspective. In some areas of the stacks, space requirements made it necessary to make no circulation in the past decade the starting point for selection.

In addition to the consultation with individual faculty members, HD-Push also led to a new round of broader efforts to seek input from the faculty. There were letters to chairs of academic departments, group meetings with selectors and faculty members, meetings with groups of faculty in similar disciplines, and updates on the project to all members of the Faculty of Arts and Sciences. Librarians received a modest amount of feedback from a general mailing; the greatest amount came from one-on-one conversations. It is clear that storage in fact provides an opportunity for furthering cooperation between librarians and faculty. The issue is of keen interest to many faculty members, and conversations about storage and the criteria employed foster, on the one hand, understanding of library issues and, on the other hand, enhanced understanding of trends and methodologies in disciplines.

Conclusion

Although storage began with the types of materials that could be housed at the Harvard Depository with minimal loss to the library's users, particularly those materials for which electronic cataloging records were becoming available, the situation has now changed. Records are available for all materials, and the material stored at HD goes ever deeper into the collection. Widener, the site, increasingly houses two kinds of books and serials: (1) the most frequently borrowed; (2) those most essential for the in-house research and consultation of scholars and students.

Everyone—librarians, faculty, university administrators, and students—recognizes and accepts the inevitability that an ever-diminishing portion of the collection will be housed on-site. This raises two kinds of concerns. One is the growing cost of storage and retrieval. The other is the question of intellectual access, as storage cuts more deeply into the collection. Some members of the faculty urge that digital technology is the solution. They do not so much urge the digitization of texts, as the extension of the cataloging records through the provision of additional metadata about content.

There is yet one other issue that needs to be moved higher onto the agenda: selection for ongoing storage. Harvard has clearly taken the course of individual selection of items for HD, and by criteria other than the purely mechanical. Despite this, storage selection has been seen basically as a project. First there was a "dotting project," described briefly above. Then, there was the work of Kenneth E. Carpenter, and it was seen primarily as being relatively short-term, in part because of anticipating (unwisely) that digital technology would soon reduce the number of new publications in print. Then came the HD-Push project. The need at this stage, one that all libraries using storage will eventually face, is to put selection and processing for storage on a programmatic basis. That is a difficult challenge, given that storage is a complicated reality.

11

The Yale University Libraries Experience

Margaret K. Powell

The movement of library materials to off-site shelving facilities raises numerous collection management issues. Much has been written about weeding collections, but, as Wendy Lougee ruefully remarks in her 1990 article, "Remote Shelving Comes of Age," "Like a distant and unpopular cousin, discussions of storage often seem relegated to behind the scenes conversations of worst case scenarios and compromised virtue"(p. 93). Making decisions to move materials to off-campus shelving, it turns out, is not always the same as making decisions to discard materials. For one thing, the scale and scope of these decisions are much larger than the scale and scope of weeding projects, which can often be made a routine part of collection management. For another, transferring parts of collections to an off-site facility forces librarians and curators to face a whole range of high-visibility issues while debating the advantages and disadvantages of on-campus versus off-campus locations. In the following pages I will address some of these in the context of Yale's planning for its new Library Shelving Facility and from the perspective of the coordinator of selection for this new facility.

In October 1996, in response to the findings of a 1994 space planning report, Yale's Working Group for an Off-Campus High-Efficiency Shelving Facility issued its *Final Report* to the President and the Provost, recommending that the University build an off-site facility that would house 2 million volumes initially in a first module and allow for additional modules to be added as (or before) needed. By relieving impossibly crowded conditions in the library stacks, this facility would allow the on-campus collections to become more browsable and more accessible; the building itself would "provide optimal environmental conditions for long-term preservation of library materials" (*Final Report*, p. 12), and the design would be based on the model of the Harvard Depository (that is, books would be shelved by size, not by subject, and would be tracked by an inventory bar code system; browsing would not be possible). Because of several imminent renovation and restructuring projects, the new facility would open for operation June 1, 1998—less than two years from the date of the report—and would be ready to receive materials at the rate of between 250,000 and 500,000 volume-equivalents a year. The aim would be to reduce the on-campus collections by about 20 percent, and to maintain the resulting number (somewhere around 8 or 8.5 million volumes) at a steady state, so that ongoing collection growth would be taken up by the off-campus facility.

From a selector's point of view there were other crucial recommendations: that no material be transferred to the new facility until appropriately represented in the online catalog; that the selection of appropriate material be the job of the librarians already carrying collection development and selection responsibilities; that the materials selected be the least-frequently used parts of the collection; that these materials "particularly benefit from the optimal environmental conditions and the high security provided at the facility"; and that no discipline's materials and no format be *ipso facto* exempt from consideration (*Final Report*, p. 14). Furthermore there should be campus-wide consultation and discussion about the new facility and what should go into it.

I'd like to discuss the issues raised by the task of implementing the recommendations specific to selection. These can be broken down into several deceptively simple questions: What goes in? Who decides what goes in? How do we identify what goes in? And, not least, how are faculty consulted and brought into the decision-making process?

What Goes In?

A.   Infrequently used material. The selection criterion of infrequent use is one whose purpose is easy to grasp but whose precise definition (not to mention implementation) is difficult to agree upon. To take full advantage of the low cost of off-campus shelving, a library should transfer only those materials that will not be needed often; each retrieval and return cycle costs money and is potentially damaging to the book. Clairvoyance is the goal: the ability to predict future use of any given item. If we could ensure that nothing transferred off campus would ever be called for again, in one sense our job would be well and truly done; in another, of course, such lack of use might raise questions about our acquisition decisions! As anyone who has read the professional literature on this topic knows, there are many studies offering formulae to predict future use from past use and recommending the implementation of these formulae to aid weeding or removal to storage. And clearly if a book has not been used in the last 20 years it is *likely* that it will not be asked for in the next 20. But it is not *certain*, and it is even less certain in a research library where faculty and students have an inconvenient habit of discovering hitherto untapped areas of inquiry and dragging dusty books out into the light.

Even if one could with certainty predict future use from past use, what does use mean, and how is it measured? There are circulation data available from an online system (but how far back does this system go?), and there is information retrievable from date-due stamps (again, how far back would it need to go to be meaningful? and where is the time to consult book after book for this information?), but these data do not measure in-house use. They tell us nothing about the faculty member who stands at a shelf of journals to check citations, for instance, or the student making photocopies. There have been various approaches taken to measuring in-building use (taking surveys, keeping reshelving records, checking for dust), but in an undertaking as large as Yale's, for example, these quickly become unwieldy. As Robert Hayes remarks in a 1981 article, "there is a fundamental difference between use of the library as a place to get books that one wants to read and use of the library as a research tool. The former use can be measured by circulation; the latter, by nothing so simple" (Hayes: p. 216).

B.   Material that would most benefit from an optimal preservation environment. It only makes sense that a building whose environment is state-of-the-art, the best in the country for books and other research materials, and whose security is tight, should contain things whose condition and characteristics call out for such protection. At first glance this would suggest as prime candidates older materials, as well as fragile, rare, valuable, or controversial items. But what happens when this criterion, preservation in its largest sense, comes into conflict with the previous criterion, use? What about those eighteenth-century books now housed in the general stacks and used steadily? How much wear-and-tear will trips to and from the repository cause to materials identified as fragile? How long before the cost of retrieving items cancels out the economic benefit off-campus shelving was designed to provide? And what sort of special treatment (cleaning, boxing, repair) will this older, fragile, rare material require as it is transferred, and how much will it cost?

Just these sorts of questions have precipitated a long-needed conversation at Yale about the materials in our general collections that in many other libraries would be under lock and key and the watchful eye of special collections reading room attendants. Until now, we have often had no alternative between transferring material to the Beinecke Rare Book and Manuscript Library—already pressed for space itself—and retaining it in the open stacks, particularly vulnerable to the vicissitudes of time and use. The off-campus shelving facility has offered a fine opportunity to rethink the disposition of and service for these wonderfully problematic items, and we have been able to find ways to identify and better govern this material (familiarly designated "semi-rare"). Now the ownership of many of these "semi-rare" materials is being transferred to the Beinecke Library; depending on date, they will either be housed in the Beinecke or transferred to the Library Shelving Facility. In either case, the materials will be used only in the Beinecke's supervised reading room.

C.   Only material appropriately represented in the online catalog. From the beginning the library has pledged to the Yale community that nothing will be transferred to the off-campus facility unless or until there is a suitable record for it in the online catalog. If we make parts of the collection physically inaccessible by shelving them off-site and in no call number order, then we have an obligation to replace the ability to browse actual shelves with the ability to browse virtual shelves, online. At present, Yale's online catalog contains records for 40 to 50 percent of the library collections; the library has embarked on a long-awaited project to convert most of the rest of its records (some 4 to 5 million titles) from paper to electronic form, using the more complete records in the official catalog—not shelf lists—as the source file. What an incomplete online catalog means for the process of identifying material for the off-campus facility cannot be underestimated, and my advice to anyone contemplating these two projects is very straightforward: finish retrospective conversion first.

Who Decides What Goes In?

In most cases, the bibliographers, curators, and other selectors who have responsibility for building and maintaining collections in their subject fields have ultimate responsibility for selecting material for off-campus shelving and for defining the shape of the on-campus collections. They know the faculty, they know the needs and patterns of scholarship in their fields, and they know their collections. In other cases, the responsibility for selecting materials to be transferred off-site may be lodged elsewhere. As the previous chapter describes, at Harvard for some years one librarian (not a bibliographer) was responsible for selection for the Harvard Depository from the Widener Library stacks. His long experience with the library system and the academic curriculum, and his ongoing conversations with the faculty, made this method successful.

At Yale, on the other hand, the principle of distributing responsibility among all the selectors has been in place from the start, but we have had to work to make sure that no part of the collection was orphaned—left without a selector—and, conversely, that no part of the collection would have several claimants. We have called this process "carving up the baby." Decisions are particularly problematic for some pieces of the general collection, especially older science and technology materials (the science selectors are concerned mainly with new materials in their branch and department libraries, the history selectors are already overburdened) and area studies materials (the area curators select from their regions and often in non-Roman scripts, and the Western-language material comes in through the good offices of the other selectors); it was unclear how to divide the responsibilities. Finally, against the specter of a case-by-case discussion for several million volumes, we decided to adhere pretty strictly to a subject division (defined by call number ranges), regardless of imprint date or language, urging consultation whenever necessary.

Once we had divided up the universe so that each and every book theoretically has a selector attached to it, we affirmed the exceedingly discipline-specific nature of the actual selection decisions. The correct material to transfer in one discipline will not be so in another. A chemist's research patterns are quite different from a historian's, and those again different from a political scientist's or a literary scholar's. It became clear that each selector, in consultation with his or her relevant faculty, would need to develop individual sets of criteria for selection, based on the curriculum, trends in scholarship, research interests of our faculty, and other information gathered from the Yale user community.

How Is the Material Identified?

Depending on one's philosophical stance, there are perhaps two ideal ways to identify material for off-campus shelving. One is to go into the stacks, pushing a book truck and armed with years of institutional and scholarly and bibliographic experience, and simply pull what "should" go. This approach has been used to good effect at Harvard's Widener Library and certainly does justice to the complexities of the collections and the people (present and yet to be) using them. The other, more expedient way is to block out entire categories of material, by call number or format, and decree that they shall all be transferred. The University of Kansas implemented such an approach, transferring only older or dead serials, and at Emory the decision was made to move long runs of ceased journals from the A and Z Library of Congress classes. This second method may be simplistic but it is blessedly easy to execute and to communicate. Reality in Yale's case lies somewhere between. We have been precluded from the latter model (wholesale relegation of classes of materials) by our first principles—nothing shall be exempt, no discipline shall bear a disproportionate burden—and by the decision to tackle retrospective conversion using the official catalog not the shelf list for reasons of completeness and evenness of treatment. Because records are being converted by main entry alphabetical order, not by call number order, and because we can transfer no books until their records show up in the online catalog, identifying an entire class of material for transfer is not possible until the conversion of our catalog is finished. We are precluded from the former (the stack trawl) by limits of selector time and, again, by the incomplete state of our online catalog (how do we know what is online and thus ripe for transfer when we're rolling book trucks through the stacks?). In a smaller, fully converted library, either of these solutions would work: item-by-item selection is certainly a possibility when not grappling with several million volumes, and, in fact, some Yale selectors may elect to take this route, but the incompleteness of our online database is a very real stumbling block.

As it turns out, our working plan for selection includes more than one methodology and depends for its implementation on the coordination of such factors as construction schedules, retrospective conversion, budgets for staff time, and the refashioning of the mission and purpose of several libraries within the system. Our first proposal (which follows) has two major advantages: it exploits our automated system as much as possible, thereby avoiding exceptionally time-consuming and expensive item-by-item selection, and it allows each discipline to draw up its own criteria. Selectors from across the system, through consultation with their respective faculty and graduate student communities, determine criteria against which to identify material to transfer to the off-campus shelving facility. These criteria are discipline-specific and translatable into formulae or algorithms that would in turn generate reports from, first, the existing online catalog and, second, the weekly or monthly loads of newly converted records.

Ideally the criteria are chosen and cast in terms of fairly limited data fields: location, call number, date, date of last use, and so on. For instance, as the librarian for literature in English, I might decide to transfer pre-1820 imprints, older, relatively unused literary criticism, and unused twentieth-century fiction exclusive of anthologies. Using the fields in the Notis bibliographic, holding, and item records, it is possible to identify the books that fit these characteristics.

At this point in our thinking we realized that what we were proposing had a very high "Systems Premium" attached (all those reports from a notoriously recalcitrant database (Notis) would cost the Library Systems Office a great deal in terms of time and focus, thereby taking effort away from other projects), so we began to ask whether we could reach library-wide agreement on several selection criteria in order to reduce the systems burden. Date, for example: could we decide that all materials published before 1850, say, would find a home in the off-campus facility? Or format: could we transfer all periodicals before a certain date or all periodicals available electronically? It soon became clear, however, that while such criteria universally applied would simplify some things, we could not force everything into this Procrustean bed. Some selectors and disciplines use date as an important criterion; others do not.

Our solution to this stalemate—the selectors' need for many reports against the limited time and staff of the Library Systems Office—was an inspired compromise. The selectors agreed to look first at books classified in the Library of Congress system, not the older materials still classified under Yale's own scheme, as the most likely to be represented in Orbis (the online catalog) with full bibliographic records. We asked the Library Systems Office to run a report against Orbis to find all LC-classed books in the Sterling stacks with no item records and published after 1800. (Lack of an item record indicates that the material has not circulated since Yale adopted its first electronic circulation system and that it was acquired before 1989; books published before 1800 had become the responsibility of the Beinecke Library and thus subject to another set of reports.) This one huge report was then sorted into Microsoft Access files according to each selector's responsibility. The individual files were loaded into an Access "Selectors' Tool" devised by the Systems staff and mounted on a server from which the selectors copied their own files to their workstations. Then the selectors reviewed their files to identify material not appropriate for transfer to the Library Shelving Facility. The inappropriate materials were tagged as such and the reviewed files loaded back onto the server. Once the files were back on the server, Shelving Facility staff retrieved them and generated pick slips for the material selected for transfer.

The Selectors' Tool was the result of active collaboration between the Library Systems Office and the selectors. It has been a real success, solving several problems at once and becoming part of the LSF selection routine at Yale. Most obviously, it has allowed us to tackle a big part of the collection right up front, even before finishing retrospective conversion, by giving selectors a method of reviewing large groups of materials as a substitute for looking at the books themselves. The Tool allows filtering and sorting on many of the Orbis data fields (e.g., author, title, date, language, content, subject), providing selectors with many possible views of their collections. This approach promises to continue to be useful in identifying material even after retrospective conversion is finished and the more obvious candidates have been transferred to the LSF. In fact, the Selectors' Tool has been so successful that it has been adapted for several other collection management projects at Yale. (For a full description of the Selectors' Tool, see http://www.library.yale.edu/%7Elso/databaseadmin/select/index.html.)

I have gone on at such length about the problem of identifying materials for transfer to show, first, that for large, older, heterogeneous collections no one method may be sufficient and, second, that the planning process can reveal unforeseen conflicts resulting from the collision of initially unrelated policy decisions (e.g., the decision to convert the paper records and the decision to build—and fill!—an off-campus shelving facility in a much tighter timeframe than that of the conversion project).

How Are Faculty Consulted?

The short answer here is, early and often. Otherwise there will be ill will and suspicion; otherwise it will seem that the librarians are conspiring to send "their" books away; otherwise the whole process will appear mysterious and threatening. Several of my colleagues across the country sent cautionary messages: "What I have learned is that we do much better when we let our faculty know as far in advance as possible of our plans, and when we listen to their complaints and then adjust our plans"; and, "One piece of advice that I offer—be sure to involve your faculty. It takes longer but you will have fewer unhappy people if they are involved in the review process." Beyond the public relations angle, of course, we need faculty help to determine what should make up the on-campus collections and what can happily be transferred off-site. Their knowledge and expertise are invaluable. From the very beginning, faculty have been involved in Yale's off-campus shelving initiative: they served on the Working Group that recommended building a facility, they serve on the Advisory Committee on Library Policy, and they continue to be consulted and asked for help as selectors draw up profiles of their on- and off-campus collections. There are several points to make here, and an anecdote to relate.

A. Rhetoric. When talking about selecting for off-campus shelving, we all fall into the trap of negative rhetoric, referring to "sending some books off" (as if to their deaths), "saving" or "keeping" others, "putting the burden" on some parts of the collections, and so on. Perhaps the most extreme example of this is the language used in some library literature: "stock control," "dead stock," "block relegation," "final extraction" (J. A. Urquhart and N. C. Urquhart). And certainly the spin put on this process in a 1997 *Chronicle of Higher Education* article is no exception: "In the new model of the research library, unused books are out, computers are in," and "Universities see off-campus warehouses as the best way to house bulging collections" (Young, p. A27). This, it seems to me, is a good example of how *not* to talk about this issue! At Yale we have very consciously avoided terms like "storage" and "warehouse," choosing to name the building the Library Shelving Facility. While it is true that for many users the ideal library would probably have all its physical holdings immediately accessible, on open shelves for consultation and retrieval, an off-campus facility can offer very real benefits, and the faculty need to hear about them: on-campus collections that are more coherent and better suited for browsing, off-campus shelving that offers an optimal environment and responsive service, a pledge to return materials to campus when use patterns change, and a delivery commitment (within 24 hours to any one of many on-campus sites) that can be an attractive addition to stack-browsing.

B. Strategies. There are many ways to involve faculty in this process, from holding campus-wide informational forums, speaking to department meetings, and asking for faculty advisory groups, to posting lists of likely candidates for transfer and making the books themselves available for review. Early on in our planning process we held a series of forums to introduce the Arts & Sciences faculty to the concept and to hear concerns. We also gathered library selectors together to discuss strategies and answer questions in two special forums. As the library liaison to the English Department, I asked the Chair to put together a small advisory group, which met during the summer to talk about possible categories for transfer. I brought a list of my thoughts, as well as stacks of background documentation, and was prepared to make a hard sell. The group—three senior full professors and one assistant professor, representing different periods and schools of thought—brushed aside my opening gambit with "we've read all that, we know all that, let's talk about the collections," and proceeded to take my recommendations and broaden them: where I had suggested 1800 as a cut-off date, they wanted 1850; where I talked vaguely about "older" periodicals, they suggested keeping on campus periodicals only from 1950 forward. The big lesson here is that the faculty have much to contribute to the selection process and are, as one of them impatiently said to me in another context, "reasonable human beings."

Conclusion

Planned carefully and managed effectively, off-campus shelving facilities provide splendid conditions for long-term preservation and security as well as relief and rationality to the on-campus libraries. As evidenced by Yale's development of the Selectors' Tool, the enforced collaboration among librarians can result in wonderfully creative solutions to the problems at hand, with unlooked-for wider applications. And finally, the planning for these facilities can provide an opportunity for librarians and faculty to work together to define the direction and shape of the collections, both now and for the future.

References

Bellanti, Claire Q. "Access to Library Materials in Remote Storage." *Collection Management* 17, nos. 1-2 (1992): 93–103.

Burrell, Quentin L. "A Note on Ageing in a Library Circulation Model." *Journal of Documentation* 41, no. 2 (June 1985): 100–115.

Burrell, Quentin L. "A Third Note on Ageing in a Library Circulation Model: Applications to Future Use and Regulation." *Journal of Documentation* 43, no. 1 (Mar. 1987): 24–45.

Burrell, Quentin L. "A Simple Empirical Method for Predicting Library Circulations." *Journal of Documentation* 44, no. 4 (Dec. 1988): 302–14.

Creaghe, Norma S. "Hard Copy in Transition: An Automated Storage and Retrieval Facility for Low-Use Library Materials." *College & Research Libraries* 47 (Sept. 1986): 495–99.

Harloe, Bart. "The Politics of Weeding: New Myths and Old Realities." *Academic Libraries: Myths and Realities*, 263–68. Association of College & Research Libraries, 1984.

Hayes, Robert M. "The Distribution of Use of Library Materials: Analysis of Data from the University of Pittsburgh." *Library Research* 3, no. 1 (Spring 1981): 215–60.

Hayes, Robert M. "Measurement of Use and Resulting Access Allocation." *Library & Information Science Research* 14, no. 4 (Oct.-Dec. 1992): 361–77.

Kent, Allen, et al. *Use of Library Materials: The University of Pittsburgh Study*. New York: Marcel, Dekker, 1979.

Kountz, John. "Industrial Storage Technology Applied to Library Requirements." *Library Hi Tech* 5 (Winter 1987): 13–22.

Lazorick, Gerald J. "Patterns of Book Use Using the Negative Binomial Distribution." *Library Research* 1, no. 1 (1979): 171–88.

Lee, Hur-Li. "The Library Space Problem, Future Demand, and Collection Control." *Library Resources & Technical Services* 37, no. 2 (1993): 147–66.

Lougee, Wendy P. "Remote Shelving Comes of Age: Storage Collection Management at the University of Michigan." *Collection Management* 16, no. 2 (1992): 93–107.

McGrath, William E. "Correlating the Subjects of Books Taken out of and Books Used within an Open-Stack Library." *College & Research Libraries* 32, no. 1 (Jan. 1971): 280–85.

Silverstein, Craig, and Stuart M. Sheiber. "Predicting Individual Book Use for Off-Site Storage Using Decision Trees." *The Library Quarterly* 66, no. 3 (1996): 266–93.

Slote, Stanley J. "Identifying Useful Core Collections: A Study of Weeding Fiction in Public Libraries." *The Library Quarterly* 41, no. 1 (Jan. 1971): 25–34.

Slote, Stanley J. *Weeding Library Collections*. Littleton, CO: Libraries Unlimited, 1975.

Tague, Jean, and Isola Ajiferuke. "The Markov and the Mixed-Poisson Models of Library Circulation Compared." *Journal of Documentation* 43, no. 3 (Sept. 1987): 212–35.

Trueswell, Richard W. "User Circulation Satisfaction vs. Size of Holdings at Three Academic Libraries." *College & Research Libraries* 30, no. 3 (May 1969): 204–13.

Urquhart, J. A., and N. C. Urquhart. *Relegation and Stock Control in Libraries*. Boston: Oriel Press, 1976.

Wortman, William A. *Collection Management: Background and Principles*. Chicago and London: American Library Association, 1989.

Yale University. Working Group for an Off-Campus High-Efficiency Shelving Facility. *Final Report*. October 1996. Available online. http://www.library .yale.edu/Administration/Shelving/historical1.html

Young, Jeffrey. R. "In the New Model of the Research Library, Unused Books Are Out, Computers Are In." *The Chronicle of Higher Education* (Oct. 17, 1997): A27.

12

Preparation for Transfer

Lee Anne George*

Once material has been selected for transfer to the high-density shelving facility, a number of steps must be taken to prepare the item and the corresponding catalog record for the change in location. Typically, these steps are the responsibility of the staff in the owning, or client, library. They include cleaning the item; determining whether it needs any conservation treatment; adjusting property and inventory tracking marks; editing or creating the bibliographic, holdings, and item records for the material in the online catalog; and packing the material for shipment to the shelving facility.

Factors That Influence Procedures

A number of factors influence the policies and procedures for preparing items for transfer to high-density shelving facilities. These include the mission of the shelving facility, the categories of materials deemed suitable for transfer, and their format and condition. A review of the descriptive literature from a dozen Harvard–style shelving facilities shows that such facilities typically have a mission to relieve overcrowding in the client library's stacks; to house important, though infrequently used, items that the client institution plans to hold permanently; to protect them in a clean and secure environment; and to provide reliable access to those items.

The descriptions stress that the shelving facilities are intended for *library* materials, though university archives and other documents that have significant historical value to the client institution are generally accepted too. Some facilities promote their suitability for older or fragile items, or those that need additional security to prevent theft or mutilation. A number of facilities advertise that

---

they accept all formats and media, as long as they meet the minimum library materials criterion. (Everyone draws the line at office supplies and equipment and hazardous chemicals.) The result is that most of the items sent to high-density shelving facilities are books, bound serials, record storage cartons, and other paper-based media.

The majority of these media was originally shelved in open library stacks. Since the shelving facility is designed to be an extension of the stacks, policies reflect an assumption that the transferred materials already have the property marks, security tags, spine labels, bar codes, and level of catalog records that are customary for an active, circulating university library collection, and that these are appropriate for transferred items, as well, with a few exceptions.

Protecting the Item and the Shelving Facility Environment

Almost every transfer policy requires that materials entering the shelving facility be clean and well supported. This ensures that the optimal environmental conditions are maintained in the facility and that the material neither causes nor receives harm in the tight shelving conditions, or during accessioning, retrieval, and use. In most cases, the client library staff is responsible for wiping or vacuuming materials and weeding out any that show evidence of mold, insect infestation, or sticky accretions. In addition, they remove any bookmarks, forms, paper clips, sticky notes, or rubber bands that may have been left in the item by staff or users. They are also responsible for deciding whether fragile, brittle, or unbound materials need to be tied, wrapped, enveloped, or encased. While most shelving facilities accept fragile, brittle, and unbound materials, only one or two have the expertise and other resources to provide conservation services such as these. Most facilities will return to the client library material that could suffer damage during accessioning or subsequent use. There are two additional benefits of making cleaning and conservation the first step in the transfer process. The client library's staff work area is kept clean, and it creates a suitable surface for attaching a bar code.

Another possibility to consider is to establish a book-cleaning program at the shelving facility itself. Yale's Library Shelving Facility has such a program in operation, and it was designed in part in response to limitations on space for cleaning on campus, but also for reasons of productivity.

Item Tracking

The bar code is the single most important element for tracking and retrieving material that has been transferred to the shelving facility. The item bar code is the link between the physical item and the catalog record and between the physical item and its tray and shelf location in the shelving facility. It is typically the basis for the retrieval process. In facilities that use an inventory control system that is separate from the online catalog, the item bar code serves as the link between the two systems.

Almost invariably, the client library staff is responsible for attaching the item bar code and linking it to the catalog record. The shelving facility staff creates the link with tray and shelf bar codes. The type of bar code, who supplies it, where it is attached, and how many are attached varies widely. Some of the variation seems to depend on whether the shelving facility serves the libraries and departments of a single institution or of multiple, independent institutions. Some depends on whether the shelving facility uses a stand-alone inventory control system or relies on the integrated library management system of the client libraries. Part depends on where the library chose to place bar codes on circulating items. Part seems to depend on how good the adhesive is on available bar codes.

The major considerations for bar code placement are: what is the retrievable unit, the item or a set; and what promotes efficient processing? If users will most often want to retrieve an individual item, then the bar code should be attached to the item or its protective enclosure. If the user will want or need to consult a collection or set of materials, they can be boxed and the bar code attached to the box.

Shelving facilities that stress high-efficiency during accessioning, retrieval, and reshelving recommend placing the bar code on the outside of the item, typically on the upper left corner of the front or the upper right corner of the back of a book. With the bar code in this location, a whole book truck full of material can quickly be scanned into the inventory control system (see Figure 1), or charged out of and back into the shelving facility, simply by tilting the item out from the tray.

Figure 1. Scanning Bar Codes. Courtesy of Yale University.

Bar code design decisions affect the efficiency of the client library's circulation staff. When users return materials that have been retrieved from the shelving facility to the library, it helps to provide a cue to the circulation staff that the item should be returned to the shelving facility, rather than to the stacks. Various approaches have been taken to achieve this. Often, a bar code that is different from the circulation system bar code is attached to the item during the transfer process. This bar code may have the code or name of the shelving facility on it. It may have a combination of the client library's and shelving facility's names. It may be a different size. It may have a different number of characters or a prefix of numbers that identifies the shelving facility. Whatever design is used, this visual cue can improve the circulation staff's sorting efficiency during the discharge process. Most circulation systems will provide an additional visual or audible flag when the item is discharged too.

Bar Code Placement

The upper left corner bar code location works well for books in good condition, bound serials, envelopes, phase boxes, microfilm boxes, and other similar enclosures. Books with vellum covers, covers that have artifactual value, bumpy covers, or leather covers suffering from red rot should not or can not have a bar code attached directly to the cover. These should be wrapped and tied and the bar code should be placed on the wrapper. Alternatively, a strip of acid-free paper can be wrapped around the front book cover and the bar code attached to it. Some libraries place a matching bar code on the inside of the cover, while others have decided that this step is unnecessary.

Volumes of bound serials should be individually bar coded. This provides better inventory control and makes shelving, retrieval, use, and reshelving more efficient. Brittle, fragile, or thin items that need additional support can be placed in an envelope or phase box, depending on their size. The bar code is then placed in the location that corresponds to the upper left corner of a book cover. A duplicate bar code on the item itself is usually not necessary and often inadvisable.

Collections of manuscripts, pamphlets, and other document sets that are represented by a collection level record in the catalog can be placed in a record storage carton. A bar code is then attached to the outside of the carton. Again, duplicate bar codes on individual items within the box is usually not advisable.

In the case of more than one title bound into a physical piece, a single bar code on the cover of the volume is sufficient. Bar codes can also be placed on the upper left corner of the front of individual microfilm boxes, videocassette cases, CD-ROM jewel boxes, and similar rectangular media cases, though some libraries choose to box collections of such media for transfer to the shelving facility.

Oversized flat items such as maps, posters, architectural plans, and works of art may require a different placement of the bar code in order to protect and not obscure the work. Decisions may need to be made on a case-by-case basis, depending on how they will be stored at the shelving facility and how they will be retrieved.

Property Marks

In general, the policy is that materials transferred to a shelving facility remain the property of the client library. For this reason, spine labels, call numbers, property marks, and security tags are usually left unchanged on materials that are being moved out of the stacks. This practice of retaining original ownership marks permits materials to be returned to the client library's stacks with minimal effort, should the use level demand it. Newly acquired material that will bypass the stacks and be sent directly to the shelving facility will usually receive the same cataloging and property marks as material bound for the stacks, but may not receive a call number and spine label until the item is transferred back to the stacks because of high use.

The Catalog Entry

When the material has been cleaned, protected, and bar coded, the next step is to edit or create the bibliographic, holdings, and item records in the online catalog. In current practice, the majority of items transferred to high-density shelving facilities either already have or receive full bibliographic records prior to transfer. The documents from several shelving facilities spell out in some detail exactly what information is expected in the record. In general, policy documents state that records should meet the prevailing local standard for full MARC cataloging for the material type and include complete holdings and item level information. A collective record is usually recommended for boxed or bundled sets. When two or more titles are bound together, individual records are usually created for each title in the volume. Some libraries accept short bibliographic records for record storage cartons. Others permit archival and special collections material to be represented by finding aids. A few facilities accept material that is not cataloged, but this is usually the exception. Some facilities refuse any uncataloged material, and at Yale for example, all material transferred to the Library Shelving Facility must have a record in the online catalog.

It is important to change or add information to the location field. For items transferred to a high-density shelving facility, the location usually contains subfields for the code that represents the client library, the name or a code for the shelving facility—or a combined code that represents both—the call number, notes, and the bar code.

The note subfield in the LOC field can be used to indicate when two or more titles are bound together in a single volume. For example, when two titles are bound together, the record for the first title might have one note that says: |n Bound with [title of second work] and a second note field for the bar code. The record for the second title would say: |n Bound with [title of first work] and would include a link to the bibliographic record number for the first title (e.g., |j AAA0001). If many titles are bound together, the note for the first title might say |n Bound in a pamphlet volume. The records for the other titles would include a field with the bibliographic record number for the first title.

Clearly, having complete bibliographic and descriptive cataloging is desirable for materials that are nonbrowsable. Users can make better decisions about whether it would be useful to request retrieval of a particular item or box from the shelving facility.

Holdings Records

Several of the surveyed policy documents stress the need for complete and accurate copy holdings information in the online catalog for material that is transferred to the shelving facility. Some even include a Not On Shelf statement for any serial volume that was not available at the time of transfer. Again, this is important for helping users determine whether a desired item is available for retrieval and use. It also is necessary for accurate inventory control.

Item Records

The item record contains information about the individual piece, including the bar code. It is vitally important to enter the correct bar code of the item being transferred into the item record. Without this data element, retrieval from the shelving facility will be next to impossible. In the case of multiple titles bound together, a single item record can be created and linked either to the collective record for the set or to the record for the first title in the volume. This item record contains the bar code for the entire volume. The subfield j data in the location field of the other titles in the volume will generate a note in the catalog directing users to this item record.

The client library also needs to set the parameters for the circulation status in the item record. Typically, the library needs to decide whether the item can circulate or must be used in-house, and to which library the item can be delivered for pick up by the user. In some cases, the client library decides the loan period and overdue fine as well. In others, all items in the shelving facility are given a standard loan period and fine. In facilities that use the client's library management system for inventory control, facility staff may enter the tray and shelf bar codes in the note field of the item record during accessioning. In facilities with a stand-alone inventory control system, this information is not entered in the catalog record.

Online Catalog Display

Since the goal of almost every shelving facility is to provide easy identification and quick retrieval of transferred items, for the most part, the records for these items display in the online catalog. Exceptions in some cases are records that don't conform to cataloging standards, and records for nonlibrary materials that are accepted for storage.

Delivering Prepared Materials to the Shelving Facility

A small number of shelving facilities are close enough to their client libraries that prepared items can be transferred on standard book trucks. Because most of the Harvard–style facilities are some distance from their client libraries, a few additional steps must be taken to complete the transfer to the facility.

Individual items need to be carefully packed into clean, sturdy cartons in such a way that they will not be damaged during shipping. Often, libraries use standard cardboard moving boxes that store flat and can be reused a number of times. Another option is a plastic tub or tote that has carrying handles and a secure lid. These can be reused for much longer, but take up more storage space. Record storage boxes can usually be transferred as is. Special arrangements will usually need to be made for oversized items.

The cartons then need to be moved to the loading dock or other pick-up location. Depending on local arrangements, either the destination will need to be marked on the cartons, or they will need to be stacked in a prearranged location for pick up by the shelving facility van or other designated courier. Most facilities have established a regular schedule for pick-ups and also make special arrangements for additional pick-ups. Upon pick-up, the material becomes the responsibility of the shelving facility.

Establishing clear guidelines for the preparation of material for transfer to the high-density shelving facility is a critical step in the overall process. Such facilities may often stress zero-defect operations and incorporate redundant processing into the workflow, but equal attention to detail and quality is required at the sending library to ensure that the whole system works to an optimal efficiency.

13

Transportation and Logistics

Donald G. Kelsey and Curtis L. Kendrick

On the surface, it would seem that the issues surrounding moving library materials into a storage center in the first place and the ongoing retrieval and subsequent transfers of material into storage are mainly logistical matters. In fact, the delivery system set up to support a storage center operation is intricately linked with the public service face of the center and should be developed with the operational, service, and public relations implications of each decision fully in mind.

It is often the case that the storage center is built five to 10 years after the need is first identified from a collection management perspective. By the time all of the political and fiscal wheels are turning in the right direction and the funding structure can be mobilized to support the construction of a storage center, the available collection space is usually bursting at the seams. Badly needed user spaces may have been cannibalized in an effort to keep as much of the collection open as possible and accessible. The library may have already been forced to move significant parts of the collection into storage sites, often far from ideal from both a collection preservation and a collection management perspective. All of these things combine, once the storage center is complete, to build enormous pressure to move a large amount of collection into the center now! This chapter will address the issues involved in determining how best to move material from the on-campus library to the shelving facility, both in terms of the typically larger-scale initial moves as well as the less frequent or lower volume ongoing moves. In addition, this chapter will discuss issues in managing the delivery and return of items requested from the facility for use by patrons.

Material Processed for Off-Site

The "move" to the shelving facility really begins once an item is processed for off-site storage. Libraries will need to consider how to handle material once it is processed but before it is moved. Collections pending transport to the shelving facility can be returned to their correct shelf location in the library. This will make them easily accessible by patrons but will require repicking in advance of the actual move. The repicking can be accomplished by working from a list of call numbers, or the books themselves can be tagged in some way on the shelf (e.g., flyer, tipped down on spine) to distinguish those that should move from among books that will not be moved to off-site. The reshelving option may require an adjustment to the OPAC at the time of moving since the location may need to be flipped from the campus location to the off-site location.

Another option for collections awaiting transfer is to move them to a staging area. Typically, this will mean that these collections must be paged by staff if needed during this interim period. Perhaps more germane is that this approach requires an adequate staging area, and for libraries just starting to transfer collections to the shelving facility, such space is likely to be in short supply.

Packing Them Up

An immediate issue that arises when a storage center plans for the movement of books to and from the facility is what means of actual packaging will be used. The advice from most professional moving companies is that boxing books is the best method. This advice is based more on the habits and traditions of professional movers than on sound wisdom regarding moving books. Books are much less substantial than they appear. A book's covers are held in place by a paper hinge, and as a book ages, its outward appearance may show few if any signs of change, but it can be very fragile and highly susceptible to accidental damage through improper handling. Putting books into cartons can be a particularly destructive experience to put a collection through, but there are measures to take to minimize this effect.

Books will move best in corrugated cartons if they are packed flat in the boxes. Rarely, if ever, do books fit into moving cartons in an efficient way when they are laid flat. There is a tremendous temptation to "be efficient" and put a few extra books in the carton turned on their fore edge to fill the carton closer to full. Books need to be loaded into cartons so that the carton is filled completely from top to bottom. It is not nearly as important that the cartons be filled from side to side as it is that the books be solid from bottom to top. This is important because inevitably the cartons will be stacked, and if they are not filled completely, the lowest box in the stack will begin to collapse under the weight of the cartons above it. (The average of 1.5 cubic feet that is standard in the moving industry can easily weigh 50 to 60 pounds when loaded with books.) If books have been turned on edge to make the packing of the carton "neater" or more "efficient," it can often be the case that a single book sticking up higher than the others in a carton is bearing all of the weight of the cartons above it, causing significant damage. This potential for damage during the time that books are riding in a moving truck from one location to another may be understood by realizing that the books are in a vibrator. Foam or other filler may be used to absorb some of the shock.

Using corrugated cartons for book moving requires training, care, and supervision as the books are packed, but also when the cartons are opened at the center destination. An alternative that could well be explored for the initial movement of materials into the storage center as well as during the operating lifetime of the center is the use of hard-shell bins. These are readily available in the industrial world where they are used for all manner of parts storage and transfer. These bins are essentially the same size as a 1.5-cubic-foot corrugated carton. They come equipped with a fitted cover, making them weatherproof. Hard-shell bins can be reused longer than cardboard cartons and can take a variety of reusable label pockets. The cost differential between buying reusable hard-shell bins at the outset as opposed to spending money on corrugated cardboard cartons that will be used mainly for the initial move is not significant. Another option to consider for moving collections is book carts. However, there are almost no library book carts designed for repeated trips over doorsills, movement on and off moving vans, and over other surface irregularities. Even if the book carts in your library are exceptionally well designed, it is a bad business decision to put them through the kind of accelerated aging experience of a library move. It cannot be stressed enough that despite the apparent sturdiness of library carts, the quality of the casters and the means of fastening the casters to the cart itself are usually fair to poor. This is true even with expensive carts. Even the heavy-duty moving carts that are common among professional movers fail over time.

Moving Them Out

Covering all of the issues relating to the use of a professional mover in libraries would take a book of its own, and a good one to consult is *Moving Library Collections: A Management Handbook* by Elizabeth Chamberlain Habich (Westport, Conn.: Greenwood Press, 1998). The focus of these comments that follow is specifically on using a professional library mover for the initial influx of materials into the storage center.

It is important to begin with a number of general observations about the professional moving industry. With only a few exceptions, most professional moving companies are engaged in all types of moves: office, industrial, residential, etc. This is an important insight because there are times during the year when all moving companies are in heavy demand for residential moves. The end of the month when many people are changing residences can be a difficult time to schedule a mover. The beginnings and ends of the local academic year also are difficult times to schedule a mover.

Expertise in library moves is sought within the industry and lodged in individuals rather than companies. It has happened that someone who has built knowledge and skills in moving library materials has been sought by other moving companies and hired away. This observation is important because the business of checking company references, if they are not closely tied to the *individuals* who have the expertise, may be a misleading, and often meaningless, exercise. During your review to select a mover, always require information about the skills of the individual in the moving company who will be responsible for your move.

A similar problem exists on a smaller scale within professional companies who have built expertise in library moves. Often the most capable individual with respect to library move planning and execution is put in a sales role in the company. This individual meets with you, convinces you that the company has the requisite expertise to be able to manage your move and then when the actual move occurs, this person is not a part of the moving team that actually executes your move. The movers who arrive to perform the move may or may not have the needed skills or supervision to do the kind of job you expect.

Using a professional mover can bring skills, expertise, equipment, and resources the library does not have. Most importantly, a professional mover brings equipment to the move specially designed to withstand the rigors of moving. It is a much better decision to contract with a professional mover for the use of their equipment and let them deal with the problems of "book cart attrition" rather than discover at the end of the move that the majority of your book carts are damaged beyond repair. A related issue regarding using book carts in a move is that most libraries do not own the number of book carts that are needed in order to have a smooth move. It is not unusual for even a relatively small move, say in the range of 10,000 volumes or less, to need 50 or more book carts in order to maintain a smooth workflow. Larger moves can easily require the use of 100 or more carts. Even if the library owns a significant number of serviceable book carts, freeing them all for exclusive use of the library move means shutting down other operations in the library for the duration of the move.

Now that we are finally paying proper attention to the potential for repetitive-motion injuries in the workplace, another strong reason for engaging professionals for a library move is that they come to the job better trained and better conditioned physically for this kind of very intensive physical activity. Full-time stack management staff members are probably engaged in the most intensive book handling of all library staff as a routine part of their jobs. The very narrow range of physical activity and the repeated grasping of a handful of books are a classic opportunity for the onset of pervasive repetitive-motion injuries. Even if the library staff is relieved of the physical aspects of the library move, there are still more than enough important roles for them to play supervising the proper loading, unloading, and handling of the collections in transit.

Accessioning materials to a storage facility usually means transferring collections from libraries organized by a classification system into a size-sorted, bar code system for inventory control. Because of this process there is an interval between the time any given item leaves its place in the library and the time it is fully accessioned and physically in its new location in the storage center when the item may be inaccessible. *May* is the operative word in the previous sentence because having materials in an inventory control limbo is not necessarily a result of the accessioning process itself. If large quantities of materials are loaded into boxes and piled in the corner of the receiving space in the storage center until the accessioning staff can get to them, then for a time they will most certainly have dropped into an organizational "black hole."

The rate at which materials can be accepted at the storage center and not fall into this collection management limbo is determined by two things: the rate of accessioning and the ability of the storage center to house materials waiting to be accessioned in a way in which items may be found should a particular item be needed between the time it leaves the library and the time it is accessioned. A well-designed storage center either sets operational limits right at the outset for how much material it can accept in a given period of time, or it is designed with a generous holding area to accommodate the influx of larger amounts of material without compromising the ability to locate items waiting for accessioning.

When a mover is employed to transport high number of items at one time, there likely will be a period when a specific item cannot be located unless some special measures are introduced to provide a method of location. Arguably, since much of what is typically transferred to an off-site facility is low-use material, it may be acceptable for there to be a period of time (a few days, perhaps) during which material is not accessible.

For some collections such as university archives, this inaccessibility may be unacceptable. Some movers have agreed to create a data file of bar codes associated with transported objects, and this capability can be used to design a temporary system to locate items prior to being accessioned into the facility. For example, the movers initially used at the Yale University Library Shelving Facility used portable bar code readers to scan bar codes of both individual archival boxes and bins containing other materials such as books consolidated for the move. Library staff maintained listings of what items were in the bins. The placement in the facility of the boxes and bins was noted. A simple spreadsheet was used to list the bar codes by location, and this permitted facility staff a fairly easy way to search for a container bar code and to identify the general location of a specific item. This system reduced the number of items that needed to be handled to find a specific item. The strong motivation to design such a measure is to support the principle that the facility is not a "black hole" where items will be inaccessible, whether short or long term, but each institution will have to weigh for itself the benefits versus the costs and complexities of establishing an in-transit/in-process tracking system.

The greatest cost benefit in using a professional mover is derived from a move plan that enables the move to take place in the shortest elapsed time possible. Often competent library movers will suggest moving the collection in more than one "stream" at a time. This means having two or more teams working at both the origin and the destination moving streams of materials simultaneously. The economics of such a move plan do not reduce the move costs by half, but they do substantially reduce the total costs over moving the collection in a single stream by reducing overall supervisory overhead. Such a multistream approach to moving materials into a storage center requires that the resulting volume of delivery be matched with the accessioning rate to handle the increased influx of materials into the center. Otherwise, confusion and potential delays at the receiving end of the system are likely.

The very speed and efficiency that a professional mover can bring to the task may turn out to be the strongest reason for not contracting an outside mover. One model that may be worth considering is to use a professional mover for the high-volume moving typically necessary when the shelving facility first opens. This period, which may be referred to as "load-in," may last months or in some cases over a period of years. Once the initial load-in is complete, the volume of transfers tends to taper off. This may be the time to consider other approaches, including establishing in-house alternatives to contracting out the moves. Regardless of the decisions about how initially to move large amounts of material to the shelving facility, how best to ensure the rapid and reliable delivery of requested items to where they will be made available to library patrons will likely involve a separate decision path. This facet of the suite of transportation services is quite likely to involve local staff and resources.

Retrieval Deliveries

Ensuring the rapid and reliable delivery of requested items from the high-density shelving facility back to campus is a primary service objective of the operation. The first set of questions to ask as the delivery system is being designed relates to the community the center will serve. What is the service audience for the center? Does the center serve a single campus? Does it serve a number of campuses within a single organizational entity? Does the center serve a number of organizational entities? What is the geographic distribution of the libraries served by the center? If the sending entities are administratively and/or geographically distributed, then it may not be possible to harmonize the varying needs. Options in these cases will include each entity establishing its own transportation infrastructure, the center itself fully managing the delivery system, or subcontracting all or part of the work to a third-party service provider. If the sending libraries are more centralized administratively and geographically, it might make sense to develop in-house expertise since there will be scale economies of one transportation department serving many libraries.

Geography is an important factor in determining which transportation models to consider. The distance from the facility to the depositing libraries, the number of stops, and the distance between them must all be considered. Other factors in determining routes include the existence or lack of loading docks and elevators, whether inside delivery is necessary or if delivery to a loading dock is sufficient, and how nearby is parking.

While there are many possible models for how to approach setting up a delivery system, three appear to be most common among high-density shelving facility operations.

Transportation Model 1

In this model the shelving facility is at a remote distance from campus. Courier vans carry material back and forth between the shelving facility and multiple libraries on campus. Courier vans may also pick up small amounts of new material being transferred to the facility. This model may work well if there are not a lot of stops along the route so that the entire route can be covered in a single shift.

Transportation Model 2

Courier vans carry material back and forth between the shelving facility and a hub on campus. Material is off-loaded for redistribution to libraries on campus. Often the hub is actually the main library. This model will likely be considered less desirable than model 1 since it requires double handling of the material. However, it may be necessary if there are many stops along the route, or if the stops are such that each one requires a lot of time. Factors increasing the amount of time at a stop include lack of a loading dock, lack of an elevator, and no nearby parking.

Transportation Model 3

This model may be appropriate if the shelving facility is not too far distant from campus. In this model the shelving facility is just one stop on a preexisting campus route. This model can be very effective. It is important, however, to make sure that the service level being promised by the shelving facility can be supported by the existing operation. If the existing service is not dependable, often neglects stops, or has the reputation for losing things, then these issues will need to be resolved in order for this transportation model to be a viable consideration.

Regardless of which model is selected, there are steps in the planning process that will be common to all. Table 1 provides a template for the planning process for the distribution system.

Table 1. Planning Steps for a Distributed System

	Time	Cubic Feet of Material Unloaded	Cubic Feet of Material Loaded
Load Van at Facility	X		X
Travel Time to Stop 1	X		
Unload, Deliver and Load at Stop 1	X	X	X
Travel Time to Stop 2	X		
Unload, Deliver and Load at Stop 2	X	X	X
Travel Time to Stop n	X		
Unload, Deliver and Load at Stop n	X	X	X
Travel Time Back to Facility	X		
Unload at Facility	X		

It generally is a good idea to have the same people who are making the deliveries be responsible for loading the van. This will give thcm a better sense of how much material is going to each stop and will help in planning the day. Moreover, they will also know where everything is in the van.

In assessing the total time for the route, planning can be done on the basis of an average day or on the basis of a peak day. If the average day is used, then managers must be prepared for what to do when a peak day hits—either with a backup capacity or flexibility to award overtime. If a peak day is used for the planning assumptions, then managers should have other tasks at the ready to assign to courier staff when their time is not fully used by their delivery responsibilities. Another criterion in determining the amount of time at each stop will be the decision regarding delivery to a mailroom or loading dock versus inside delivery to a service desk. Inside delivery is more secure and typically results in material being available for users more quickly, while delivery to a loading dock or mailroom is more expeditious for the delivery staff.

In assessing the total cubic feet of material moved, the obvious limiting factor is that at no time along the route can the total amount of material loaded into the van exceed the capacity of the van. It certainly makes sense for the same van that is delivering requesting items to pick up returned items from the libraries. In estimating the load levels these returns need to be accounted for, as will new accessions if the transportation model is one where new accessions are picked up by the courier service. While communication between the facility and the libraries is key, established limits for how much material may be transported each day may also be helpful for staff in the field. Such limits, which may be viewed as guidelines, will give staff firm footing upon which to refuse part of a pick-up if the amount of material won't fit in the van.

Overlaying all of the planning efforts is the issue of existing delivery services. In an academic setting it is common for the campus or library to have in place some sort of regular delivery system. It is possible that existing networks can be expanded to include the deliveries to and from the storage center. In evaluating the efficacy of using existing services, it is important to understand what the system is designed to handle, and to ensure that the service level provided would adequately meet the service standards established for the shelving facility. Timing is also critical in scheduling the shipment of items retrieved from the facility for delivery to readers. For example, when a facility is dependent on another transport system, whether a library or campus delivery system or a commercial vendor, the scheduling of retrieving and preparing needed items should be coordinated with pick-up schedules in order to meet service delivery goals.

Whether using a preexisting transportation capacity or developing its own, in order for the storage center to maintain a level of delivery service equivalent to what might be procured through outsourcing, the center will need to plan for a minimum level of redundancy in the service. Such redundancy may include having an extra vehicle on hand to keep the service operating when the principal vehicle requires routine maintenance or repair, or budgeting for the emergency rental of trucks, assuming they are available on short notice. It is important for several members of the staff to be trained and equipped with a valid driver's license, to cover the service in the event of illness or vacations for the regular delivery staff. These required levels of redundancy should already be built into any thriving delivery service. Taking advantage of such a separately maintained service, while it gives up a small measure of individual control by the storage center, may be the most economical method of setting up the center delivery system. The practice of outsourcing is also becoming more and more common on college and university campuses. The world of courier delivery systems has proliferated nationwide over the last decade. In most cities there are frequently a half-dozen or more competing delivery services that are more than eager to take on the delivery function for the storage center. The advantage of considering to outsource the delivery system is that all of the issues related to the selection, customizing, maintenance, and replacement of delivery vehicles are someone else's problem. The storage center management can contract for services on a fee basis and may be able to reduce substantially the cost of this part of the operation over fitting up and operating the delivery service in-house.

Conclusion

The allure of all of that empty space in the new storage center sets up its own siren song. As a consequence, the thought of hiring a professional moving company to come in and quickly and efficiently move a large amount of collection into the storage center is very appealing. In the face of the initial pressure to relieve the space shortage in the libraries served as quickly as possible, taking time to think through the whole receiving and delivery system may seem overly elaborate and time-consuming. The design of this delivery system is going to be needed regardless of when it is put in place, and getting it organized and operational from the very first day of center operation has enormous benefits with respect to the public service image the center is able to present to its users.

The move of the collection into the center can seem deceptively simple—not simple with regard to the large volume of material that needs to be moved from bulging library buildings, of course. But in the whole scheme of things, it is easy to underestimate the design and organization of the delivery system for the storage center, including the initial move, not thinking of these as integral parts of the center's operational design. There is an erroneous perception that once the initial move is over, the relatively minor matters of how materials will move back and forth between the storage center and the libraries it serves will be a simple matter, one that will fall into place with relative ease. Administrators may be convinced that the routine delivery service can easily shirttail on an existing campus delivery system. There will be no need to put on additional staff "just" to handle deliveries. However, the design and operation of the delivery system is more than a planning nicety; it is critical to the successful operation of the center.

14

Computer Systems

Joel J. Felber, J.D.

This chapter will examine systems-related issues faced by institutions planning high-density shelving facilities. Proper computer hardware and software planning and implementation provide part of the infrastructure necessary for efficient operations. An accurate and well-designed computer system ensures that materials can always be located, a condition that increases confidence levels in the community. Inventory accuracy and preventing an item's loss is the paramount consideration in operating a high-density shelving facility. This chapter will describe in detail the planning effort and implementation program for automation support of Yale University's Library Shelving Facility, which may help planners of other facilities in their system design efforts.

Software Selection Committee

Initially, a software selection committee at Yale outlined and evaluated the needs of its libraries in relation to the proposed library shelving facility. After considerable research and discussion, the committee generated a list of hardware and software specifications to be submitted to vendors for evaluation and response. The committee then evaluated the vendors and rated relative quality, price, support, and ability to meet the specification. At first the committee speculated that many vendors would be available for evaluation and that a process of elimination would occur revealing the most cost-effective and promising finalist. As of 1998 and given Yale's desired specifications and budgetary restrictions, however, only three vendors offered software applications suitable for Yale's needs. Differences among these vendors included price, performance, support, and reputation in the industry.

The committee decided early on that a third-party vendor, not in-house developers, would be selected to provide the inventory application software. The committee determined that the cost associated with designing, programming, and implementing an in-house system was higher than purchasing one from a third-party vendor. As discussed above, Yale produced an extensive list of software requirements and desirables and submitted the compilation to bidding vendors. The vendors were charged with responding to each item and indicating whether their software and hardware systems could furnish the particular features. Work-around solutions were requested if specific features weren't available and vendors were asked to describe in sufficient detail how all features were implemented. Vendors were also asked to respond to other application details including cost estimates, installation timelines, professional references, hardware requirements, licensing information, and maintenance agreements.

Once the committee received responses from vendors, a series of telephone interviews commenced with users of the particular applications. The users were asked to provide candid evaluations of vendors' systems, vendor responsiveness, and to state whether the vendor had delivered the application within promised budgets and timelines. The committee considered continued maintenance and technical support important elements in its overall evaluation, and so users were asked to evaluate the nature of a vendor's continued support, for example, user-groups versus individual attention. User-groups typically have regularly scheduled meetings. Users of a particular software application convene at these meetings to learn of new software upgrade features, express concerns, suggest changes, and generally to have an opportunity to interact. Some software companies offer user-groups in lieu of individual support and maintenance arrangements. Yale considered a user-group to be a less preferred maintenance support option because of the likelihood that individual attention in a custom support contract would be met. Eventually, like Cornell University, Yale elected to purchase the Library Archival System written and supported by Generation Fifth Applications (GFA), a company located in Maine. This system was developed in conjunction with Harvard University. As owner of the LAS, Harvard has an agreement with GFA allowing the company to sell this system to others.

GFA's product offered the most features from Yale's software selection committee's specification list at the most affordable price. In addition, GFA repeatedly promised to customize the application to meet Yale's needs, and GFA had a successful track record of installations in other university settings. A series of telephone and face-to-face interviews with GFA ensued prior to the final decision to purchase. Interviewing prospective vendors, especially in person, is very helpful to assess whether delivery is likely and also to develop a personal rapport especially in the case of small business software developers, such as GFA. The GFA product continues to undergo revisions and customization at Yale in response to refinements in operational requirements.

An integration of different software and hardware systems comprises GFA's Library Archival System. The package employs a variety of hardware and software, with most of the software written by GFA and some purchased from other third-party vendors. GFA recommended and sold much of the hardware and software for the facility, and GFA helped administer the implementation of the computers, data terminals, and printing devices. While future shelving facility owners or companies may develop a single comprehensive software and hardware system, it is probable that some version of this model that includes over five third-party software applications will continue to be employed. The heterogeneous system provides a great amount of flexibility and remains cost-effective.

The software applications support the facility's operations. Bar code data identifying items (e.g., monographs, serials, maps, drawings, film, video, digital media, trays, and shelves) are entered in a computer workstation terminal prior to shelving of the item in the facility. During shelving, item locations are entered into a portable data terminal (PDT) and then uploaded to a workstation for continued data processing. The data entry drives an accurate database of the facility's inventory and enables users to look up an item's characteristics, status, and location quickly. Item requests made by patrons are printed, having been automatically ordered by aisle, shelf, and position, thereby ensuring efficient retrieval in the facility. Under the Yale model, the campus-wide library information management system (LIMS) is modified by programs written in-house to perform data updating and retrieval tasks. Finally, daily backups and a redundant archival system developed by Yale are implemented to guarantee continued retrieval of items in the event of a system outage.

Testing the Application

At Yale, the inventory application software was configured to operate in a test mode months before being installed for live operations at the facility. This enabled systems staff to familiarize themselves with the workings of the system and also helped to train facility staff in the various components of the application. Yale installed two workstations in a testing room and entered a large and diverse selection of items into the system. The diverse sampling represented the various collections of items scheduled for shelving at the facility and enabled testing of many of the different modules in the system. Additionally, the diverse sampling and extended testing process exposed bugs such as scanners and portable data terminal compatibility (problems recognizing bar-code symbology) that could be addressed before putting the system into production. Additionally, a model workstation design had evolved after completion of testing, and once implemented, an image of the workstation was made and burned into a computer disk (CD) for replication. At Yale, all of the workstations at the shelving facility were configured to perform all of the tasks at the facility.

After the testing process was complete and appropriate modifications to the application were finished, the system went into production. Facility staff were trained and closely monitored to ensure accuracy and proper use of the system by GFA personnel for a full week after going into production. In-house Yale systems staff were also on-site or on-call during the early operations of the facility to make necessary adjustments, report errors, answer questions, and provide technical details for GFA.

Hardware: Overall

The shelving facility uses a combination of computer hardware devices to maximize efficiency. Computers, portable data terminals (PDTs), bar-code scanning and printing equipment, office printers, and network hardware operate in combination to produce the overall system. The use of PDT docking stations and network hardware enable communication paths between shelving facility local devices and campus-wide systems. These paths provide fast, accurate and efficient transportation of data. Some of the programs that transport the data were developed by Yale to provide automatic transfers and eliminate end-user errors. In addition to forwarding data from application to application, remote technical support for in-house systems staff and third-party vendors is enabled. By accessing the workstations or the file server remotely via the Internet or local intranet, repairs can be made without any, or hopefully without significant, interruptions. Issues of security were raised and handled for all remote access to the computer systems. To further Yale's security procedures, remote access is restricted by user TCP/IP address, user name, and associated passwords. Whenever system resources can be accessed via remote communications, security should be a high priority.

The shelving facility's staff is trained in specific operations of the LAS to ensure proper use of the system. Yale employs a hierarchical system of restricted user access to the LAS, determined in part by the qualifications and employment level of the user. This hierarchical system of access reduces the number of users in many areas of the LAS, which consequently reduces the potential for damaging mistakes. Additionally, "hackers" are locked out of the system and unable to wreak havoc upon the database. Restricting staff to small, specific portions of the system results in greater familiarity and also faster, accurate operations with fewer data processing errors. As in any computer environment, staff will have to be trained periodically as new technologies are introduced and made available in the facility.

Hardware: Personal Computers

Personal computers running Microsoft Windows NT operating system are networked together and coupled to Yale's campus-wide network. This enables two-way functionality: staff at the LSF can access campus systems, and on-campus staff, particularly systems staff, can access the workstations at the LSF. While most of the workstations at the LSF are configured identically to perform the same set of operations, some workstations are configured somewhat uniquely to perform specific tasks. For example, one computer is connected to the docking station and used to download data from the portable data terminals (PDTs) and upload the data to the GFA application. Other specialized tasks performed by individual computer workstations include bar-code production and running office desktop applications, for example, word processing, spreadsheet, and database applications. The configuration schemes produce efficient use of hardware and software, as well as guide employee activities. All of the computers are networked, and the workstations are configured so that in the event that one becomes disabled, another can be substituted to perform its specific tasks. As discussed above, a model workstation was developed during the initial setup and an image of that workstation's drive was made for "cloning" purposes. Using the image of the model workstation to clone the others simplified the task of setup and installation.

The GFA software application uses the UNIX operating system and requires a dedicated server. Currently, that server is a Sun® Microsystems computer, running Sun® Microsystems Solaris® operating system version 2.6. For redundancy, the server computer has mirrored drives and in the event one hard drive fails, a mirrored drive can instantly take over and continue operations uninterrupted by the crash. As discussed above, directory and file permissions are configured for security purposes and those permissions are managed in-house by Yale's Library Systems Department. All of the workstations at the shelving facility run 3270 terminal emulating software to enable connection to the Sun® Microsystems server computer. Access to the Sun® Microsystems computer is restricted by IP address of the workstations, and users are added and removed periodically. The use of the 3270 terminal emulating software enables any computer with a TCP/IP connection and proper permissions to access the server and run the inventory application. This is immensely useful for connecting and working on the system, in addition to troubleshooting, testing, and performing other remote LSF computer operations.

Hardware:
Portable Data Terminals

The portable data terminals are wireless devices for remote use while items are being shelved and retrieved. Data entry in the form of pressing keys on the PDT alphanumeric keypad and by scanning bar codes with an attached bar-code scanner on the PDT enables accurate and fast item, tray, and shelf data collection. Two types of PDTs were evaluated by Yale, one with an integrated bar-code scanner built into the PDT, and another with a detachable bar-code scanner that connects via a cable and plugs into the PDT. The integrated model was slightly more expensive, and Yale staff decided it was also less appealing to use. GFA indicated that users from other installations felt the integrated model was easier to use, which suggests the choice of model is subjective. Testing different models is therefore suggested.

As mentioned above, the PDT has a hardware interface to a computer via a docking station and computer cable. The PDT has a programmable memory chip enabling custom programming for data collection applications. These programs are written on the PC, and then downloaded and embedded on the chip via the docking station. At Yale, the docking station plugs into the computer through a serial port. The portable data terminals rest in slots in the docking station, which simultaneously charges the terminals' batteries. Once the data from the shelves are collected and the PDT is resting in the docking station, data can be downloaded to the computer.

Hardware: Bar-Code Scanners

The use of bar-code scanners improves accuracy and efficiency in LSF operations. By using a bar-code scanner, staff are not required to type individual codes via a keyboard and be prone to data entry errors and associated data problems. To accommodate different types of bar codes and differing procedures, Yale uses three different types of bar-code scanners for LSF operations. One type, discussed above, is used with the PDT and connects to the PDT via a cable. This first type of bar-code scanner is used during the shelving and retrieving of items inside the facility. The second type of bar-code scanner attaches to the computers for processing of the items into the inventory application. This second type of scanner is used for all items and their respective trays that are processed in the inventory application. The third type is connected to the workstation dedicated for bar-code production and is unique in that it is capable of reading an older type of bar code (codabar) that is discontinued. The second two types of bar-code scanners connect to computers through a cable shared with the keyboard and are configured by scanning special configuring bar codes included with the scanner.

Hardware: Printers

Yale's LSF uses two specific types of printers. One type is a traditional office laser printer, and the other is a specialized bar-code printer. Yale prints thousands of tray and item bar codes monthly, thus a standard office printer would be ineffective for bar code production. Yale currently has two dedicated bar-code printers for printing bar codes needed for trays and duplication of individual item bar codes. Two bar-code printers were needed because the size of the bar-code labels differs significantly for the tray bar codes and the item bar codes. Rather than change the labels inside the printer for items or trays each time one or the other require printing, one bar-code printer is used only for items and one is dedicated only for trays. Per GFA's suggestion, shelf bar codes were purchased from third-party vendors for financial savings and ease of use. The office laser printer is used for reports and output from desktop applications, for example, word processors, spreadsheets, and databases.

Software: Inventory Application Software

The inventory application manages the data for all of the items in the facility, including item locations in the facility, dates shelved and retrieved, item characteristics, owning institutions, item restrictions, and item status. Potentially millions of items will be shelved at the facility, and so item accuracy remains a paramount concern. However, performance rate is also critical as the facility's inventory grows significantly each week. Thus far, after two years of operations, no system performance degradation has been realized. To maintain acceptable rates of production, the system is not adversely affected by volume or multiple users and proper design of the user-interface and the application's back-end has balanced the needs for efficient data entry rates, application performance, and overall accuracy.

Much of the data entry and data edit operations in the GFA application are performed by using bar-code scanners. During data entry, items are scanned twice: once by one staff member and again by another staff member. The system has internal checking mechanisms to ensure that items are not scanned incorrectly or skipped, and the system requires the items to be scanned twice in order to operate. The system prompts users in the event some data entry error has occurred and hard copies of reports are generated of every entered item.

The system provides a variety of efficient mechanisms for data entry and management. For example, the system performs efficient retrieval means for items. Currently, item requests for retrieval are processed twice a day and the system automatically generates the list of items in an order that is most efficient for retrieval. The design enables staff to work through the facility once to retrieve all items on the work order without having to return to an area previously visited during that retrieval run. Additional examples of efficiency include a design engine for redesigning the "front-end" of the application. Yale redesigned the menu choices and ordering of menus to reflect more accurately the operations at the shelving facility as well as to accommodate Yale's system of user restrictions. Different password groups have been designed to restrict users from accessing the entire system. Summary reports also are generated from the LAS and demonstrate processing rates, selection totals, and ownership statistics. LAS reports print daily to confirm successful entry and processing of items.

Software: PDT

The portable data terminals are programmable for data entry. Programmable PDTs are very desirable because of the need to accommodate custom operations to ensure fast and efficient data entry. From time to time, Yale modifies the PDT programs to reflect changes in the shelving facility's operations. There are a variety of portable data terminal software applications available on the market. GFA suggested and Yale agreed to purchase a software application from a company named AccuScan® whose product is called Data Harvester®. As is typical of the programmable PDT applications in the market, the PDT data entry applications are developed on a PC using a relatively simple interface. Data types, message prompts, and menu choices are designed and added to the interface, which is eventually saved and downloaded to the PDT. The programs enable staff to enter data such as dates, owning libraries, tray information, and shelf information remotely at the shelves in the facility, and then return the PDTs filled with data to the computer where the data are uploaded. At Yale, PDT data entry applications have been developed for items placed directly on shelves ("trayless items"), for trays full of items that are placed on shelves, for items returning to the facility after being retrieved, and for the creation of new shelves.

An illustration of the setup and use of the PDT (see Figure 1) may help the reader gain an understanding of some of the logistics behind its use. The setup of the PDTs is not complicated. Initially, the PDTs require flashing of the read only memory (ROM) chip to enable operation. This is done by turning on the power of the PDT while pressing down two or three keys on the keypad. Once the memory is flashed, certain communication parameters have to be set, for example, baud rate of transfer, parity, start and stop bits. After proper configuration, the PDT is ready to receive a data entry application developed on the PC. The PDT is placed in its docking station, and the predesigned application is downloaded into the PDT. After the data entry applications are downloaded into the PDTs, the PDT can be used for data entry.

Each day, after staff have used the PDT in the facility and entered item, tray, and shelf data, the PDT is placed in the docking station and the data are uploaded

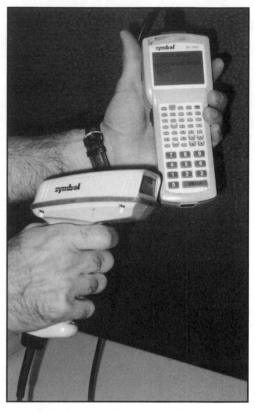

Figure 1. Setup and Use of PDT. Courtesy of Yale University.

by selecting choices in the third-party application on the personal computer. Once the data are uploaded from the PDT to the PC, a final step is required to send the data to the inventory application. Yale uses an FTP (file transfer protocol) client on the PC to send the data to the LAS. To simplify operations, batch files were written to launch the FTP session and move the data to specific user directories. These batch files are represented by icons on the computer desktop, and simply double-clicked to invoke the operation, thereby eliminating the need for data entry and potential keystroke errors. Upon successful completion of the FTP process, staff select a menu choice in the inventory application to upload and process the file that was sent. This system of scanning items in the facility, uploading the data to the PC in the facility, and then uploading the data to the GFA inventory application is efficient, cost-effective, and fast. This component of the entire automated shelving and retrieval process is in large part responsible for the accuracy of Yale's inventory application.

Software:
In-House Programming

In addition to the GFA inventory system, Yale has written some innovative software that interfaces with the facility's inventory system and with the library-wide OPAC database, a Notis system. These programs, described in detail below, are scheduled to run regularly and are installed on Yale's IBM System 390 in addition to personal computers inside the shelving facility, depending upon the applications. The programs provide improved efficiency in processing item requests for retrieval from the LSF and for updating Yale's LIMS for items that have been shelved or returned to the LSF. A data archival mechanism has also been developed to enable continued retrieval of items in the event the GFA inventory system becomes unavailable. These innovations save valuable staff processing time, increase accuracy, and provide increased confidence in the overall system because items are easily located and a disaster recovery plan is in effect enabling retrievals from the shelving facility even in the event of a system outage.

One of the in-house developed programs is written in the C programming language and updates the LIMS by changing the location value of the item to a code indicating the shelving facility, the owning library, and a circulation code. This update reflects that the item has been successfully shelved at the facility. The program was developed to eliminate the need for one staff member to scan an item when it leaves an owning library and another staff member to scan the item when it is received at the facility (indicating the item has been successfully transported). With this inventive software, staff and patrons can reference the LIMS to see if an item has been sent to the shelving facility and when that item has been received and processed. This innovation has saved Yale significant amounts of staff time and associated costs.

A second program (also written in C) updates the LIMS to reflect that an item has been successfully returned to the facility once it was retrieved for a patron. This enables staff in owning libraries to reference the LIMS to see if an item has been returned to the shelving facility once it has been retrieved and then returned by a patron. This program saves staff time and costs by enabling staff to check the LIMS to find information about a borrowed item rather than having to call the shelving facility to receive the same information.

Guidelines and instructions for processing records in the library management system are accessible from Yale's Library Shelving Facility Web site http://www.library.yale.edu/lsf/. Staff members at Yale can look up instructions on the Internet for changes to procedures, or to refresh their memory and understanding of specific issues. Data entry in Yale's LIMS is performed prior to running some of these programs in order for the programs to perform correctly. The data entry instructions are also published on the Internet. Additionally, the programs produce data logs and saves them on an additional computer for future reference. These logs are available for review by staff and ensure that errors were handled correctly and that the programs ran correctly.

The third program sends data files to the inventory system. These data files are created from Yale's LIMS where items are requested for retrieval and delivery within campus libraries. Once formatted, the files are sent via file transfer protocol (FTP) to the inventory system. A file processing daemon runs regularly (every 30 seconds) on the inventory system server (Sun® Microsystems computer) and when a file is FTPed over, the daemon starts a process that imports the data and updates the inventory application accordingly. The inventory system then produces retrieval reports (pick lists) of requested items. The file processing daemon and the import and printing routines were developed by the vendor.

The in-house developed programs, in conjunction with the customized inventory system, save a significant amount of staff time and processing costs, as well as providing increased accuracy. The result is often increased confidence of library patrons, faculty, departments, and staff. Increased confidence in the system within the library community brings ancillary benefits of reduced resistance to the off-site shelving concept.

Software: Backup

Yale uses IBM® ADSM to back up the contents of the Sun® Microsystems server nightly. The system is brought down, backed up, and then restarted. Workstations at the facility are backed up manually by LSF staff using client software for the ADSM backup. Additionally, Yale recently developed a redundant data archival system that allows for retrieval of items. The inventory system is queried to output item information (shelf, tray, item characteristics) to a file and that file is imported into Microsoft Access. A useful interface enables staff to find specific items and to print retrieval reports similar to the inventory system. Recently, Yale had a temporary problem with a primary communication line, but retrieval of items out of the facility was still made using the Access redundancy system.

Software: Selection of Materials

Yale developed an application for selection of materials to be shelved at the facility. Data parameters are entered in a configuration file, which is used to retrieve specific items out of the library-wide OPAC database. Parameters include the number of times an item has circulated, its publishing date, class code, status value, encoding level, owning library, and other specific item characteristics. The data are extracted into an ASCII data file, which is sorted and imported into Microsoft Access. The data are imported into an application designed to assist selectors with narrowing down the sampling to a manageable number. By applying filters in Access, selectors can refine the collection from over 100,000 items to several thousand or less. The MS Access application has a user interface for viewing and printing the data. Files of selected items are then turned over to shelving facility staff who print paging slips used to retrieve the items from the library stacks.

Software: Space Management

Yale has developed an application for monitoring space used in the shelving facility. This application enables the manager at the facility to determine where to put materials on shelves already identified for a specific library. Additionally, new shelves can be reserved in the facility for owning libraries by locating available space in the shelving facility. This application is in an early stage of development, and can evolve into an integrated application using both spreadsheets and a database. Currently, the application is an alternative to manually printing charts and tracking shelf occupancy.

Conclusion

Once an application has been selected, extensive testing should occur to work out bugs and operation-related issues during continued planning and implementation. Additionally, security concerns should be raised and resolved prior to applications being placed into production. Proper computer hardware and software planning and implementation can significantly benefit shelving facility operations. A shelving facility systems selection committee is recommended for informed decision making and effective planning. Vendors need to be evaluated by engaging in extensive discussions with them and by conducting interviews with users of systems. Vendors should provide assistance with integration and management of the varied hardware and software components. Some custom programming may have to be written to perform specific tasks in different environments. Customization and continued support should therefore be negotiated with vendors. Yale and third-party vendors provide technical support for the facility seven days a week, 24 hours a day, in the event the automation process fails. As a direct result of automation at the facility, there exist enhanced efficiencies, improved reader services, and overall satisfaction at Yale.

15

Managing a
Remote Storage Facility

June L. DeWeese

Managing a high-density storage facility presents special opportunities and challenges for librarians. This chapter will discuss some of the workflow issues in establishing efficient and effective procedures and present implications for managers in planning for and operating a facility.

Processing Materials at the
Home Institution

An earlier chapter described in detail the processing procedures and guidelines necessary to have in place at the sending library. From the perspective of the storage facility it is important that:

♦ All items are bar coded, and that there is a bibliographic or other record indicating the bar code number associated with the item.

♦ Mechanisms are in place so that staff at the sending library knows that an item retrieved from the facility and used by a patron should be sent back to the storage facility rather than the campus stacks after use. This can be as simple as a forced acknowledgement flag in the circulation system, or may include a particular bar code prefix, series or imprint, special placement of the bar code on the book volume, or some other designation.

♦ Each item is cleaned before it is shelved. This may happen at the sending library before the item is sent, or at the facility itself. Some institutions use a hand-held vacuum or a lint-free cloth, but for a discussion of a state-of-the-art approach to book cleaning, see The Yale Book Cleaning System.

♦ Procedures are established for dealing with materials that are brittle, have red rot, or which need other types of special care. For example, the University of Missouri requires that all books with deteriorating leather bindings (red rot) or very brittle paper be enclosed in an archival-quality polyethylene bag, phase box, or archival polyester dust jacket.[1]

♦ Workflow is documented for how to handle material that for some reason cannot be shelved at the facility. Examples include items without a bar code or items with a duplicate bar code.

**The Yale
Book Cleaning System**

The environment at the storage facility must be kept free from dust, mold, red rot and other contaminants, which might threaten the entire collection. At its Library Shelving Facility, Yale University has established an area between the loading dock and processing area where four workstations are devoted to cleaning. They use a specially designed, closed vacuum system utilizing hand-held, soft bristle brushes connected to flexible hoses. Residue from items is deposited in drums located on the loading dock. Each station is powered by a 4.0 horse power motor housed in the mezzanine section of the building in order to reduce the exposure of staff to noise.

Source: Michael DiMassa, "Re: Some Depository questions . . . ," e-mail to June L. DeWeese, May 11, 2000.

Such guidelines will help ensure that once materials arrive at the storage facility, the workflow will proceed efficiently and that each item can be processed into the collection using the same routines.

Processing Materials at the Remote Storage Facility

After material is prepared by the sending library and transported to the storage facility, it must be processed at the facility. The focus of this book is on high-density storage facilities. Two of the underlying principles for these operations are:

1. Books are stored in book trays by size to make maximum utilization of the cubic space available; and

2. Access to stored material is via a hierarchical series of bar codes, with item bar codes linked to tray bar codes, and tray bar codes linked to shelf bar codes.

In order to maximize the space available, the most efficient way to store books is by height and in trays that generally fit two deep on a wide shelf. There may be variations on that method for very large books or very small books or nonbook media. Shelving by size uses all available space most effectively.

When books are received at the storage facility, the first step in processing is to determine the size of the books by using a template designed to ensure uniform sizing. Unlike measuring with a ruler, the template determines the range of height and width of books, which will fit in various size trays and corresponds to the various size shelves throughout the facility. Templates are generally divided into nine or ten categories. The dimensions may vary somewhat depending upon the facility but will generally be within the range as shown in Table 1.

Table 1. Book Sizing Template Dimensions

	Book Height in inches	Book Width (spine to fore-edge) in inches
A	7.5	5.75
B	8.0	5.75
C	8.5	6.75
D	9.5	6.75
E	10.5	8.00
F	11.5	8.00
G	12.5	9.75
H	13.5	9.75
I	14.5	12.5
J	16.5	12.5

Each section on the template is generally painted a different color in order that one may do the sizing more easily by relying upon the color boundaries. Any book that crosses over into any larger size color is automatically grouped with the larger size. It should be emphasized that width is defined in the use of a template as the distance between the spine and the fore-edge of the book. Depository staff will probably want to discuss with consultants who may be from currently operating facilities or other experts in the field about the actual construction of the templates. There is no substitute for actual experience in the construction and use of a template. See Figure 1 for a photograph of a book sizing template.

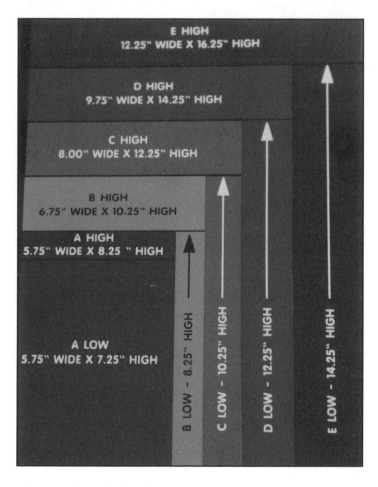

Figure 1. Book Sizing Template. Courtesy of Yale University.

Trays

In high-density storage facilities regular monographs and bound journals typically are placed in corrugated paper trays for storage two deep on shelves, which are 36 inches deep and 53 inches wide. These pH^2 neutral trays should be purchased flat, tied in manageable-sized bundles for manual lifting, and stored on empty shelves set aside in the storage facility for this purpose. (See Tips for Purchasing Trays.) All storage facility designers should set aside several sections in the shelving area for the storage of trays. For the facility planned by the Research Collections and Preservation Consortium, a collaborative enterprise of Columbia University, the New York Public Library, and Princeton University, the facility will have an area designed for the storage and setup of trays. This group found this to be necessary due to the large volume of material to be transferred to the facility. The trays should be organized in the storage area by size for ease of pulling and assembling as needed. Microforms and other nonbook materials may require trays of sizes other than those depicted in Table 2. Consulting staff at facilities that store those types of materials is advised. Five sizes of trays are typically needed in a storage facility that shelves only monographs and serials. They should be labeled from A–E.

Table 2. Cardboard Dimensions for Trays

Tray	Size in Inches
A	21.739 x 36.104
B	24.896 x 38.229
C	24.646 x 40.729
D	33.896 x 44.229
E	41.771 x 43.479

Tips for
Purchasing Trays

It is important that trays meet the standards for acid-free cardboard. Each new order of trays should be tested for pH level before any of the trays are used. The paper in the trays must have an 8.0 pH or greater in order to preserve the paper in older books and to prevent or slow deterioration as long as possible. It is possible to use the Fisher Scientific's pH indicator paper (Hydrion indicator paper) to do spot testing. The process consists of putting the pH paper below a book page, allowing a drop or two of water to leach through the page onto the pH paper, and then reading the pH. Alternatively, one could use a licensed chemical laboratory using TAPPI procedure T435, "Hydrogen Ion Concentration (pH) of Paper Extracts—Hot Extraction Method."* If the testing process is cost-prohibitive or not available, a letter from the paper manufacturer stating what they guarantee the pH to be is acceptable.

An economical way to purchase trays is by the tractor-trailer truckload. Because a purchase of this magnitude requires a bidding process in most institutions, the ordering of trays should be timed to allow for the usual lead-time that local Purchasing Departments require. It is not unusual for three or more months to elapse between the time that an order is placed and the trays are received. Because of the requirement in many states that in-state companies be used, it is very important to work closely with purchasing agents to be certain that if in-state companies cannot meet the exact pH requirements that it is possible to contract with an outside paper producer to provide the material used to make the trays. A longer lead-time for delivery can be anticipated if an in-state firm subcontracts the making of the cardboard to a firm in another state. The price of trays will vary with the size of the tray, and also with market conditions. Typical tray prices as of 1998 were in the $0.60–$1.00 per tray range. In the late 1990s paper prices skyrocketed, and consequently, the cost of trays increased. Tray prices will also vary with the quantity ordered. Some storage facilities, like the Harvard Depository and the Washington Research Library Consortium, have had success in executing joint orders. Vendors have been willing to reduce the per tray price and to ship the right quantities of trays to each facility.

---

*Procurement/Materials Management, University of Missouri, "Bid Request and Bid—Book Storage Trays" (Columbia, MO: University of Missouri, 1997), unpaged.

As assembled each tray has the outer dimensions in inches as shown in Table 3.

Table 3. Dimensions of Assembled Trays

Tray	Height	Length	Width
A	6.250	17.813	6.313
B	7.313	17.813	7.375
C	8.563	17.813	8.625
D	10.313	17.813	10.375
E	12.938	17.813	13.000

Trays are often labeled with a sticker containing the letter of the alphabet corresponding to its template size for ease in shelving, and bar code prefixes may also be used to designate one type of tray from another.

Accession and Verification

High-density storage facilities offer an opportunity to organize work in a manner that is both highly efficient and highly accurate. Typically, after loading volumes into trays, the contents are counted and the full book trays are brought to a station for a process that is called "accessioning." During the accessioning process, the inventory control system (which may be the library OPAC or a dedicated inventory control system) is updated to reflect the new items transferred to the facility. This is accomplished by scanning the bar code of the tray, and the bar code of the item to associate a unique item with its tray.

While processing procedures vary from institution to institution, most include an important step of quality control, which may be referred to as "redundant processing." Because books are shelved by height and accessible by bar code, it is very important to be certain that every book in every tray is accounted for at the time of processing. After the accessioning process, a verification process is executed. During this step, essentially a replication of the accessioning process, each book is scanned a second time. After this verification stage, ideally performed by a different person from the one who did the original processing and at a different workstation, a match is run to make sure that the same information that was entered during the accession process was entered during the verification process. This duplication minimizes the probability of human or machine error. Any errors are reported and must be corrected, and when error-free, the books are ready to be shelved.

Shelving

Before trays can be shelved in the storage area of the facility, the shelving itself must be appropriately configured. Since the high-density storage system is one that maximizes the efficient use of the cubic space, the shelving layout must reflect this goal as well.

A planograph is a document that shows the ideal placement of shelves according to size in a storage facility. It should be provided by a consultant experienced in storage facility construction and management. Based upon national averages of the size of books in other storage facilities currently in operation or on data from the local institution if that data are available, the planograph will allocate space for shelves throughout the storage facility. If an institution plans to store archive boxes, books too large for conventional trays, microformat materials or other nonmonograph items, all of those items and their unique sizes should be taken into consideration when the original planograph is drawn.

It is very important to determine the placement of the shelving during the planning process in order that the shelving can be permanently placed according to the planograph when it is first installed. The goal of any storage facility staff should be to move as few shelves as possible after the first installation. Once the planograph has been drawn and approved, each shelf should be put into place by the shelving installers, cleaned, and left in that location.

The storage facility staff may find making a chart of each range of shelving helpful. Whether the chart is on paper or computerized in some way, the purpose of the chart is to enable the staff to know at a glance which shelves, in all sizes, are filled and which remain available throughout the building. If the chart is on paper, as each shelf is filled, they can be lined off of the chart. The University of Texas at Austin uses eight large charts. Each "is constructed of a large resin-coated velox print dry-mounted on light-weight yet durable Gatorboard and coated with heavy-duty matte laminate. The charts are mounted two-deep in four rows on a 327"-wide wall at the LSF [Library Storage Facility]."[3] At Yale University, for example, an Access-based database is maintained from which staff can determine where an appropriately sized shelf is available. Whatever method the staff chooses to use, it is very important to monitor both the space used and the space remaining and be able to quickly determine where available shelves are for each size tray. Looking at the actual shelves and trying to determine either space used or space remaining is inefficient because of the height of the building and the compact nature of the shelving.

Once accessioned, books and other materials are ready to be shelved in the stacks of the storage facility. In many facilities currently in operation, when a batch of new accessions is brought into the stacks, the target shelf bar code is scanned with handheld scanners, followed by the bar code of each tray (or in some cases the item itself). The data on the handheld scanners are uploaded into the OPAC or the inventory control system, and the accession process is complete. The inventory system has a record that the item has arrived at the facility and where it is located. There is an electronic link between the unique item bar code and the unique tray bar code, and an electronic link between the tray bar code and the unique location bar code.

Errors

In spite of all the best planning and procedures, staff working at the facility, as well as staff preparing items for shipment at the sending library, will occasionally make errors. As an added check it is useful to have a verification process to compare records of what was sent against records of what was received. This is particularly critical if there is a significant lag between the time an item is prepared for shipment and the time it is actually shipped to the storage facility. The most practical way of handling this is to compare computer files of what was sent and what was received. The sending library can issue a file against which a comparison will be run by the storage facility and the storage facility should create and send a file back of what was accessioned and the sending library can then run the comparison. Starting either way, this is an important part of the overall processing stream.

Managers must also articulate what procedures should be followed in the event that a requested item cannot be located at the storage facility. The following not-on-shelf search procedures may be helpful in thinking about this problem:

♦ Examine other books in the tray or on the shelf where the item is recorded to be located; the bar code may have fallen off.

♦ Search nearby shelves—above, below, across the aisle, etc.

♦ Notify requestor, as it is probable that at this point the requested item will not be delivered within the target timeframe established for the service.

♦ If an inventory control system is used, it may have a history file to indicate any activity associated with the item. This file should be reviewed.

♦ Check the inventory control system and OPAC again to make sure the item is not charged out of the facility or already charged out to a patron.

♦ Check all processing areas and partially filled trays.

♦ Search trays and shelves storing other items belonging to the same library that were moved, shelved, or reshelved the same day or close to the same day as the missing item.

♦ Search trays and shelves storing other items belonging to any library that were moved, shelved, or reshelved the same day or close to the same day as the missing item.

♦ Conduct inventory of all trays and shelves storing items belonging to the library that owns the missing item.

Staffing

Operating a high-density storage facility is different in many ways from running a traditional library since most remote storage facilities are indeed remote and are not located on or near the main campus of the institution or institutions whose books are deposited there. These facilities are frequently not open to the public or are only open to the public by appointment. Technical service tasks comprise the majority of the functions performed at a remote storage facility, but there is always a public services component since some of the materials do circulate.

To run a remote storage facility efficiently, there must be a capable, competent manager on site. Often, that manager reports to a librarian on the campus under whose jurisdiction the day-to-day operations are conducted. Since the librarian is rarely on-site and usually does not visit the facility daily or even weekly, the manager must be able to handle all of the day-to-day supervision and operation of the facility. There are exceptions to this scenario, however. The Washington Library Consortium provides permanent offices for its entire management team at the facility. Most places, like Harvard and the University of Missouri, have an on-site manager at the remote storage facility and the supervising librarian is located on the campus of the institution responsible for the operations.

Many challenges exist in hiring staff to work in a Harvard–style facility. Some of those include the following:

♦ the remoteness of the work site

♦ the temperature and humidity factors

♦ the extremely high shelves

♦ the physical stamina required to lift trays and shipments

♦ the routine but exacting nature of processing materials into the collection

♦ the requirements for providing high-quality service

♦ the safety and logistical issues related to using the forklift truck, such as driving, maneuvering trays at distances as high as 30 feet off the ground, and charging batteries and performing routine maintenance checks. (See Appendix A: Forklift Safety.)

Managers also need to be sensitive to the fact that staff working at a storage facility may often be working in isolation, and that the same few people will see each other and only each other day after day. Moreover, the physical location of the facility may be in a place where it is inconvenient to exercise break time away from the job site. In order to mitigate the isolation that staff working at the storage facility may feel, those who are administratively responsible for the storage facility must be aware of the isolation and work with the staff of the facility to find creative solutions to that problem. For example, Yale depository staff is responsible for retrieving from the campus stacks and preparing materials to be transported to their facility. The University of Missouri depository staff rotates the duties of taking materials to the central mail facility and the Ellis Library on the Columbia campus each day, and regularly attends staff meetings, social events, seminars, and other meetings on the main campus. Hiring student assistants to assist with tasks such as unpacking tubs, measuring books, assembling trays, sorting books, and other related processing duties will also provide an opportunity for full-time employees to interact regularly with other people at the work site. It is also important for on-campus managers to take every opportunity to promote the efforts of staff who may be working at a remote site. Staff at the Harvard Depository, for example, were recipients of the annual university-wide "Harvard Heroes" award for the year 2000 in recognition of their outstanding effort in service to the university. Managers and staff at each storage facility will need to address the issue of staff working at a remote site and find solutions to the isolation issue that best fit their own institutions.

Managers must also work closely with the staff on the campuses who are depositing material into the facility as well as the staff requesting items on behalf of patrons. In order for the processing workflow to be as efficient as possible, there must be a steady flow of materials from the home institutions to the facility. If the facility holds more than one institution's materials, the depositing efforts must be coordinated so that each institution has its materials processed expeditiously and equitably with regard to the number of items deposited and the priority with which they are processed. There should be at least one contact person in each institution that deposits materials in the facility designated to regularly communicate with the depository manager about the efficient flow of materials to the facility. Some sites, such as Yale, have staff responsible for all elements of the processing function from identity to shelving at the library storage facility. This way, the facility manager regulates the flow of materials and can ensure that no backlog will exist.

Services Provided

As with any library service operation, the management team for the off-site storage facility will need to work with its patrons (in this case typically staff from the depositing libraries) to establish and manage expectations for services. A Service Level Agreement is a document that specifies the types and levels of service provided to each library that deposits materials in the storage facility, the lines of responsibility for the facility, and any management-related issues deemed necessary such as dispute resolution and mediation. Such an agreement can be very helpful in establishing the guidelines for service and clarifying the expectations that each library has. Service Level Agreement content will vary from institution to institution and should be tailored to meet local needs. Generally, however, the agreement should describe the lines of responsibility for management of the facility and list the services to be provided by the facility staff. A good service level agreement typically states what services the storage facility staff will provide and may include expectations about the time involved in performing some or all of the tasks. For example, the University of Missouri's document states that the UMLD (UM Libraries Depository) staff will provide the following services:

> [L]ibrary materials will be processed and prepared for storage, including measuring, barcoding, traying, and shelving the books; each book will be recorded as held by the UMLD in the MERLIN library catalog [the online catalog used by the four campuses of the University of Missouri System who deposit materials in the UMLD]; each book that is needed by a patron will be retrieved from the stacks, acclimatized, processed for the patron, put in-transit, and shipped to the pick-up location specified by the patron. The staff will also discharge books that are returned, determine if any repair/mending is needed and arrange for it with the owning library, and reshelve materials. The staff will be responsible for preparing overdue notices, recall notices and bills for replacement costs as needed.[4]

The agreement should also include turnaround time expectations, specifying the average time to be expected between the time a request for an item is made and the requesting library receives the item. It may also include other components such as limits to liability for damage or loss of collections, the length of time between receipt of an item to be added to the collection and that item being shelved in the facility and available for patrons' use, and other specific performance measures against which the facility's service performance can be measured.

The types of services that are included in the service level agreement should ideally be determined by the staff of the storage facility in cooperation with the staff in the depositing libraries, who actively seek feedback from their patrons. These services may specify communication and delivery methods such as the use of fax, e-mail, ARIEL, photocopying, or telephone. The agreement should also address whether patrons can be served on-site and if so, under what conditions, or if all materials will be delivered to the requesting libraries for patrons to use there. The role of interlibrary loan should also be addressed to determine whether materials at the storage facility would be available for interlibrary loan to and by all depositing libraries or just the library that originally deposited the book. The interlibrary loan service at a remote storage facility should be consistent with service expected at academic libraries in the United States but can be modified to meet the needs of the specific institution or institutions served by the facility.

Service Level Agreements can be very helpful in articulating the service program for the facility and will help to assure those whose collections are being shelved off-site that their collections are under appropriate stewardship. The service delivered by the facility in terms of accuracy and reliability—essentially meeting the terms of the Service Level Agreement—will also promote the perception that the off-site facility "works." Managers of storage facilities will also want to do all that they can to demonstrate that the collections are well cared for in terms of meeting the HVAC control targets, establishing training programs for handling books, and working with colleagues to develop an emergency preparedness program. Every storage facility should have written emergency procedures to follow in case of severe weather (tornado, hurricane, rain and flooding), earthquakes, fire, medical emergencies, assaults and robberies, apparent intoxication, staff disorderly conduct, and other emergencies. A list of persons who must be contacted in case of emergency should be filed with the appropriate university officials, including the police department. A written plan can prove to be invaluable if the unthinkable does occur and staff is faced with a disaster of any kind. (See Appendix B: University of Missouri Libraries Depository Emergency Procedures.)

Management Data

Planning and implementing a high-density storage facility presents an opportunity to design an operation optimized for workflow and isolated from many of the political considerations that often infuse decision making at even an operational level on campus or at the home institution. Shelving facilities are highly focused operations; they typically do not offer a wide breadth of services, but it is critical that those they do offer are done well. There should be an exacting level of attention paid to process and workflow issues, and planners may find it useful to look beyond the library literature to the discipline of warehousing, transportation, and logistics for expertise. Groups such as the Council of Logistics Management and the Warehousing Education and Research Council offer programs that may provide valuable insight into planning a storage facility.

The nature of the work is such that it lends itself to managing and continually improving production rates. The number of items processed per day varies from facility to facility depending upon the number of staff available, processing procedures, and the range of tasks staff perform (e.g., whether the persons processing also unload the tubs, size the books, construct the trays, and shelve the trays, or if those tasks are shared with others). It is useful for managers to track information about the volume of work output performed (e.g., number of items accessioned and retrieved), and the effort required (e.g., time to perform tasks, amount of supplies needed), in order to gauge efficiency and the impact of any changes introduced to improve productivity.

Conclusion

Over the past 10 years, the number of remote storage facilities has increased dramatically. Management, training, logistical and safety issues are always among the topics discussed when managers of pioneer facilities share their experience and advice with those persons who find themselves confronted with the responsibility of managing a new facility. Procedures vary somewhat from institution to institution, but the combined experiences of those who manage the first facilities constructed (Harvard being the first model for all of those who have followed) are most valuable for colleagues just beginning to put materials in storage. Contact with experts in those facilities during the planning, construction, and early implementation phases has proved to be most helpful to persons just entering this exciting arena of service to library patrons.

Notes

1.   University of Missouri Library Directors Committee, "University of Missouri Libraries Depository" (Columbia, MO: University of Missouri, 1997), 6.

2.   *Random House Webster's Dictionary of American English* (1997) defines pH as "a symbol used to describe the amount of acidity or alkalinity of a chemical solution on a scale of 0 (more acidic) to 14 (more alkaline)."

3.   The General Libraries, The University of Texas at Austin, "Library Storage Facility Information Packet" (Austin, TX: University of Texas at Austin, 1992), 77.

4.   University of Missouri Library Directors Committee, "University of Missouri Libraries Depository" (Columbia, MO: University of Missouri, 1997), 3.

Appendix A: Forklift Safety

Many safety issues are involved in running a remote storage facility. Safety issues must be a top priority when shelving extends 30 feet high and when forklift trucks are needed to access many of those shelves. Driving the forklift truck requires training and compliance with OSHA (U.S. Occupational Safety and Health Administration) standards. See the OSHA Regulations 29 CFR 1910.178 and also the safety standards from ASME B.56.1: "Safety Standards for Low Lift and High Lift Trucks."

Many safety issues also arise in the charging and maintenance of the battery of the forklift. Battery-charging products, if mishandled, can cause serious injury or death and can cause damage to buildings and other equipment. Precautions must be taken to avoid electrical shock. All aspects of the equipment used to charge the battery must be checked by a competent electrician upon installation and at regular intervals throughout the time of use.

Each person handling the battery should be aware of the danger of burns and other bodily injuries caused by contact with the metal conductor that carries the electrical current. Battery acid can also burn human skin. In accordance with safety guidelines at most universities, there must be a shower with active water near the charging area.

Every person working in the storage facility should know how to respond in case of accidents and injuries resulting from interacting with the battery or forklift truck.

The possibility of injury also exists any time staff is involved in lifting heavy trays of books. Each person should be trained in proper lifting and bending techniques and should observe those techniques at all times. Ergonomic furniture is also very important for persons using computer terminals for long periods of time to process materials into the storage facility.

Safety issues involved in moving shelves, sometimes in very high areas, include the risk of cutting and pinching hands, hitting oneself or others, dropping the shelves from great distances, and causing injury by lifting and twisting one's torso while holding the shelf. Installing and moving shelves are best left to those persons professionally trained in this area; however, if it is necessary for staff at the facility to adjust shelf placement, they need to be aware of actions that may cause accidents.

There may be institutions whose safety requirements dictate that facility staff wear hard hats and steel-toed shoes while in the stacks area. Many existing facilities do not have such a requirement but do observe safety precautions such as prohibiting staff other than those persons on the order picker from being in the same aisle as the order picker. Any time there are two or more persons in the stack area, each person should know the location of all persons in the area. Such precautions make the possibility of someone on the floor being struck by a falling object or accidentally run over nearly impossible.

Where safety issues are concerned, training and vigilance are very important. Safety must be the highest priority for all staff at all times. Conducting periodic safety meetings with staff is a recommended routine to stress the importance of taking safety precautions and developing an accident-free attitude.

Appendix B: University of Missouri Libraries Depository Emergency Procedures*

Contents

1.0 Weather/Tornado Warning
2.0 Fire Alarm
3.0 Rain/Flooding
4.0 Emergency Evacuation
5.0 Medical Emergency
6.0 Personal Emergency
7.0 Assaults and Robberies
8.0 Drunkenness and Disorderly Conduct
9.0 Earthquake

1.0 WEATHER/TORNADO WARNING

1.1   The city will sound the warning siren prior to severe weather or when a tornado warning is in effect. Campus Police will broadcast a warning over police radios. Turn on weather radio located in manager's office.

1.2   Manager or authorized personnel will verify the situation if weather does not appear to be threatening and will notify all personnel.

1.3   When the sirens sound during severe weather, or when notified by authorized personnel, all staff should assist in evacuating all personnel and building occupants to the janitor's closet (the most secure interior room). It is important to keep people away from windows and the danger of shattered glass.

1.4   Anyone trying to leave the building should be warned of the danger by authorized personnel and encouraged not to leave until after danger has passed.

1.5   In case of injury, follow medical emergency procedures (below).

1.6   If a fire results, follow fire procedures (below).

1.7   Personnel may return to the work areas upon clearance by the manager or authorized personnel. Since storms are normally of a short duration, it is each employee's responsibility to return to work in a timely fashion at the end of the weather emergency.

---

*Reprinted by permission of the University of Missouri Libraries Depository, 2001.

2.0 FIRE ALARM

Upon hearing· alarm, authorized personnel should check alarm panel for origin of alarm. If necessary, personnel should begin to evacuate the building by the nearest exit. Alarm panel can be re-armed by pressing the *acknowledge* button and then the *reset* button. Both Campus Police and Campus Fire Protection are automatically alerted when the fire alarm is activated.

3.0 RAIN/FLOODING

Protect any library material threatened by leaks or flooding. Plastic sheeting is kept in janitor's closet. Notify Depository Manager if necessary.

4.0 EMERGENCY EVACUATION

When evacuation must occur for any other reason, the manager or other authorized personnel will notify Campus Police. All staff should assist and follow instructions in clearing building. Personnel should use the nearest exit and meet at the edge of LeMone Industrial Blvd. near the *UM Libraries Depository* sign.

5.0 MEDICAL EMERGENCY

Call Campus Police (911). *DO NOT MOVE AN UNCONSCIOUS PERSON* except when in immediate danger of fire, etc.

6.0 PERSONAL EMERGENCY

Obtain name of person to contact, get relevant details, and notify manager or authorized personnel.

7.0 ASSAULTS AND ROBBERIES

Notify Campus Police at 911.

8.0 DRUNKENNESS AND DISORDERLY CONDUCT

Same as 7.0, above.

9.0 EARTHQUAKE

If quake is felt, *EVACUATE STACKS IMMEDIATELY!* Evacuate building if possible or take cover under sturdy furniture and cover head and neck. Stay away from windows. Do not run through areas with falling debris. Since aftershocks may occur, *DO NOT RETURN TO WORK* until authorized by manager or other authorized personnel. Give help if asked.

10.0 EMERGENCY CONTACTS

Contact Michael or June as soon as possible during or following an emergency.

	Work	Home	Pager
Michael Kelty	xxx	xxx	xxx
June DeWeese	xxx	xxx	xxx
Campus Police	xxx	xxx	xxx
Fire Protection	xxx	xxx	xxx

10/98

10.0 EMERGENCY CONTACTS

Contact Michael or June as soon as possible during or following an emergency.

	Work	Home	Pager
Michael Kelty	xxx	xxx	xxx
June DeWeese	xxx	xxx	xxx
Campus Police	xxx	xxx	xxx
Fire Protection	xxx	xxx	xxx

10/98

16

Access to Collections

Bruce Hulse

Introduction

While the high-density storage facility has emerged as the solution of choice to the space problems faced by research libraries, the decision to move materials to such facilities has not been always well received by library users. Faculty in particular have long been advocates of keeping library materials on campus, in open stack arrangements conducive to browsing. Economic realities have normally prevailed in this controversy; the prohibitive cost of building traditional library space, as compared to high-density storage, has in most cases been the deciding factor in the decision to move materials into storage. The access services provided by storage facilities provide the necessary link between the end user and the stored materials. The quality of these services has had a significant impact on the acceptance of the high-density facility by research library users.

While the use of technology and modern materials handling techniques may strike many as a rather cutting-edge approach to an age-old problem, in the area of service to end users the high-density facility represents a reversal of sorts. Most research libraries abandoned the closed stack model many years ago. The high-density facility is by definition a closed stack environment. Retrieval of materials from the shelves is mediated in all cases; the timeliness with which users can gain access to materials is therefore entirely dependent on the efficiency of the services provided. These services are in most ways analogous to those traditionally provided by libraries. Materials are delivered physically, as is the case with interlibrary loan, or via facsimile transmission. Many facilities offer on-site access to materials, and some also circulate materials directly to eligible borrowers. What distinguishes the storage facility service environment is the absolute requirement for mediated retrieval, coupled with the sensitivity to timeliness, which the removal of materials from the open stacks engenders.

Given these factors, storage facilities have necessarily focused a great deal of effort on ensuring timely physical delivery of requested materials. But physical delivery is not the whole story. Many facilities provide telefacsimile delivery of articles. Over time, technology has increasingly been employed to offer new and innovative means of access to stored collections. It should also be noted that not all services are aimed at the library user. Some facilities also offer storage services to university departments outside the library, serving as record centers in addition to providing library storage. However, the primary role played by the high-density library storage facility is physical storage of library materials, and it follows that the primary service goal is the provision of quick, reliable delivery of library materials upon request. It is in meeting this goal that end user acceptance is achieved.

User Populations

Since the primary service provided by storage facilities is delivery of materials to end users, it is worth asking who makes up this population. Most storage facilities are associated with a specific library or library system. The primary clientele of these facilities is typically the same as that of the library, and access privileges to materials in storage parallel those to the same types of materials in the library. A significant number of facilities serve library consortia (such as the Northeastern Ohio Cooperative Regional Library Depository); again the primary clientele of the consortium member libraries forms that of the facility, though policies regarding intrainstitutional requests may be more complex. Whether materials can be requested by users affiliated with any consortium member library typically will depend on the nature of the materials: general circulating materials normally can be lent directly to any library in a consortium, whereas special collections materials would need to be requested through the owning library.

Outside of a facility's primary clientele, service to end users is most often provided through the library owning the materials requested. The potential exists for direct service, particularly in filling interlibrary loan requests. As information technology is used increasingly to provide delivery of requested articles and documents from storage facilities, the potential for storage facilities to serve as document delivery centers to a broader clientele is also increased. The potential needs to be further explored for cooperation between storage facilities in providing online document delivery as an alternative to storing multiple copies of the same material.

Request Mechanisms

As noted above, storage facility services are in large part analogous to traditional library services. Traditionally, requests for interlibrary loans were mediated by library staff. The same applied to most requests for materials in high-density storage. Increasingly libraries are moving towards nonmediated request mechanisms that allow authorized users to place interlibrary loan requests without mediation, and this same trend is occurring in storage facilities. Not all materials are suited to this approach; rare books, archival materials, and other special collections items are examples of materials where mediation of the request is a logical requirement. (This is of course true with these types of materials whether stored off-site or held within the library.) Mediation to submit requests plays no useful role, however, for materials that would normally be housed in open stacks. Given the sensitivity to timeliness in the off-site storage environment, and the relatively well-defined primary clientele for most storage facility services, the shift towards nonmediated requests seems a natural direction for storage facilities.

The typical storage facility offers a variety of options for communicating request information. In the case of mediated requests, this can include the traditional range used by libraries, including fax, telephone, and written requests. The use of online request mechanisms is becoming increasingly common. These can include e-mail requests, Web forms (often available to the end user) and request mechanisms based on the online catalog of the libraries owning the material. Online does not necessarily imply nonmediated. (Requests via Web forms may be reviewed by library staff before being forwarded to the facility, for example.) However the online approach is the best mechanism to support nonmediated requests. Request mechanisms based on the online catalog interface are particularly effective in supporting this goal, as users are authenticated via the library management system without staff intervention.

One minor drawback to using the online catalog as the request interface is that most OPACs are designed to request titles, rather than items. This means that staff at the storage facility do need to determine the bar code for the item in storage via the library management system to determine the item's location in the inventory control system (in some cases the library management system serves both purposes). This is typically a manageable workload, though that will obviously be dependent on the volume of requests being handled. Some facilities, such as Yale's, incorporate an interface that transmits the bar code and delivery information from the OPAC to the location inventory system at the facility. This results in the inventory system producing pick lists without requiring staff to search for locations of items requested. The software, designed in-house, links a NOTIS-based OPAC with the GFA inventory system.

Since OPACs operate at the title level, they also cannot provide sufficient specificity for article level requests, staff typically having to determine if the volume requested is in fact in storage and, if it is, if the citation itself is correct. A mechanism for notifying the end user in cases where the citation is incorrect also needs to be set up. At the Washington Research Library Consortium's facility, for example, requests are initiated through the OPAC (Endeavor's Voyager software) and then processed through back-end software developed in-house. This Web-based software includes a "bad citation" option that forwards the request back to the requestor's home library for resolution. Nonmediated mechanisms increase the ease with which end users can place requests for items in storage. Another area in which it is desirable to reduce mediation is that of informing end users of the status of requests. The use of online mechanisms (e-mail, secure

Web pages, OPAC) to provide status information directly to the end user is becoming more common and is a valuable enhancement to storage services.

Retrieval

Retrieval of materials in the high-density storage facility is the one service activity that is entirely unique to that environment. A distinct set of skills is required, both to locate materials in the high-density shelving scheme through the automated inventory control system, and to operate the order picker to physically retrieve them. (The latter task is one not all potential employees are comfortable performing, due to the heights involved.) Retrieval of materials from the high-density storage environment is therefore a highly specialized task in comparison to retrieval from traditional library shelving arrangements.

Efficient retrieval relies on proper organization of the workflow, as in any environment. In the high-density warehouse the need for organization and scheduling of retrieval activities is heightened, due to the use of the lift and the time consumed in maneuvering it into and out of the aisles. In facilities using a stand-alone inventory control system, the design of the system is integral to the organization of the retrieval workflow, producing pull slips in an efficient sequence for retrieval.

Where the library automation system is used as the inventory control system for the facility, having properly sequenced pull slips is not a given. If pull slips are not automatically sorted, it is up to the staff to organize requests appropriately. Perhaps the most unusual concept to be applied to the retrieval process is Johns Hopkins University's Comprehensive Access to Print Materials (CAPM) project, in which the potential for robotic retrieval of materials is being explored. In this model the entire process, from end-user initiation of the request to physical retrieval from the shelving will be handled automatically, with shelf location being transmitted to a robot that performs the actual retrieval.

While retrieval by humans is likely to be the norm for some time to come, the use of automated processes to efficiently organize workflow has considerable benefits where the volume of retrieval is high enough. In environments with lower retrieval volume (e.g., at the Washington Research Library Consortium's facility in Upper Marlboro, Maryland, retrievals average 60 volumes daily), manually sorting the requests for retrieval is not a serious drag on efficiency. In all cases, minimizing the number of runs made using the order picker is a key to efficient retrieval.

On-Site Use/Circulation of Materials

Most high-density storage facilities have made some provision for use of materials on-site, and in some cases facilities may serve as circulation service units as well, charging materials directly to end users. The level of use of these facilities varies; the most decisive factor being the proximity of the storage facility to the user population it serves. Cornell's Library Annex reports regular on-site usage; it is located near the main campus. At the Washington Research Library Consortium's facility, 22 miles from the nearest university campus, there have been a mere handful of users over the past six years.

Since on-site consultation of materials requires that an appropriate physical space be available, the decision to offer this option has a distinct impact on the facility's design. The types of materials stored, and those offered for on-site use, will determine the design of the reading room. Security issues need to be considered; if unique or rare materials are expected to be among those used, then adequate provision for monitoring their use needs to be made. If materials are to be circulated to end users, then access to the owning library's circulation system will be required. Photocopy services may also be desirable, particularly if large numbers of periodicals are stored.

If a facility is located near campus, then offering on-site use may have an impact on staffing. This is particularly true if rare or unique materials whose use must be monitored are available for use on-site. It is important to keep in mind that the nature of the high-density storage environment makes quick, on-demand retrieval of requests costly. Many facilities therefore encourage users to provide advance notice in order to permit staff to pull items requested for on-site use in the course of their normal workflow. This arrangement is important for both the end user, who may obtain needed materials without undue delay, and the staff, since staffing levels are typically low in comparison with the traditional library environment.

Library staff themselves may be significant on-site users of the storage facility. For many projects, such as creating finding aids for archival collections, it may be more practical for staff to work at the facility than to shuttle materials back and forth between the facility and the library. Access to the library management system must be available for a storage facility that will need to support staff activity.

Physical Delivery of Materials

Physical delivery of materials is a vital component of storage facility services. Even if a high percentage of delivery can be accomplished electronically, for many materials in storage this is not a feasible alternative. Materials that may be physically delivered from storage are typically more varied than is the case with those normally handled by traditional ILL services. Delivery of bound volumes and photocopies of journal articles are common to both services. But storage facilities often house large amounts of archival materials, and may house rare or unique materials as well. These also need to be delivered, and special handling is often required. More truck space may also be necessary as a typical request for archival materials may result in delivering many boxes simultaneously. Transporting 30 boxes for one request is not unusual and may overload routine library delivery system's truck capacity. Similar considerations may apply to nonprint media. In traditional ILL services the determining factor on the types of materials handled is typically circulation policy. In the storage environment the determining factor is the range of materials housed in storage. In most cases all materials must be deliverable. Delivery may be through a dedicated service (handling only materials moving to and from storage), or it may be handled through an existing intercampus or interlibrary service. The desirability of maintaining a dedicated service is dictated by a number of factors: the volume to be handled, the distance involved, and the number of service points to which materials are delivered. If a facility handles interlibrary loan requests directly (rather than through the library's ILL department), then in addition to the locally run service, arrangements for postal or commercial delivery service pick-ups must be made.

Physical delivery of materials is generally a mediated service, requested items being delivered to one or more service points on campus. It would be feasible for facilities to offer delivery directly to campus offices or faculty mailboxes in the case of nonreturnables (e.g., journal articles). This sort of service would typically be offered as part of a broader campus delivery system (such as the University of Michigan's 7-FAST service[1]) rather than one dedicated to the storage facility. Removing materials from an environmentally controlled facility into the ambient outside temperature for delivery presents some preservation concerns. Many facilities remove materials from the storage module a minimum of 12 hours before delivery to allow for a more gradual change in temperature to take place before the item is taken out of the building. For most materials, this fits neatly into the normal workflow; materials are pulled by late afternoon for delivery the following morning. Nonprint materials that are especially sensitive to temperature changes, for example, motion picture film, may require factoring additional acclimatization time into service procedures or temperature controlled delivery containers for optimal preservation.

Facsimile Delivery of Materials

A variety of technologies is used to support facsimile transmission of articles and other documents from storage facilities. This is more often than not a mediated service, with documents being transmitted to a library for distribution to end users. However facsimile transmission offers greater potential for nonmediated delivery at a reasonable cost than does physical delivery, and there is a growing trend to exploit this potential.

Traditional fax transmission is the best-known form of facsimile transmission and has been in use the longest. One advantage to fax is that a significant percentage of end users have fax machines in their offices or homes, and this offers the option of nonmediated end user delivery for some requests. The primary disadvantages with fax transmission are costs, especially for long-distance transmission, and the relatively large size of many articles and documents as compared to the average fax.

An alternative to fax is RLG's ARIEL document transmission software. This software, which uses the Internet to transmit digitized copies of documents, is in widespread use in the research library environment. The primary advantage of using ARIEL for document transmissions is reduced telecommunications costs, since the Internet is employed (in most cases a university's existing connections to the Internet will be used). This is particularly useful in those cases where documents are transmitted to remote users in areas that would be subject to long-distance charges if fax were employed. ARIEL also offers better image quality than fax. A minor disadvantage is that the initial setup costs are higher than those associated with fax, as a computer and scanner are required. The primary disadvantage with ARIEL, until the introduction of the open source Prospero software package (discussed below), has been that the software needed to be installed on both the sending and receiving end, requiring this to be a mediated service in most environments.

A promising new option being implemented at a number of facilities is Web-based document delivery. In this approach documents are scanned (as with ARIEL, which may in some cases serve as a front-end, using the Prospero[2] electronic document delivery software to convert files for Web-based retrieval) and then transferred to a secure Web site where the user may sign on and retrieve them. Users are typically notified via e-mail that the document is ready for their use. The documents are normally removed from the Web server after a specified period of time; this, in connection with the security provisions restricting access to the user who requested the document, is a feature intended to assure compliance with copyright laws. Cornell University's Library Annex is one of the first storage facilities to have implemented this service. Cornell's approach to Web-based delivery is to scan the documents and then convert them into the Adobe Portable Document Format (PDF); end users need to install the Adobe Acrobat reader (available free of charge) on their machines in order to read or print the documents. PDF, a common standard for providing documents through the Web, will be familiar to most Web users. Given the high percentage of library users who have Web access, this means of delivery offers the great potential for increasing the level of nonmediated delivery to the end user.

In planning for storage services, it is important to recognize that the infrastructure required to support facsimile transmission is typically already in place at the libraries being served by a storage facility. Where the majority of the requests are being handled by a central library service point, it may make more economic sense to transfer materials to that point for copying or scanning, rather than duplicating the infrastructure at the storage facility. A drawback with such an approach is increased turnaround time for filling article requests. Where multiple sites are being served by a single storage facility, handling facsimile requests directly from the storage facility is a more practical approach.

Staffing

Determining the appropriate level of staffing for storage facility services will depend on the size of the stored collection, the services to be provided, and the nature of the materials selected for storage. In most cases, materials placed in storage are low-use items. Most storage facilities that store low-use materials are reporting annual retrieval rates ranging from 2 percent to 4 percent of the stored collection. If higher-use materials are stored, this percentage will naturally have to be adjusted upward.

Most facilities are able to handle retrieval with a fairly small staff. (The WRLC Storage Facility uses a single staff member to provide service from a collection of 665,000 items. A second staff member provides backup when necessary.) The Harvard Depository, with a much larger collection, uses seven full-time staff members to provide circulation services. In general, approximately 10 retrievals per staff hour (factoring in the time required to refile in addition to pulling and preparing for delivery) seems to be the norm. If article level requests are handled, the additional time required to photocopy or scan the articles will need to be factored in.

Qualifications for storage facility staff tend to be similar to those required of most library support staff. Lift operators will need training in this specialized skill. Since the trays used to hold bound volumes can be rather heavy (up to 60 pounds), staff who will be engaged in pulling materials from the shelving system will need to be able to handle this weight. (See Appendix for examples of job descriptions.)

Until a facility's collection reaches a certain critical mass, most staff will be assigned to multiple tasks, as the need for full-time retrieval and delivery staff will not be present. What constitutes critical mass in this context is dependent on the nature of the collection and the level of usage; in the typical low-use (2 percent to 4 percent) scenario, it probably does not make sense to have staff who specialize solely in retrieval and delivery until the collection size reaches 1 million or more. In collections of 500,000 items or less, one full-time equivalent staff member is typically sufficient to provide retrieval services (assuming weekday only operations), but the need for backup will require at least two, and preferably three, staff members competent to handle requests.

Performance Standards

Given the sensitivity of many researchers to the lack of direct access to materials in high-density shelving, performance standards have always been at the core of high-quality storage facility service arrangements. Standards vary somewhat from one environment to the next, though in almost all cases the minimum standard is next business day delivery for materials requested during normal operating hours. In setting performance standards, facilities need to balance the desire for quick turnaround times with the costs involved in achieving them. The primary cost factors are staffing (to perform retrievals) and the actual cost of physical delivery.

Some facilities are able to offer same-day physical delivery for materials requested by a specified time (e.g., Johns Hopkins University's Moravia Park Facility offers same day delivery to campus for materials requested by 2:30 P.M.).[3] The proximity to campus is one factor determining a facility's ability to offer this level of service. The nature of the materials stored and the expected level of use are the other key factors. To offer same-day physical delivery typically requires that the distance between the facility and the campus dropoff points per day be relatively short.

Another service for which same-day delivery is offered by many facilities is facsimile transmission of individual article copies. In this case the storage facility is essentially providing document delivery service. The ability to offer same-day delivery of articles is a relatively inexpensive service enhancement for facilities that are offering individual article delivery in the first place. The actual costs of implementing the service will depend on whether fax or ARIEL is the primary delivery mechanism. The additional labor required to transmit copied or scanned articles is minimal and certainly no more than required to prepare them for physical delivery. Facilities that are not offering article delivery at this time would naturally face increased staffing expenses for photocopying or scanning the requested materials, as well as the associated infrastructure costs. As electronic delivery of information to the end user becomes increasingly prevalent, storage operations have a strong incentive to use data transmission technologies to the greatest degree possible.

More common than same-day delivery is next-day delivery. This can be accommodated with a single trip by the delivery service vehicle, and therefore is more cost-effective. One issue that naturally arises is whether this is truly next-day delivery, including weekend service, or next business day delivery, with materials being delivered Monday through Friday. Weekend delivery is more costly, but provides faster access to stored materials (it is important that staff be available at the pick-up locations to receive and process deliveries for weekend service to be worthwhile). The costs for providing weekend delivery typically include staffing (at Johns Hopkins Moravia Park facility, where service is offered on Saturday and Sunday, this is handled by a single part-time staff member; daily weekend request totals in fiscal year 1999 ran at about 70 percent of the weekday totals) and the cost of physical delivery (this will vary considerably depending on whether internal staff are used or a contractor handles the delivery). The next business day model is still the most common, but despite the cost some facilities are now offering weekend deliveries as well.

To achieve any given turnaround time requires adequate staffing at the storage facility to ensure requests are pulled within the agreed-upon timeframe and appropriate backup arrangements for physical delivery in the event of delivery staff's being absent. High-density storage facilities have generally done an excellent job of meeting performance standards, as long as these factors have been estimated accurately. The nature of the storage system itself almost completely removes the possibility of requested materials not being found on shelf, unless they are in circulation, and therefore creates a very predictable environment in which to provide this service. In choosing the performance target for a particular environment, it is basically a question of accurately estimating the costs of reaching a given level of performance, and balancing these costs against user expectations and anticipated levels of funding.

Summary

The high-density storage environment is unlike the traditional library environment in that all retrieval must be performed by staff with the appropriate training. This creates a potential bottleneck in the provision of services that needs to be carefully addressed in planning for storage facility staffing. On the other hand, the limited number of staff with meaningful access to the storage facility creates a service opportunity, as the likelihood of the status and location information for items in the storage database being erroneous is extremely small. A high degree of efficiency and reliability in pulling requested materials is therefore achievable.

The clear trend over time has been for access and delivery mechanisms for materials in storage to move from a highly mediated model, with all requests and deliveries being made through library service points, to a nonmediated model for many types of requests, in which users can place requests directly, and, where appropriate, receive requested materials directly as well. Information technology is the key to providing nonmediated access at a reasonable cost. To the degree that storage facilities are able to exploit technology to provide such services, they will be able to minimize the impact lack of direct access to stored materials has on the timeliness with which the end user can gain access to these materials.

Notes

1.   7-FAST Delivery Service. University of Michigan. 2000. http://www.lib.umich.edu/libhome/services/7fast.html

2.   Prospero (An Electronic Document Delivery System). Prior Health Sciences Library. Ohio State University, 1999. http://bones.med.ohio-state.edu/prospero/

3.   Moravia Park Shelving Facility. Johns Hopkins University. 1997. http://milton.mse.jhu.edu:8001/library/moravia/moravia.htm

Appendix: Sample Job Descriptions

The following are the job descriptions used at the WRLC Storage Facility storage facility. Other facilities may have additional positions, for example covering staff who manage or perform physical delivery of materials (these functions are contracted to a third party by WRLC). These job descriptions are published here with the permission of the Washington Research Library Consortium.

POSITION DESCRIPTION

JOB TITLE: **Storage Facility Supervisor**

SUMMARY: Supervises daily operations of the Storage Facility, including accessioning of materials, fulfilling requests, and the delivery service; assists Director of Library Services in planning Storage Facility operations

DUTIES AND RESPONSIBILITIES:

1. Supervises accessioning of materials into the Storage Facility. Responsible for 1 FTE Storage Services Assistant, plus a variable number of contract staff (up to 12 FTE; more typically 6 FTE).

2. With assistance of Storage Services Assistant as required, receives and processes requests for materials in the storage facility (loans and copies).

3. Supervises the Delivery Service. Responsible for coordination and performance monitoring of delivery service contract.

4. Coordinates the accessioning of materials from member libraries into the Storage Facility, including monitoring the accuracy of accessioning work, and coordinating shipping and receipt of materials shipped by member libraries. Plans for shelving of materials being accessioned.

5. Works with temporary services contractor to maintain appropriate staffing levels.

6. Provides assistance to on-site users of the Storage Facility, including retrieval and charging of requested materials, and issuing change/cards for photocopiers. Monitors the reading room.

7. Maintains appropriate records and statistics for lending, photocopy, and accessioning activities. Reviews system generated invoices for accuracy.

8. Monitors supplies required for the storage operation and orders supplies as appropriate. Monitors usage and maintenance of the order selection vehicle.

9. Communicates with consortium member libraries to coordinate and resolve problems regarding request and delivery of Storage Facility materials.

10. Performs related duties and projects as assigned.

MINIMUM QUALIFICATIONS:

1. High school diploma required; college degree (B.A. or equivalent) preferred

2. Library experience preferred; experience with automated systems desirable

3. Supervisory experience required

4. Good English language communication skills required

5. Ability to handle light loads (lift 40 lbs. regularly) and operate order selection vehicle required

POSITION DESCRIPTION

JOB TITLE: **Storage Services Assistant (Support Staff Position)**

SUMMARY: Accessions materials into the storage facility; assists the Storage Facility Supervisor in coordinating the work of temporary accessioning staff; provides backup to the Storage Facility Supervisor in filling requests as needed

DUTIES AND RESPONSIBILITIES:

1. Accessions materials into the Storage Facility using established procedures; including: unpacking and sorting materials, assembling and labeling trays; creation of records for trays, updating item records for inventory control purposes, and related activities.

2. Shelves materials in the Storage Facility, using the automated lift.

3. Assists the Storage Facility Supervisor in filling request for loans and photocopies; including: printing out requests; pulling materials from the shelves, photocopying and transmitting articles, and preparing materials for delivery.

4. Assists the Storage Facility Supervisor in coordinating the delivery service; in the supervisor's absence ensures that the delivery service is running properly; arranges for backup courier as needed.

5. Performs related duties as assigned.

MINIMUM QUALIFICATIONS:

1. High school diploma required

2. Ability to handle heavy loads (lift 50 lbs. regularly; 80 lbs. on occasion)

17

Special Collections

Mary C. LaFogg and Christine Weideman

Introduction

Archivists in Manuscripts and Archives (MSSA) in the Yale University Library began planning for the move of approximately 20,000 linear feet of our holdings to the Library Shelving Facility (LSF) in September 1997. We were almost entirely out of space in the department for adding new collections, and, due to library reorganization, had also been asked to vacate one of our on-site shelving areas. The move began in December 1998, and since then, time has been devoted to problem solving and review in order to refine our knowledge of how best to make use of the facility. While some of our experiences are unique to the Yale University Library, the majority of what we learned can help other archivists and curators plan for and undertake a similar project.

Manuscripts and Archives was fortunate to have its senior collections management archivist serve as co-chair of the library-wide shelving facility implementation task force. As a result, very early in the process, vital information about the unique characteristics and needs of special collections materials was shared with library and facility administrators. This process of education and the resultant discussions among users of the facility and its managers was an important factor in the ultimate success of our efforts. Special Collections professionals at other institutions should try to become active participants in the planning for a facility so that they may influence how key issues affecting their materials are taken into consideration during the design and execution of similar types of projects.

Special Collections materials, like those in MSSA, include paper items, photographs, films, and audio and video recordings. Due to their environmental needs and the space required to house them, among other reasons, high-efficiency shelving facilities can be superb locations in which to place these materials. Before beginning a project to move materials to a shelving facility, however, archivists and curators need to delineate the assumptions upon which the move will be based, and understand issues related to facility specifications; selection, tracking, physical preparation and moving of materials; operational needs for successfully retrieving items from and returning them to the facility; and maximizing use of the facility. We will review these steps and the deliberations needed for them.

Know Your Assumptions

The first step in any major project is to develop the list of assumptions that will guide project participants in their efforts. In Manuscripts and Archives, key project participants, including the director and the heads of the arrangement and description, collection development, public services, and collections management and reader services working groups, gathered for two half-day retreats and drew up the list of assumptions to govern the move of our holdings to the shelving facility (see Table 1).

Table 1. The Addressed Project Assumptions

♦ the priority level for the department of the project

♦ the linear footage of materials to be moved

♦ the various shelving locations to be vacated

♦ whether entire collections, or just individual parts, could be sent to the facility

♦ the extent of collections tracking operations needed before, during, and after the move

♦ the systems work required for tracking and retrieval operations

♦ where physical preparation of materials was to occur, onsite or at the facility

♦ minimizing disruptions to researchers while materials were being prepared and moved

♦ obtaining needed assistance from library units outside of the department

♦ deadlines to be met

We periodically reviewed, modified, and added to the list as necessary, and made certain that the entire department understood and shared the assumptions. These crucial underpinnings formed the framework for the undertaking and guided the exploration of the remaining issues as the project advanced. (See the Appendix.)

Know Your Facility

To develop an understanding of the capabilities of a shelving facility, and to determine whether it can meet the needs of special collections, the curator or archivist needs to examine the physical environment the facility provides, the security systems it employs, its shelving capacities, the technology it uses to track the location of materials and the requests for them, and the transportation methods used to move items to and from the facility.

An important goal of the LSF at Yale was that its environment meet or exceed any of the standards available for on-campus shelving of collection materials. Yale's LSF combines a number of unique technologies to achieve a rigorously controlled environment where heating, cooling, humidification, and dehumidification maintain a constant 50°F temperature with 30° relative humidity. In addition, the air filtration system is state of the art, and every item that enters the facility is vacuumed to remove any loose dirt, further improving the overall conditions under which materials are kept.

Financially it made sense to design one shelving area with environmental systems that could provide the ideal environment for the maximum number of types of materials that would potentially be shelved there. This strategy benefited all users of the facility, but was especially valuable to special collections that contain a variety of materials often in fragile or poor condition. For MSSA this represented a chance to locate its collections in the best possible environment for maintaining and prolonging their existence.

Of equal importance to the environment was security. The building at Yale is locked at all times, with keycard access for employees only. Visitors must be let into the facility, are visible to staff, and monitored at all times. In addition, motion detectors and alarms on all perimeter doors ensure that unlawful entrance or egress is immediately detected. Finally the random shelving of materials by size provides another type of security since it is virtually impossible to know where a particular item is without the use of the inventory system. No bibliographic information is needed to shelve or retrieve items, so potential name recognition of valuable items is not likely to occur.

Knowing that the facility was environmentally ideal and secure meant the department, and other special collections at Yale, could send any of their holdings to the LSF, but could the facility handle the size and types of containers that housed the collections? MSSA, as one of the largest special collections units at the university, provided a report listing more than 30 types and sizes that represented the range of containers used for holding collection materials. The shelving consultant reviewed the list and designed the placement grid in such a way that all of the various containers could easily be accommodated.

Many of the items transferred from MSSA fit the six sizes of shelf trays used in this and other facilities. An additional size tray was designed to hold videocassettes. The depth and width of the shelving were the only limitations on what could be shelved at the LSF. Shelving is approximately 53 inches wide and 36 inches deep, with through-the-shelf shelving in a few places that extends the depth to at least 72 inches. Only one container, out of 43,700 sent to the facility, was unable to be accommodated.

Another important decision, made in the design phase at the request of special collections representatives, was to include flat drawers as part of the overall shelving design. Folios, maps, drawings, posters, broadsides, and similar types of materials could then be safely housed in drawers at the facility. This was particularly important for MSSA, because our on-site space for flat shelving is limited.

To ensure that the methods used at the facility to accession, locate, retrieve, and return items would work for both book and nonbook materials, MSSA participated in discussions leading to the request for a system and critiqued the vendors' proposals. This process provided assurances that the chosen system could handle nonbook materials. The Library also determined, during this phase, that the system employed at the LSF would interface with the Library's online catalog (Orbis, a Notis system) to generate patron requests for materials at the facility and track them. This had major implications for MSSA, since it used Orbis for bibliographic purposes, but not for circulation activities.

The decision to use the LSF also involved hard choices with respect to transportation of items to and from the facility. It would be best for the items to only be subjected to transport during the initial transfer, and then remain in an ideal environment that would prolong their existence. The reality is that the containers must be transported between buildings by truck or van and moved from shipping docks to departments by book and hand trucks to accommodate requests for use.

To minimize potential damage smaller items and books are crated in plastic totes. Book trucks are covered during inclement weather, and the shipping dock at the LSF is fully enclosed. The LSF staff has received extensive training in the handling of all library materials, but despite precautions, some container damage has occurred necessitating the replacement of a few boxes and lids. Consideration for acclimatizing special media, such as videotapes, has been achieved through the use of coolers. Wrapping of fragile books in acid-free paper has added protection while providing a safe and secure place for bar codes. Despite all of these precautions, however, a special collection may conclude that some of its materials are too fragile or valuable for inclusion in a shelving facility.

Developing Your Project Plan

After determining the assumptions on which a move of special collections to a shelving facility will be based, and gathering as much information as possible, a project plan can be drafted. Our project plan included deadlines that had to be met and was arranged in three parts. The first concerned selection of materials for the LSF, and various subcommittees immediately began to select manuscript and university archives collections to be housed there. The last step in the process involved determining how much usable shelving we would have on-site once the move was over and what type of containers it could hold. This was important because we knew that in addition to housing high-use collections, our on-site shelving would need to provide hold space for collections from the LSF requested by patrons and staff.

The second part of our project plan concerned preparing materials to be moved to the LSF. We needed to do systems work, ranging from first ensuring that our in-house location database provided complete and accurate information about our holdings, to creating records in Orbis to facilitate the circulation of materials to and from the facility. We also needed to physically prepare the materials, which included box repair, uniquely identifying each item (we used bar coding), and shifting materials from one on-site shelving area to another so that all materials to go to the LSF in the initial large move were located in the same space.

One of our assumptions from the very beginning of our project was that operations throughout the department would change. The changes affected the policies and procedures of all of our departmental working groups and in the third part of our project plan, each working group was to analyze what needed to be done in their particular areas. The public services working group, for example, developed a plan for informing our patrons about how long materials would be unavailable while they were moved out of the department and processed into the LSF, and for informing anyone who contacted us about the need to begin to request materials prior to their visits to the department. Public services and the collections management working groups developed the procedures for using the Orbis circulation system and for training staff in how to do so. The arrangement and description working group in conjunction with the collections management staff developed procedures for decommissioning bar codes when unprocessed collections were retrieved from the LSF for processing. The collections development working group had to determine how to prepare materials for direct transfer to the LSF from donors' homes and offices as needed.

Like our list of assumptions, we periodically reviewed our project plan and updated it as necessary. We found it very important to explore what could and could not be done simultaneously when we developed the plan, so that we could estimate the staffing needed at various points in the project.

Materials Selection

In addition to wanting to take advantage of the LSF to house a portion of our holdings, MSSA had been asked to vacate one of its large, on-site, shelving areas. We knew that we had to move at least 10,000 linear feet of materials to the LSF. We could move more if we chose to, and in fact one of our long-term goals was to vacate several other shelving areas that did not meet the environmental standards of the LSF. There was a minimum amount of footage that we had to select, but because we kept our long-term goal in mind, we ended up selecting more.

The team doing the selection was comprised of seven archivists with a combined 86 years worth of experience in working in MSSA. Five of them had served at least four hours per week as reference archivists throughout their tenure in the department. They began with the assumption that due to systems restrictions, we could only send entire collections to the LSF, rather than parts of collections. Certain kinds of collections were immediately designated for the LSF: those with restrictions on their use, and those for which the originals were available on microfilm. Other collections were designated to remain on-site: primarily collections each team member knew were used so often, either by researchers, reference archivists, or university staff and administrators, that to send them off-site would lead to disruptions in daily operations that we were not willing to incur.

The library-wide principle for selecting materials to be housed in the LSF was low-usage. The team had seven years worth of data about the number of boxes used and number of researchers requesting material for each of our manuscript and archival collections, and we used those figures to begin our discussions of what to select. Our selection involved running a report in which collections were organized by number of boxes requested and the number of readers. We then ran a second report that totaled the linear footage at various cut-off points in the first report. We learned that in order to meet our minimum footage, we would be sending collections to the LSF that would probably not be considered low-usage. As a result, the team discussed, individually, every collection designated for the LSF for which usage figures were higher than we were comfortable. The box and researcher usage reports were initially arranged by year and we were able to determine for many of the collections that usage had been particularly high for one or two years in the past, but not for most recent years. Team members were able to shed light about class usage of particular collections and whether the faculty members teaching the classes were still using them. Our discussions resulted in several collections designated for the LSF being kept on-site. The team also discussed every collection for which usage figures indicated it should remain on-site. The same type of analysis was done and we were able to designate several of those collections for the LSF. These discussions among team members were extremely valuable and when we were done, each team member felt that the justification for our selections was valid and in keeping with the overall project assumptions.

Shortly after selection work was completed, we learned that it would be possible to send just portions of collections to the LSF. The box usage data available were not detailed enough to indicate specific box numbers used by researchers. During its earlier discussions about selection, however, particularly during its analysis of individual collections to remain on-site, team members discussed a number of collections for which individual series within them could be sent to the LSF. A variety of reasons were given; some series had restrictions placed on their use or had been microfilmed; others were comprised of books, that were available elsewhere in the library; and others consisted of materials the donor had wanted included in the collection even though they were of limited research value. As a result of the discussions, we were able to select portions of collections designated to remain on-site, to go to the LSF.

Throughout the team's discussions, members recognized the importance of capturing more complete box and researcher usage data. They knew that we would need to evaluate on an ongoing basis what boxes were being requested so that collections could be brought back onsite if they were being heavily used. Alternatively, if collections designated to remain on-site remained unused over a period of time, they could be considered for placement in the LSF. As a result, a database was created and prior to delivering a container to a researcher, reading room support staff scan the container's bar code and enter the series number (if there is one) into the database. We are able to run reports from this database that help us monitor usage and ensure the best location of material for meeting our researchers' needs.

Materials Tracking

Tracking the location of materials in a shelving facility involves new ways of thinking about how to identify individual containers. Special collections often use a range of methods to track the location of items in their shelving areas. MSSA uses random shelving and tracks the starting location of each accession in a database that allows for searching by collection name, group number, accession number, and accession date. Once we began using the LSF, however, the concept of shelving in contiguous patterns was no longer valid. A unique identification became the key to locating any particular item. Bar codes provide this kind of identification, but bar coding was not routinely employed in MSSA for nonbook materials. Bar coding was also necessary in order to use Orbis circulation for the request and return of items to the LSF.

Items at the Yale LSF are shelved by size with no regard to parent collection. The process of accessioning associates an item bar code with a tray. The tray bar code is then associated with a shelf. During accessioning, information on the sending unit and type of material is also captured. Retrieval and return of items are accomplished in a two-step process that involves Orbis circulation functions and the LSF's software system. The challenge for MSSA was to find a way to use Orbis circulation in order to participate in the normal workflow designed for the LSF.

Materials Preparation

Before materials can be sent to a shelving facility, they must be prepared, intellectually and physically. The intellectual preparation involves developing a system that will uniquely identify each container designated for the facility. In MSSA, the department's location database master record contained fields for collection title, group number, accession date and number, series, part, and linear footage, as well as information about restrictions. Based on the library's decision to use Orbis for tracking patron requests, we determined that the container type, along with a bar code, could provide the unique identification we needed for each item. The location database was expanded to include container type and a bar code in an item record for each of the 57,700 containers in the collection.

We used duplicate and, in the case of videocassettes, triplicate bar codes for identifying items. Triplicates were needed in case the tape became separated from its container. A bar code was affixed in the same location to every item. The duplicate bar code went on a worksheet generated from the location database item records for each collection. The worksheets were then used to input, through the use of bar code readers (wands), the bar codes into the item records in the local database. A script, written in-house, uploaded container, accession, and bar code information from the local database to the Orbis database. We ended up with unique item records for all of our containers in the library's online catalog.

At the same time that the bar coding was done, a physical check of the containers was made. Broken containers were replaced or repaired as needed to anticipate the rigors of transport to and from the facility. Worksheets were annotated for any missing items and the few items on the shelves for which we had no records in the location database. Staff members from the departmental arrangement and description working group analyzed and resolved these problems.

Moving Materials

Moving materials to a shelving facility can involve the use of regularly scheduled transportation to and from the facility, or the use of hired movers. Because MSSA was asked to vacate one of our largest on-site shelving areas by a certain date, it faced the daunting task of transferring 27,000 items from on-campus shelving to the LSF in a 10-day period. A move of this magnitude required the use of a commercial vendor skilled in handling library materials. The selection of the vendor involved an assessment of how well they could guarantee the location of the items while in transit and while they awaited processing at the LSF. We had to be able to respond to emergency requests from university administrators (no matter how unlikely) for materials which were in transit or awaiting processing at the facility, thus it was very important that the mover be able to identify which pallet or commercial bin contained which bar coded items. At the time of MSSA's move, the LSF had only been operational for about a week, and the staff was processing about 500 items per day. The movers were to bring in pallets and bins as quickly as possible, so containers would be in the facility, but not accessioned or shelved for some weeks.

The vendor subcontracted with systems personnel to design a database, kept in the department and at the facility, to link item bar codes to a pallet or commercial bin. As each item was removed from on-site shelving, its bar code was scanned and associated with a pallet or bin. In this manner all items were accounted for at all times. The move itself was accomplished within the allotted time frame with a minimum of supervision. Special collections contemplating the use of the commercial vendors should be assured that some are quite capable of handling this kind of transfer and should be able to employ technology to provide tracking at all times. Planning is crucial and oversight is needed to re-solve any unanticipated problems.

Since the initial move, additional transfers of over 16,700 items have taken place. In some instances, new accessions are labeled, bar coded, and picked up when requested items are routinely brought back to the department or returned to the LSF. For larger transfers, batches of containers are prepared and shelved in particular on-site locations. The department has entered into a productive work arrangement with the LSF staff who then removes these items and transports them to the facility for accessioning. We have found that this additional work ac-tivity by the LSF staff does not adversely affect the daily production rate at the facility.

In all cases the bar code is the key to whether or not the item is ready for moving. An item without a bar code does not leave the shelf. Other preparation work prior to the move involves verification that an item record including the bar code exists in the departmental location database and in Orbis. We also need to change the location code in Orbis for an item from on-campus to the LSF prior to transfer.

Orbis requirements seem simple now, but initially resulted in much discus-sion and development work in MSSA. The database displays a location and loan code status for every item. The combination of these two elements provides a means for knowing where something is shelved and where it can be requested and used. For example, MSSA materials may only be requested by our staff and used only in our reading room. Codes that provide text in the database to indicate that an item is located in MSSA and must be requested and used there, were de-veloped in consultation with the Library System Office (LSO). This exercise was held throughout the Yale library system; it provided consistency and allows all staff to accurately interpret information in Orbis to answer patron inquiries.

The LSF software produces a list of accessioned bar codes at the end of the day. This is run in a batch job overnight to update Orbis by changing the loan code to one that tells the staff that an item is now at the LSF and may be requested according to the established rules. MSSA uses this same end of day information to update its own departmental location database, so that the location of every container, whether on-site or at the LSF, is accurately shown.

MSSA and other library units using the LSF do not prepare an outgoing inventory of bar codes prior to transfer. It is assumed that the LSF will accession 100 percent of what is transferred. It turned out that problems caused when com-piling the end-of-the-day accession file at the LSF could result in an incomplete transfer of data to Orbis. For this reason we instituted a strict accounting proce-dure to reconcile every item that is transferred. This check involves keeping a list of items sent and reviewing the Orbis database to see if the loan code has been changed. If too much time elapses, and we believe the item should have reached the LSF and been accessioned, we contact the manager and ask that a particular bar code be verified. The manager then reports the date of accession and the local database and Orbis are manually updated. At some point in time a global (library-wide) reconciliation will be undertaken to match all LSF bar codes with the Orbis database to determine if any updating was missed. This report will assist other units, who do not do their own reconciliation, to determine if some of their holdings are at the LSF but the Orbis record still indicates an on-campus location.

Deciding how to handle ongoing moves to a shelving facility will be challenging for special collections because the amounts involved and the complexity will differ from book transfers. Deciding on a workflow that provides enough checks and balances to ensure zero errors will require a commitment to quality control unlike any other used for daily operations. The consequences of errors are irreparable since the random shelving philosophy means little chance of ever locating a lost item. The department's record of which bar code identifies which item is its only means for retrieval. MSSA is satisfied that its local database and Orbis give it a redundancy that ensures recoverability should one system or the other fail.

Request/Return of Materials

Special collections units must develop a thorough understanding of how they will request materials from and return them to a shelving facility. This will generally entail systems work and training in the procedures for staff members.

MSSA must use the Orbis circulation system to request and return items to Yale's LSF. Most special collections will not be part of library circulation systems since their materials traditionally do not circulate. Nevertheless, becoming a service unit can be advantageous. Service unit status means that a department may obtain tracking and statistical data not formerly available. MSSA has not used patron files within Orbis to link collection use to particular individuals, but hopes to do so in the near future. More sophisticated analysis of collection use for security purposes and determining research trends makes this linkage desirable.

In a rather simple fashion, MSSA uses departmental charges to request items from the LSF through Orbis. Items are checked in upon receipt and charged to the department. Upon completion of use, the items are discharged, and in-transit lists are generated to indicate that items are in the process of return to the LSF. This entire operation is accomplished using the bar code.

It is critical to identify the correct bar code so that the right item is requested. The department's location database is the easiest place to find that bar code, since Orbis does not routinely display an item's bar code. Staff find the bar code in the local database and copy it to an electronic clipboard. They then begin an Orbis session and request the materials, a process that involves copying the bar code from the clipboard into an Orbis field. Upon receipt of the item in the department, its bar code is again scanned into Orbis to complete the transaction.

On rare occasion, the Orbis request system may fail due to power outages, downed network access, or other external factors beyond anyone's control. The backup method for retrieving items is to send an e-mail message, containing the needed bar codes, to the manager of the LSF. The manager can manually enter the bar codes into his system to determine locations of requested items and include the items in the next delivery to the department.

Special collections will need to consider the delivery schedule that the shelving facility establishes. Will it work for their hours of operation? A late-day delivery can be acceptable to the library since it may be open until midnight, but may not be as acceptable to the special collection department that closes at 4:30 P.M. Negotiating a twice-daily delivery schedule is difficult, but certainly makes sense for most special collections that must do whatever they can for visiting scholars and institutional officials during normal business hours.

Problem Solving/Review/Reports

Problem solving and review of operations are critical to the ongoing success of housing special collections in a shelving facility. No matter how careful the planning, there will be unanticipated problems and operational disruptions that need attention. Over time, as staff becomes familiar with new operations, they will offer suggestions for improvements and there must be a vehicle for evaluating those suggestions.

For nearly the first four months of operation of the LSF, MSSA was its only client. This was fortunate for the department as well as the facility. The LSF is available for all Yale library collections. When fully operational it was to combine, in its system's database and reports, as well as its shelving protocol, materials from all campus libraries. For the first few weeks, however, only MSSA material was accessioned. All errors, therefore, were known to be ours. This allowed the department to identify consistent problems and revise workflows to avoid these in the future. Conversely, the LSF and Library Systems Office encountered situations they had not anticipated. Addressing and resolving them meant that they were not encountered when the LSF began to accession materials simultaneously from several locations.

The department benefited from having the undivided attention of the LSF staff. Everyone approached the experience with open minds and a willingness to exchange ideas on problem solving and improvements. The strong working relationship and mutual respect for each other's operations continues to this day. Going first was tough, but it paid big dividends in the end.

MSSA continues to ask the LSF staff for new approaches to operational concerns. Finding ways to transfer materials directly from university offices or donors without first bringing them to the department; preparing and reviewing materials at the LSF prior to their being accessioned; and retrieving large quantities of items from the LSF without having to make individual item requests using Orbis are just some of the scenarios that have been explored.

Internally the department underwent tremendous evolution as a result of placing over two thirds of its holdings at the LSF. Almost all of our operations, from public services, and collections management, to arrangement and description, and collection development, were affected. Bar codes for every container in the department, advance notification to retrieve items from the LSF, use of a circulation system, and the availability of almost unlimited space for newly acquired collections caused us to rethink and redesign most of our daily operations. Our handling of space management is still evolving. Reports based upon actual usage by readers of collections will enhance the department's ability to shift collections to appropriate shelving locations. Devising strategies for temporarily locating in-use materials and finding holding areas for collections retrieved from the LSF for on-site arrangement and description will require innovative thinking and application of technological solutions.

Conclusion

Shelving facilities provide the most efficient and secure housing for special collection materials. Making the decision to use a facility and integrating it into daily operations can be enterprising and rewarding. Next to library automation, it is the most radical challenge to past practices that special collections have faced in the last 25 years. The good news is that like integrated bibliographic databases, integrated library shelving facilities will be among the best things to have happened to our collections.

Appendix: Projects to Be Completed for Move to Library Shelving Facility*

1. SELECTION: Select 28,000 ft. Develop criteria for selection by types of materials: manuscripts, archives, video archives, publications, and dissertations.

1a. Develop criteria for selection—a blend of what should go and what needs to stay (keep in mind quality of description of materials before determining whether they should be moved). Determine whether the criteria developed can be used in the future.

1b. Run reports to translate selections into linear footage. Begin by running reports to determine number of linear feet of: zero usage, restricted, microfilmed, and shelving area by type of container.

1c. Identify usable shelving, which will remain in Sterling and analyze by type of container it can hold.

1d. Modify. If selection falls short or too much is selected, determine how to proceed.

1e. Once collections have been designated for move to LSF, manuscript and university archives selection groups need to determine which collections have ORBIS bibliographic records.

---

2. PREPARATION OF MATERIALS: Will include checking container condition, bar coding containers, and resolving inconsistencies between actual materials and inventories.

2a. Survey container types/numbers throughout the department. Enter information into the locator database and verify.

2b. Locator system—what information should departmental system provide?

2c. Container preparation. All containers in the department will be bar coded (probably two per container) and bar codes entered into both locator database and ORBIS. Those materials being sent to LSF receive priority over those to remain in the department. Can proceed as soon as bar code system is in place and can proceed simultaneously with 2a.

2d. Creation of ORBIS records. We need an ORBIS bibliographic record (or something similar) for each collection/record group to go to LSF. We attach item records (there is one for each container) to the bibliographic record. Item records have to be created and will include the bar code (which will be wanded into the record) and other information, including that which makes the container unique (i.e., number, accession, series, etc.). Video Archives has to determine how it will handle tapes for which there are no bibliographic records in ORBIS. They might be grouped together and attached to the appropriate affiliate bibliographic records.

Dissertations: Currently there are records (approximately 11,000) in ORBIS for dissertations, which have been filmed. Can we attach an item record for the print version to the film ORBIS record? If not, can we do some form of derivative cataloging and take the film record and modify it so that it is a print record? Is the dissertation catalog in the retrospective conversion queue?

2d1. Determine which collections/record groups do not have ORBIS records (see Selection above)

2d2. Determine what is involved in creating ORBIS records (bibliographic, if necessary, and item) for our holdings. Determine how much of information inputting can be automated. Estimate time involved in creating records in order to determine how much staff time is required.

2d3. Create bibliographic records if necessary. Create item records. Can begin as soon as bar codes system is in place and bar codes are placed on boxes/tapes. We can begin by creating item records for those collections, which already have bibliographic records in ORBIS.

2e. Moving materials to/from the annex. Not all materials in the annex will be sent to LSF. Some materials from A and B vaults will go to LSF. We have to move those materials, which will remain out of the annex, and move those which will go to LSF from A & B into the annex. There will not necessarily be a one to one match of the space that opens up in the annex to the containers that need to be placed there from A & B. Can we move the materials from A & B and store them in the processing annex so that we only move them once, and then move the materials, that are staying, out of the annex and into the openings in A & B?

2e1. Select materials and determine footage and box types which need to be moved within the department.

2e2. Determine how move of materials should take place and how long it will take.

2e3. Complete bar coding of boxes (i.e., physically putting the bar codes on the boxes) before moving them to/from the annex.

2e4. Move materials.

2f. Establish operations flow. We need to determine the overall order in which the steps involved in creating Orbis bibliographic and item records and moving the materials will take place. We also need to establish a time frame for doing so. Begin after the discussion about what is involved in creating an item record.

3. OPERATIONS: Operations throughout the department will be affected by the move of 2/3 of our holdings to LSF. The biggest changes will be in reader services, but there will also be changes in reference, arrangement and description, and collection development. Each group will examine how our current operations will change and what new procedures and policies need to be established.

XI. Bibliography

18

Citations and Web Sites

Helen R. Goldstein

Citations

Ash, Lee. "Selection of Materials for Storage: Policies and Problems." In *Yale's Selective Book Retirement Program*, 7–16. Hamden, CT: Archon Books, 1963.

Bellanti, Claire Q. "Access to Library Materials in Remote Storage" (University of California Southern regional storage facility). *Collection Management* 17, nos. 1–2 (1992): 93–103.

Benedict, Marjorie A., Michael Knee, and Mina B. La Croix. "Finding Space for Periodicals: Weeding, Storage, and Microform Conversion." *Collection Management* 12, nos. 3–4 (1990): 145–54.

Boll, John J. *Shelf Browsing, Open Access, and Storage Capacity in Research Libraries*. Champaign, IL: University of Chicago, 1985.

Boll, John J. *To Grow or Not to Grow?* New York: R. R. Bowker Co., 1980.

Boss, Richard W. "Facilities Planning for Technology." *Library Technology Reports* 31, no. 4 (July–Aug. 1995): 389–483.

Boss, Richard W. "Appendix: Prominent Space Planning Formulas" (Library Facilities Planning for Technology). *Library Technology Reports* 31, no. 4 (July–Aug. 1995): 477.

Bright, Frank. *Planning for a Movable Compact Shelving System*. Chicago: American Library Association, 1991.

Buckland, Michael K. "Little Used Duplicates, Cooperative Collection Development and Storage." *Collection Management* 13, no. 4 (1990): 39–52.

Chepesiuk, Ron. "Reaching Critical Mass: Off-site Storage in the Digital Age." *American Libraries* (April 1999): 40–43.

Choudhury, Sayeed. "A Proposal for Comprehensive Access to Off-Site Library Print Materials. Submitted to the Andrew W. Mellon Foundation by the Milton S. Eisenhower Library, The Johns Hopkins University, 11 May, 1998." Available: http://dkc.mse.jhu.edu/CAPM

Clark, Lenore, ed. "Guide to Review of Library Collections: Preservation, Storage, and Withdrawal." *Technical Services Quarterly* 9, no. 3 (1992): 85.

Cogan, Sarah and Bullard, Rit. "The Automated Retreival Collection at Bruce T. Halle Library." *Library Hi Tech* 18 no. 2 (2000): 142–43.

Cooper, Michael D. "The Sensitivity of Book Storage Strategy Decisions to Alternative Cost Assumptions." *Library Quarterly* 61, no. 4 (Oct 1991): 414–28.

Cooper, Michael D. "A Cost Comparison of Alternative Book Storage Strategies." *Library Quarterly* 59, no. 3 (1989): 239–60.

Crampon, Jean E. "Moving to Storage: Balancing Technical and Public Services Needs." In "Preserving the Past, Looking to the Future," *International Association of Aquatic and Marine Science Libraries and Information Centers*, edited by Elizabeth Fuseler. 19th Annual Conference, Bethesda, MD, 1993.

Creaghe, Norma S., and Douglas A. Davis. "Hard Copy in Transition: An Automated Storage and Retrieval Facility for Low-Use Library Materials." *College & Research Libraries* 47 (Sept. 1986): 495–99.

Crosbie, Michael J. "Library Science." *Architecture: The AIA Journal* 79, no. 7 (July 1990): 103–6.

Ehrlich, Martin. "Criteria for Not Discarding Books from a Public Library." *The Unabashed Librarian* 78 (1991): 26.

Ellsworth, Ralph E. *Economics of Book Storage in College and University Libraries*. Metuchen, NJ: Association of Research Libraries, 1969.

Feinman, Valerie Jackson. "From Attic to Annex: The Story of an Off-Campus Storage Facility." *Serials Librarian* 5 (Summer 1981): 49–57.

Foot, Mirjam. "Housing Our Collections: Environment and Storage for Libraries and Archives." *IFLA Journal* 22, no. 2 (1996): 110–14.

Fraley, Ruth A. *Library Space Planning: A How-To-Do-It Manual for Assessing, Allocating and Reorganizing Collections, Resources, and Facilities,* 2nd ed. New York: Neal-Schuman, 1990.

Fraley, Ruth A. *Library Space Planning: How to Assess, Allocate, and Reorganize Collections, Resources, and Physical Facilities.* New York: Neal-Schuman, 1985.

Frodl, Hermann. "Opening of the New Subterranean Storage Addition of the Austrian National Library" (German). Original title: "Die Eroffnung des neuen Tiefspeichers der Osterreichischen Nationalbibliothek." *Biblos* 41, no. 4 (1992): 185–90.

Fuhlrott, Rolf. "Cooperative Storage: Lightening the Burden of Libraries." *Libri* 30 (Dec. 1980): 321–27.

Fussler, Herman Howe. *Patterns in the Use of Books in Large Research Libraries.* Chicago: University of Chicago Press, 1969.

Gerencher, Joseph J. "An Inexpensive Horizontal Map Storage Facility (moveable shelves at Moravian College)." *Bulletin* Special Libraries Association, Geography and Map Division 141 (Sept. 1985): 2–6.

Gleaves, Edwin S. "The Cost-Effectiveness of Alternative Library Storage Programs." (Book Review). Monash University. Graduate School of Librarianship, 1983. *Collection Management* 6 (Fall-Winter 1984): 136–38.

Gorman, Michael. "Moveable Compact Shelving: The Current Answer." *Library Hi Tech* 5:4, no. 20 (Winter 1987): 23–26.

Gorman, Michael. " A Box Where Sweets Compacted Lie: Compact, Subcompact, and Miniaturized Libraries and the Myth of Browsing." *American Libraries* 15 (Apr. 1984): 210–11.

Graham, Barbara, Curtis Kendrick, and Joseph Urtz, "The Design and Operation of Off-Site Storage Facilities in Support of Preservation Programs." In *International Conference on Conservation and Restoration of Archival and Library Materials, Erice, 22nd–29th April 1996*, edited by Carlo Federici and Paola F. Munafo, 133–44. (Rome: Istituto centrale per la patologia del libro, 1999).

Gyeszly, Suzanne D., Marifran Bustion, and Jane Treadwell. "Infrequently Used Serials: A Space Utilization Project." *Collection Management* 12, no. 1 (1990): 109–23.

Habich, Elizabeth Chamberlain. *Moving Library Collections: A Management Handbook.* Westport, CT: Greenwood Press, 1998.

Harrar, Helen Joanne. "Cooperative Storage Warehouses." Ph.D. dissertation, Rutgers University, 1962.

Hauser, Hans-Jorg. "Reserve Storage or Library Storage: Concerning the Storage of Book Collections in Academic Libraries" (German). Original title: "Ausweichmagazin oder Speicherbibliothek: zur Auslagerung von Literaturbestanden aus wissenschaftlichen Bibliotheken Zeitschrift fur Bibliothekswesen und Bibliographie." 30 (Sept.–Oct. 1983): 371–89.

Henshaw, Rod, and Cordelia Swinton. "The Penn State Annex: A Model for Implementing a Successful Collection Storage Program." *Technical Services Quarterly* 7, no. 4 (1990): 11–19.

Hickey, C. David. "Serials Derelegation from Remote Storage." *Collection Building* 19, no. 4 (2000): 153–60.

Hirsch, JoAnne. "Sidebar: California State University Northridge Builds High Tech Storage Facility." *Library Hi Tech* 8, no. 3 (1990): 90–91.

Kendrick, Curtis. "High-Density Storage Libraries: The Harvard Depository Model." In *Solving Collection Problems Through Repository Strategies: Proceedings of an International Conference Held in Kuopio, Finland, May 1999*, edited by Pauline Connolly, 53–65. (Boston Spa, UK: International Federation of Library Associations [IFLA] Offices for UAP and International Lending, 1999).

Kennedy, James, and Gloria Stockton. *The Great Divide: Challenges in Remote Storage*. Chicago: American Library Association, 1991.

Korevaar, J. D. "A Central Depository for Little-Used Literature in the US (with Selection Criteria of the Law School Library)" (Dutch). Original title: "Harvard Depository Inc.: een centraal depot voor weinig gebruikte literatuur in de Open." (April 21, 1989): 131–33.

Kountz, John. "Industrial Storage Technology Applied to Library Requirements." *Library Hi Tech* 5:4, no. 20 (Winter 1987): 13–22.

Lougee, Wendy P. "Remote Shelving Comes of Age: Storage Collection Management at the University of Michigan." *Collection Management* 16, no. 2 (1992): 93–107.

Lucker, Jay K. "Library Buildings: Their Current State and Future Development." *Science & Technology Libraries* 13, no. 1 (Fall 1992): 3–16.

MacRitchie, John. "From the Sticks (Weeding and Discarding Books)." *Scottish Libraries*. 35 (Sept.–Oct. 1992): 5.

McCormick, Edith. "NYPL, Columbia, Princeton Cooperate on Storage Site." *American Libraries* (May 1999): 16–17.

Merrill-Oldham, Jan. *Library Storage Facilities: Management and Services.* Association of Research Libraries, Office of Leadership and Management Services. SPEC Kit no. 242. Washington, DC: ARL, Systems and Procedures Exchange Center, May 1999.

Meyboom, Leen. "The Randtriever at Erasmus University, Rotterdam—1969–1990: Two Decades of Change in Mechanical Books Storage." *Library Hi Tech* 8, no. 3 (1990): 83.

O'Connor, Phyllis, "Remote Storage Facilities: An Annotated Bibliography." *Serials Review* 20, no. 2 (1994): 17–26.

Palladino, Grace. "Out of Sight, Out of Mind: Shelving by Height at the Library of Congress." *Chronicle of Higher Education* (June 11, 1999), B6-7.

Pallier, Denis. "Conservation, Communication, Weeding: The Library Storage Problem Presented at an ABF Pre-conference Seminar, Valenciennes, Sept. 1990" (French). Original title: "Conservation, communication, elimination: le probleme bibliotheconomique des silos." *Bulletin des Bibliotheques de France* 35, no. 5 (1990): 282–86.

Payne, Lizanne. "The Washington Research Library Consortium: A Real Organization for a Virtual Library." *Information Technology and Libraries* (March 1998).

Peterson, Kenneth G. "New Storage Facility at Southern Illinois University." *College & Research Libraries News* 51 (Jan. 1990): 39–43.

Poole, Connie. "Guide to Budget Allocation for Information Resources and Guide to Review of Library Collections: Preservation, Storage, and Withdrawal." *Bulletin of the Medical Library Association* 80, no. 1 (Jan. 1992): 53.

Quinn, Aimee C., and Michaelyn Haslam. "Open Government, Closed Stacks: Onsite Storage of Depository Materials (New Automated Storage and Retrieval Systems at California State University, Northridge and the University of Nevada Las Vegas)." *Government Information Quarterly* 15, no. 2 (1998): 221–28.

Roth, Harold L. "A Study of Library Storage and Augmented Service Facilities for the State of Washington: Final Report." Great Neck, NY: Rothines Associates, 1976.

Rusli, Agus. "A Temporary Storage in a City of Intersections: Evanston Public Library." *Journal of Architectural Education* 47, no. 3 (Feb. 1994): 135.

"The Relegation and Storage of Material in Academic Libraries: A Literature Review." Centre for Library and Information Management, Dept. of Library and Information Studies, Loughbourough University, 1980.

Rowse, Dorothea E. "The Storage of Science Journals at the University of South Africa." *South African Journal of Library & Information Science* 52 (Aug. 1984): 105–8.

Seaman, Scott, and Donna DeGeorge. "Selecting and Moving Books to a Remote Depository: A Case Study." *Collection Management* 16, no. 1 (1992): 137–42.

Seeds, Robert S. "Impact of Remote Library Storage on Information Consumers: "Sophie's Choice?" *Collection Building* 19, no. 3 (2000): 105–8.

Silverstein, Craig, and Stuart M. Shieber. "Predicting Individual Book Use for Off-Site Storage Using Decision Trees (at Harvard College Library)." *Library Quarterly* 66 (July 1996): 266–93.

Singh, Bawa Jeet. *Optimal Subdivision of Service Functions to Alternative Facilities Based on Usage Patterns: Application to Book Storage in University Libraries.* Ann Arbor, MI: University Microfilms International, 1978.

Spyers-Duran, Peter. *Secondary Access Storage of Books in Small and Medium Sized Academic Libraries: A Proposal for an Experimental Model.* Boca Raton, FL: Florida Atlantic University, 1973.

Steele, Virginia. *Remote Storage, Facilities, Materials Selection, and User Services.* Association of Research Libraries, Office of Management Services. SPEC Kit no. 164. Washington, DC: ARL, Systems and Procedures Exchange Center, 1990.

Stockton, Gloria. "Northern Regional Library Compact Shelving Facility." *DLA Bulletin* 3 (March 1983): 6–7.

A Survey of Compact Storage Facilities and Collections in the Member Libraries of the Association of Research Libraries (ARL): A Preliminary Report. Ithaca, NY: Cornell University Libraries, 1978.

Strayner, Richard. *The Cost-Effectiveness of Alternative Library Storage Programs.* Australia: Graduate School of Librarianship, Monash University, 1983.

Tanis, Norman, and Cindy Ventulah, "Making Space: Automated Storage and Retrieval." *Wilson Library Bulletin* 61 (June 1987): 25–27.

Theilig, Richard. "Remote Possibilities (Moving Older Periodicals to Campus Storage Facility: Experience of University of Arkansas Medical Sciences Library)." *Library Mosaics* 8, no. 6 (Nov.–Dec. 1997): 14–15.

University of California, Los Angeles. Planning Office. "Southern Regional Library Compact Shelving Facility. Final Environmental Impact Report." Los Angeles: UCLA, 1981.

University of Texas at Austin. General Libraries. *Library Storage Facility Information Packet.* Austin, TX: General Libraries, University of Texas at Austin, 1994.

VanBrimmer, Barbara, Elizabeth Sawyers, and Eric Jayjohn. "The Randtriever: Its Use at The Ohio State University." *Library Hi Tech* 8, no. 3 (1990): 71.

Ventgen, Carol. "Library Facility for 2000 and Beyond (Workshop Report at the University of Iowa, 1994 PNLA Conference)." *PNLA Quarterly* 59 (Fall 1994): 27.

Victorian Association for Library Automation. "Robots to Knowbots: The Wider Automation Agenda." *Proceedings,* 9th Annual Conference and Exhibition, Melbourne, Victoria, Jan. 28–30, 1998.

Walsh, Tom. "Storage Is Where You Find It (Ellis Library Looks to Example of Leavey Library at USC)." *American Libraries* 28 (April 1997): 54–56.

Young, Jeffrey R. "Three Research Libraries Plan Vast New Facility to Store Little-used Books." *Chronicle of Higher Education* (Apr. 6, 1999).

Young, Jeffrey R. "In the New Model of the Research Library, Unused Books Are Out, Computers Are In." *The Chronicle of Higher Education* 44, no. 8 (Oct. 17, 1997): A27–A28.

Storage Facility Web Sites

University of California, Northern Regional Library Facility
http://www.lib.berkeley.edu/NRLF

University of California, Southern Regional Library Facility
http://www.srlf.ucla.edu

Columbia University, Annex and Prentis
http://www.columbia.edu/cu/libraries/indiv/butlcirc/offsite

Cornell University, Library Annex
http://www.library.cornell.edu/newannex

University of Florida, Storage Collections
http://web.uflib.ufl.edu/toolbox/accserv/lad.html

Harvard University, Harvard Depository
http://hul.harvard.edu/hd

Johns Hopkins University, Moravia Park Off-Site Shelving Facility
http://www.mse.jhu.edu:8001/library/moravia/moravia.htm

University of Michigan, Buhr Shelving Facility
http://wwwlib.umich.edu/libhome/services/buhr

University of Minnesota
http://kinglear.lib.umn.edu/mlac/mlac.asp

Northeastern Ohio Cooperative Regional Depository
http://web.neoucom.edu/~jscalf

Ohio University, Southeast Ohio Regional Library Depository
http://www.library.ohiou.edu/libinfo/depts/circ/annex

Penn State University, Academic Activities Building and Aaron Building Annexes
http://www.libraries.psu.edu/pubinfo/librannexes.html

University of Pennsylvania, High Density Storage Facility
http://www.library.upenn.edu/storage/storage.about

University of Pittsburgh, UPARC Storage Facility
http://www.library.pitt.edu/services/requests/uparc.html

Southwest Ohio Regional Depository
http://www.lib.muohio.edu/libinfo/depts/sword

University of Texas, Austin, Library Storage Facility
http://www.lib.utexas.edu/dataware/cgi-bin/web_evaluate

Tri Universities Group Annex
http://www.tug-libraries.on.ca/info/annex/index

Virginia Tech
http://www.lib.vt.edu/services/circ-reserve/storage.html

Washington Research Libraries Consortium
http://www.wrlc.org

University of Waterloo, Library Annex
http://tug.lib.uwaterloo.ca/info/annex/index.html

University of Western Ontario
http://www.lib.uwo.ca/DBW_rdl.htm#what

Yale University, Library Shelving Facility
http://ww.library.yale.edu/Administration/Shelving

Other Related Web Sites

Council of Logistics Management
http://www.libertynet.org/clm/clm/clm.html

Warehousing Education and Research Council
http://www.werc.org/

Index